FRAUDSTER TALES

Vijay Narayan Govind is a senior finance professional with over three decades of experience in financial auditing, fraud examination and information systems. He works closely with companies and business entities, advising their boards and audit committees on risk, controls and processes. Govind serves on the boards of trade and industry bodies and is actively involved in various service and cultural organizations.

FRAUDSTER TALES

History's Greatest Financial Criminals and Their Catastrophic Crimes

VIJAY NARAYAN GOVIND

PAN

First published 2024 by Pan
an imprint of Pan Macmillan Publishing India Private Limited
707 Kailash Building
26 K. G. Marg, New Delhi 110001
www.panmacmillan.co.in

Pan Macmillan, The Smithson, 6 Briset Street, Farringdon, London EC1M 5NR
Associated companies throughout the world
www.panmacmillan.com

ISBN 978-81-19300-97-6

1 3 5 7 9 8 6 4 2

Typeset in Petersburg by R. Ajith Kumar, New Delhi
Printed and bound in India by Thomson Press India Ltd.

Matha, Pitha, Guru, Daivam – the forces that shape us and enable our expression

Contents

Author's Note

Crimes have fascinated us as a subject since time immemorial, though the more violent ones have typically attracted the most attention. This distinction is also evident across the literary spectrum, with murders and street crimes taking up the majority of narrative space, leaving little room for what are commonly referred to as white-collar crimes.

The chief reason was that while such crimes have also been around for long, they gained public interest only much later. In fact, it was as late as the 1940s when Edwin Sutherland, a pioneering American criminologist (since recognized as the father of white-collar crimes) kindled academic interest in the topic for the first time. Even so, his postulation that '*white-collar crime may be defined approximately as a crime committed by a person of respectability and high social status in the course of his occupation*' was originally seen as a controversial affront to the upper classes and summarily rejected.

Nevertheless, spurred by a new world order that demanded greater equity, later criminologists reaffirmed Sutherland's theory. They stated that perpetrators of white-collar crimes frequently lack characteristics associated with a typical 'street criminal' – archaically referred to as a 'blue-collar criminal' – such as poverty, neglect, low self-esteem, alcohol or drug abuse. On the contrary, white-collar criminals usually grew up in good homes and neighbourhoods and graduated from colleges with some idealism, until they found themselves in occupations where these transgressions became acceptable. The schemes employed were generally very inventive and did not involve any violence. However, they could also potentially have far-reaching consequences for a larger number of people. Interestingly, in all such cases, apart from the perceived pressure and opportunity to commit fraud, there was a tendency to rationalize the act, completing the recognized concept of 'fraud triangle'. Many experts believe that this type of criminal behaviour is primarily learnt through a person's interactions with others rather than being an innate human tendency.

Unfortunately, the fact that people in positions of power are induced to commit crimes of this nature has led to serious shortcomings in deterrence and punishment. The technical complexity, combined with the gloved hands of the powers that be, has significantly slowed progress against them.

The famous economist John Kenneth Galbraith once observed that '*the man who is admired for the ingenuity of his larceny is almost always rediscovering some earlier form of fraud*'. As an amateur student of white-collar crimes, I've always believed that telling true stories is an effective way to explore this complex subject.

The ten true stories selected in this book emphasize the same exploration. Despite my best efforts to mine all relevant facts through my research, there may be multiple versions of these cases due to the elusive nature of the subjects and periods to which they refer, and I have tried to weave together whatever seemed most plausible to me, sans any bias. To a limited extent, I've exercised some creative licence, where I felt it might improve the telling. Original statements, recordings and notes have been reproduced verbatim in italics to distinguish them from those made up for dramatic effect.

An important aspect I'd like the reader to remember is that the value of money has changed significantly over time, and applying a consistent measure to quantify the frauds in today's worth is nearly impossible. I can assure you, however, that all these frauds were significant enough at the time to send major ripples through the systems they challenged, with many of them serving as catalysts for key legal and regulatory reforms.

In this light, I once again express my sincere hope that you will enjoy reading the rest of the book and, of course, I will be grateful for any feedback.

1

William Chaloner

The Coin Connoisseur

> '[The criminal] shall be strangled, being hanged up by the neck between heaven and earth ... then is he to be cut down alive ... his bowels and inlay'd parts taken out and burnt ... his body to be quartered, and the quarters set up in some high and eminent place, to the view and detestation of men, and to become a prey for the fowls of the air.'
>
> – SIR EDWARD COKE, Chief Justice of the King's Bench, pronouncing punishment for counterfeiting offences in the seventh century

By the middle of the seventeenth century, traditional blacksmiths in Birmingham's once-thriving forges found themselves struggling. Mechanized processes churned out nails, horseshoes, pots and locks at a pace their hands could not match, prompting them to seek new opportunities. To their delight, a lucrative venture emerged that exceeded their expectations.

The groat, a coin worth four pennies, occupied a humble place in the British monetary system. Though seemingly insignificant for large transactions, the constant need for petty change, particularly among traders, kept them in high demand. Recognizing the Royal Mint's inability to meet this demand, the blacksmiths seized an opportunity. Many farriers abandoned traditional horseshoes and similar products in favour of crafting these counterfeit coins, known in clandestine circles as 'Birmingham groats'. Their craftsmanship was so impeccable that only a true expert could tell them apart from the genuine coins, gradually flooding the market with counterfeits.

It was around this time that William Chaloner arrived in Birmingham. Born into a family that owned a small weaving unit in Warwickshire, he had no formal education but could read, write and speak fluently. His father had initially intended to bring him into the family business, but the boy's ambitions clashed with their modest way of life. When William showed his disregard for morals and ethical standards, the family decided to send him away to find employment. The ideal opportunity arose with a blacksmith in nearby Birmingham, where his father arranged an apprenticeship at a small nail-making unit, affording William the chance to learn the trade.

To the young man's surprise, the apprenticeship took an unexpected turn. Much like many other smiths in Birmingham, his employer was deeply involved in the production of counterfeit groats. He welcomed the new intern's eagerness to delve into the intricacies of coining, who swiftly mastered the craft. But Chaloner yearned to move to London, a city teeming with tales of opportunity. Suddenly, to the elderly smith's dismay, his best assistant decided to leave. With little money for transport, he undertook the long journey on foot.

Upon reaching the outskirts of the sprawling city, worn and weary, Chaloner found himself adrift. Making do with what he could get from odd jobs, he sought stability. Given his background, jobs in metal and related fields seemed promising. Despite his earnest efforts, securing employment proved elusive, even after offering to toil extra hours for meagre wages. The problem, he realized, was that all jobs – be it metalworking, craftsmanship or small trades – were firmly controlled by powerful guilds operating as quasi-unions, accessible only to those who could afford their fees upfront. With naught but holes in his threadbare trousers, this option was not available to William Chaloner, spurring him to continue his pursuit.

Out of sheer desperation, he came up with a daring plan. Since sex trade was popular in London and the suburbs, Chaloner used his metalworking skills to create a one-of-a-kind product. After numerous trials, he designed a tin watch that doubled as a dildo and pitched the concept to a watchmaker. Though the man agreed to manufacture it, he stipulated that Chaloner be solely responsible for marketing it.

While promoting the product in London's lower echelons, Chaloner met many people involved in the city's dark underbelly and made useful connections. Although the watchmaker took the lion's share of the profits, Chaloner was relieved to finally earn enough for a regular meal and a place to sleep.

This was when something new caught his attention.

On the outskirts of the city, many unqualified 'practitioners' treated people for various ailments. Surprisingly, despite several deaths, a much higher proportion of the sick appeared to be getting better. Chaloner concluded that the cause was most likely their own curative systems, not the 'treatment'. But importantly, they all appeared to be perfectly willing to pay exorbitant fees for this.

Chaloner reasoned that combining medical treatment with elements of magical healing would allow him to make lots of money. He chose a remote area of town for the operation and hired a cunning aide to spread the word about a new local doctor who also possessed some mystical abilities. After painting his ragged old suit to look presentable for the role, 'Dr William Chaloner' officially began his 'medical practice'.

He soon perfected the art of dispensing medicinal and miraculous cures. Fortunately, many of his 'patients' recovered on their own, just as he had anticipated. The practice quickly spread. Chaloner was overjoyed that he was finally earning enough for a decent living. Moving beyond therapeutic remedies, he began to persuade people that he could call on divine intervention to solve their problems, even forming magical alliances for unmarried women seeking a suitable partner. Along the way, he met a young woman named Katharine Atkinson. Following a brief courtship, they married and started a family in the suburbs.

Despite his overall success, Chaloner grew frustrated with his inability to expand this con beyond a certain point and sought to devise a new strategy. Bringing together a group of his shady friends, he presented his scheme. The plan called for a few of them to steal some valuable items and hide them in a remote, predetermined location. The victim would then learn from unknown sources that there was a famous spiritualist in their area who possessed magical retrieval abilities. Subsequently, they would be taken to the chambers of the 'great' Dr William Chaloner. The mystic would then visualize the stolen goods in his 'inner eye' and, predictably, the eager victim would find everything intact at the divined location. Chaloner was not wrong in estimating that the targets would be willing to pay a large fee for this ostensibly valuable service.

For a while, everything went as planned. But then, a disgruntled associate leaked information about the scheme. As a result, authorities set up a trap to capture the trickster while he was working. Chaloner, on the other hand, received a tip from an inside source and fled the city right away. However, he was forced to leave everything behind, including his family and all of his savings. Once again penniless, he resurfaced in Hatton Garden on London's Holborn side – a bustling commercial district where he hoped to avoid detection and lay low for a while. He landed a job at a small workshop that specialized in japanning – a lacquer process that involves painting cheap tin and paper pulp furniture to look like expensive East Asian curios. Many of these items would be gilded to give them a golden sheen and justify their high prices. Despite the low pay, he persisted, keeping an eye out for better opportunities.

The world of coins

After a while, his attention shifted to Britain's coinage system, particularly as he learnt about the issues surrounding the circulation of silver coins.

Historically, all coins in the British currency system were handcrafted, and astute players quickly discovered a critical flaw in their manufacturing. They noticed that the edges of these coins were always smooth, allowing anyone with a basic understanding of metals to easily clip small amounts of silver from the sides without being detected. Some silver could also be collected by placing such clipped coins in a bag and vigorously shaking it, a technique known as 'sweating' the coins.

Over time, many smiths improved these techniques, shaving off generous quantities of silver. But as this practice became rampant, the administration realized that the quantity of silver in each coin was rapidly depleting and instituted stringent checks to catch offenders. The punishments were severe, with Queen Elizabeth I even ordering that clippers be publicly burned at stakes rather than hanged to deter others.

Following his restoration in May 1660, King Charles II acknowledged that the only long-term solution to this problem was to automate coin production. For this mission, he commissioned a team of experts led by Pierre Blondeau, an eminent French engineer, and the Roettier brothers, renowned Dutch engravers. During this three-year process, the Royal Mint made a crucial decision to equip the new coins with rough, jagged edges to prevent clipping. However, replacing all the coins in circulation with the new machine-minted ones proved to be a time-consuming task that was still underway when Chaloner arrived in Hatton Garden.

In the meantime, the hand-made coins had to serve as legal tender and Chaloner quickly observed that despite all efforts, people continued to engage in clipping. He was drawn to the opportunity, confident that he had the necessary skills to board this ship. After a short time, though, he realized that there were far too many people in the trade and that the risks outweighed any potential silver gain.

Even though he had decided to quit, he couldn't shake off the strong suspicion that there might be ways to profit from the valuable coins in circulation. The challenge was to think of something unique, with a focus on new coins that were considered tamper-proof.

Chaloner learnt everything he could, including the mint's manufacturing processes, and was soon convinced that, unlike the old coins, there were no simple methods for removing the metal from machine-minted coins. The only option was to try and recreate the entire coin itself. This was clearly not easy, and previous attempts had produced crude imitations that were easily identifiable. Many of these entrepreneurs were arrested and executed in public.

Nevertheless, he was unwilling to let go of his new obsession. Diving right in, Chaloner studied every possible aspect of modern minting techniques, eventually mastering the entire currency system and coining. He also managed to obtain information about how the large moulds and mechanized presses at the Royal Mint produced high-quality coins at a rapid rate.

Now his mission was to build the infrastructure needed to produce the same type of coin. But even the most basic facilities required for such a project, such as a good screw press and allied equipment, warranted a significant investment. With little money on hand, Chaloner decided to return to clipping old coins, at least until he could raise the funds to finance his venture.

Furthermore, he was aware of the technical difficulties involved in minting the coins. The most important challenge was how to successfully replicate the rough, jagged edges of the counterfeit coins without being detected. The Royal Mint, Chaloner knew, accomplished this by employing experts trained in the use of a specially designed milling tool with custom-made moulds. These processes were also difficult to reproduce. In fact, many before him had failed in their attempts to replicate the coins.

Determined to find a solution, Chaloner carefully cast his net, looking for an expert who was willing to collaborate. Eventually, he discovered veteran goldsmith Patrick Coffey, who seemed ideal for the job. Coffey had never worked at the Royal Mint, but he had ample experience working with mechanized facilities, including the use of milling techniques to craft ornamental gold coins with similar rough edges. When he agreed to join the team, Chaloner assigned his brother-in-law, Joseph Gravener, to work closely with the master smith and learn the intricacies of producing flawless counterfeit coins.

Another issue raised by Chaloner was the Royal Mint's recent practice of engraving images on coins with special dies created by Dutch engravers. It was difficult to produce such high-quality dies locally. Just when he was at a loss for what to do, Chaloner met Thomas Taylor, an expert engraver. Chaloner was convinced by Taylor's work that he could recreate the etchings and invited him to join the team.

One of the most difficult aspects of the venture was sneaking counterfeits into the market. Chaloner enlisted the help of some of his old gangster buddies and handpicked a savvy couple – Thomas and Elizabeth Holloway – to lead the team.

Once everything was in place, Chaloner ran several rounds of trials to ensure that the 'silver' French pistoles produced at his 'mint' matched their real counterparts before beginning full-scale production.

To his delight, the coins were received well in the markets, with no one suspecting they were anything but authentic. As cash flow increased, Chaloner expanded his line of products, introducing new coins like the 'gold' English guineas.

Quickly, the challenge became how to produce enough coins to meet the increasing demand. With money pouring in, Chaloner's lifestyle shifted dramatically, influencing the way he dressed and moved. After purchasing an exquisitely furnished house in an upmarket area of Knightsbridge, Chaloner's hobbies grew more extravagant in nature, including a fondness for changing mistresses frequently.

Things proceeded smoothly until law enforcement closed in on one of his team members. When officials apprehended William Blackford, a trusted member of the inner circle in charge of coin distribution, Chaloner was concerned. Upon learning that Blackford had agreed to confess their wrongdoings in exchange for leniency from the death penalty, Chaloner quickly gathered his belongings and fled.

Managing to evade all attempts to apprehend him, he resurfaced in public only after learning that the authorities, frustrated by their failure to catch Chaloner, had accused Blackford of lying and decided to execute him. Effectively, this decision also brought a closure to all proceedings against Chaloner.

Despite the narrow escape, he couldn't shake the desire to restart the halted counterfeiting operation. But he decided to wait a little longer until the situation improved. Of course, there was still the issue of not having enough capital on hand to resume operations. Eventually, a change in the royal regime created an opportunity to raise some funds quickly.

During the Glorious Revolution of 1688, James II of the Stuart dynasty had been forced to abdicate. Power passed to his daughter, Mary II, and her husband, William III of Orange. The new monarch was determined to wipe out all traces of Jacobitism, offering large rewards for information on those plotting to overthrow his rule.

With good money in sight, Chaloner began looking for Jacobite supporters to report to the administration. By feigning support for the movement, he could gain their confidence and gather information. Later, when they were prosecuted, Chaloner would receive a fat reward. This game, however, came to an end when he crossed paths with Coppinger.

Coppinger was a small-time criminal who had been reported to the administration by Chaloner. Knowing the latter's counterfeiting history, Coppinger filed countercharges. But he was unable to back up his allegations against Chaloner and was executed for his anti-monarchy activities, as Chaloner proved.

With Coppinger's execution and the money earned through the rewards, Chaloner felt ready to return to his favourite business – counterfeiting coins. The entire English currency system was reeling under severe stress, which made re-entry an even more appealing prospect.

The most recent challenge to the monetary system was the sudden rise in value of silver in neighbouring nations such as France and the Netherlands. This led speculators to exploit the situation, melting down large quantities of silver coins and selling them as silver in Paris and Amsterdam. As a result, England experienced a severe coin shortage, leading to a national crisis. Everyone felt the heat of the fiscal tightening, from large corporations to small merchants and ordinary citizens. The strain worsened with the impending war between King William III and Louis XIV of France.

Monetary experts and senior officials, like William Lowndes, Secretary of the Treasury, were scrambling for solutions. The experts agreed on the necessity for quicker, more effective routes to restore the money supply, fearing a looming economic downfall without them. Facing continuous failures, they turned to independent experts.

Amidst the chaos, Chaloner saw an opportunity to resurrect his business. Except, now he was consumed by a new ambition. He believed that by leveraging his knowledge of the currency system to address its current issues, he could not only establish himself as an expert but also potentially secure a high-ranking official position. The overriding aspiration was to helm the Royal Mint.

Chaloner set about compiling documents on the country's monetary systems and proposed numerous solutions to its currency dilemmas. Unexpectedly, he even advocated for stricter counterfeiting controls. His ideas were widely disseminated, ensuring that they reached the top bureaucrats. However, his efforts ended in disappointment when his studies and recommendations were ignored, as he was not considered credible to advise on such complex matters.

Yet, one individual took serious note of his submissions. Charles Mordaunt, a former Lord of the Treasury marginalized during William III's reign, sought retaliation against his main adversary, the current chancellor of the exchequer, Charles Montagu. Mordaunt saw Chaloner's writings as ample fodder to highlight flaws in the monetary system and managed to push these observations to the highest authority. He even arranged for Chaloner to present his findings to the king's high privy council.

Seizing this chance, Chaloner criticized numerous flaws in the system, especially those regarding the mint's structure and processes. The council acknowledged many of his suggestions, agreeing that a comprehensive review of the mint's coining systems was urgently needed. Unfortunately, Chaloner's final proposal to entrust the mint's future affairs to him did not garner any support. Disappointed, he ended the meeting without achieving his ultimate goal. As these events were taking place, however, another development was unwinding, set to completely revolutionize the British currency system.

Brainstorming in unlikely circles

The Secretary of the Treasury, William Lowndes, turned to distinguished individuals from various professions for solutions to resolve the problems plaguing the financial system. This group included an extraordinary mathematician and physicist too, albeit unrelated to finance. Known for his ego and peculiarities, he was a Fellow at Trinity College before becoming a professor at Cambridge. Although his university lectures were not particularly well-received, some of his theories had gained recognition in the scientific and academic communities, one of which was famously inspired by an unpredictably falling apple.

Even though Isaac Newton had no direct connection to monetary systems, Lowndes wrote to his brilliant friend from Trinity hoping that he could provide him with some insights. Newton, intrigued by the unusual query, investigated the issue and responded promptly.

He offered two solutions. First, that only a comprehensive recoinage of all hand-minted coins could terminate the clipping threat permanently. While this was not an entirely new idea, he suggested melting down all the older, clipped coins and refashioning them into new unclippable machine-minted coins.

The second recommendation was to undertake a full-fledged currency devaluation. This entailed marking each coin down exactly to its silver content value, thus eliminating the present arbitrage that made coins appealing as bullion, especially across borders.

Although Lowndes liked both the ideas, his attempts to set it in motion were met with substantial opposition, particularly from the wealthy, who feared that a devaluation of money would disproportionately affect them. Ultimately, Lowndes had to abandon this option, but he chose to proceed with the recoinage plan.

It was intrinsically clear from the start that the recoinage process would be complex and time-consuming. Melting existing coins was relatively straightforward, but manufacturing enough new machine-minted substitutes was a colossal undertaking. Experts predicted that the operation would take at least ten years to complete. Meanwhile, the coin availability continued to decline, indicating a deepening financial crisis. The situation worsened when King William III, already in a war, refused to cut spending and demanded more money. Attempts to extract new revenue sources, like tax hikes, faced fierce public backlash, and the British government could feel the pressure intensifying.

By mid-1695, the authorities had few options and decided to act on the long-pending proposal to issue paper currency. Whenever suggested previously, this concept had been met with opposition, particularly from bankers. They questioned how a worthless piece of paper could be compared to bullion. However, as the financial crisis grew worse, King William III was left with no choice but to sanction the use of paper money. Originally intended for government expenditure, its use expanded when this limited approach failed to address the escalating issues. Only the Bank of England was authorized to issue paper currencies, and specialists ensured the use of specific paper and ink patterns to prevent duplication.

Other plans

William Chaloner had other plans and was already plotting an assault on the new type of currency. He devoted time and effort to study the new processes and, by the time the bank began issuing paper currency on a larger scale, Chaloner had found a printer and arranged to obtain the exact materials needed to create perfect replica notes.

But only months into this endeavour, bank officials detected counterfeit notes in circulation and traced them back to the printer, who quickly confessed. Before Chaloner could comprehend what was going on, he was placed under arrest.

Chaloner maintained that he was simply stress-testing the new currency systems as an expert to assist the administration in identifying any flaws. He was also confident that he would not face prosecution due to the absence of laws governing paper currency counterfeiting. Even so, he refused to rest. Using his sources, he obtained information on certain fraudulent payments from the Bank of England to a city orphanage charity, threatening to publicize it if his case was pursued any further.

Chaloner not only got off scot-free, but he also received a reward for exposing the fraud! Nevertheless, this incident put a stop to his prospective venture into paper currency. While contemplating his next move, he came across an unexpected development.

His inflammatory speech before the privy council had instigated the Royal Mint to investigate the illegal coining activities in the country. And Chaloner's name was also featured in their list of suspects.

He was arrested again and taken to Newgate Prison for questioning. During the interrogation, he learnt that only a few small-time criminals had alleged his involvement in coin-related matters, even though investigators had found no substantive evidence to convict him. Emboldened, he vowed to use his arrest to his advantage, even while awaiting trial.

From prison, he sent a confidential petition to Charles Montagu, Chancellor of the Exchequer, reiterating the flaws he had observed in the currency system. Using his experiences, he described the process of producing counterfeit coins from debased blanks and distribution channels used for them. To back up his claims, he elaborated on the involvement of his former associates, such as Patrick Coffey and Thomas Carter, while subtly hinting at his own contribution under the vague alias 'Chandler'.

The chancellor was deeply disturbed by the petition, particularly the allegations of counterfeiting at the Royal Mint through the bribery of officials. Given the petition's apparent authenticity, he decided that an investigation was imperative. Chaloner was summoned before a committee of the Lords Justices, where he reaffirmed the content of his petition. He repeated that someone with his coining expertise was required to resolve the critical issues. Taking these submissions seriously, the committee agreed that the currency systems needed urgent repair. They also declared the immediate need for a full-time warden at the Royal Mint. Owen Wynne had resigned over six years ago, and his successor, Benjamin Overton, had only been in office for a year. Given the ongoing large-scale recoinage activities at the mint, the committee unanimously agreed that a competent leader was necessary. But to Chaloner's profound disappointment, the committee also reiterated that they did not believe he was the right candidate for the role.

Leading the search, Charles Montagu and his team found a large number of qualified candidates who worked at the mint or in other prominent positions. But all of them were found to be either inefficient, corrupt or both, rendering them unfit for such an important position. Experts also believed that at this critical economic juncture, the ideal candidate would be someone who could think and act differently than the average bureaucrat or economist.

Montagu, after reviewing Newton's previous currency reform recommendations to Lowndes, began to believe that the scientist could be a candidate for the position. When he proposed the rather unusual idea, it was opposed by a number of officials, some of whom were vying for the position themselves. However, Montagu decided to proceed after some of the most senior members of the administration agreed that it was worth exploring. Without seeking Newton's approval, the official paperwork was started, and in April 1696, King William III issued a formal order appointing Isaac Newton as Warden of the Royal Mint. Newton, surprised by the unexpected directive, briefly considered declining. But this was a royal decree that could not be refused. The more he thought about it, the more intrigued he became by the prospect of taking on such a different role than his previous academic pursuits.

Newton's appointment as Royal Mint warden sparked a series of rapid changes. He soon established himself as an integrated leader, spending time working closely with the workers, including at hot smelters and presses. On identifying the major issues confronting the mint and, since he wielded complete authority, Newton implemented corrective measures across the board. Unwanted incidents, such as accidents and fatalities, were significantly reduced, while transparency replaced inefficiency and corruption. Changes permeated all levels, and productivity levels skyrocketed. One critical mission was to oversee the recoinage activity so that the task could be completed well ahead of schedule.

Clash of experts

Chaloner was paying close attention to all the recent developments at the mint. Even after Newton's appointment, he held out hope for a senior position. When no opportunity emerged, he sought a direct meeting with the head.

In his first meeting with Newton, Chaloner echoed his previous arguments about financial concerns and requested the opportunity to serve the mint. If Newton was hesitant to hire a senior figure, he proposed assigning a trained employee, Thomas Holloway, to work for him at a lower salary. Newton listened attentively but had reservations about Chaloner's integrity, suspicious of the latter's unusually strong desire to gain access to the mint.

Newton's suspicions were not unfounded. Chaloner knew that running his operations would be easier if he or a trusted individual were part of the mint's official structure.

When his pleas to Newton failed, Chaloner made another attempt. Informed of a House of Commons committee reassessing the mint's state, he requested an audience with them. Again, he exposed irregularities and fraud at the mint, reiterating the allegation of original master dies being smuggled out for counterfeiters with insider assistance. He even subtly criticized the warden, citing the absence of sufficient skills and knowledge to manage such complex issues. As always, he concluded with a renewed offer to assist the mint in any suitable capacity. To his advantage, the house committee was largely convinced of the systemic flaws Chaloner had pointed out and issued stern directions to the warden for necessary resolutions. Though it echoed its previous view that Chaloner's direct involvement was unnecessary, the committee went on to suggest that Newton could consider hiring Chaloner as an independent expert to advise him.

Thoroughly convinced of Chaloner's malevolent intentions and perturbed by his veiled personal attacks, Newton decided to retaliate. One of his key responsibilities as the warden was to bring currency criminals to proper justice. So far, his focus had been on more pressing issues, leaving this to the other law enforcing officials. But after the latest showdown, Newton decided it was time for serious action.

He promptly ordered an investigation into Chaloner's repeated claims of official dies being misused and directed his men to gather information about the man and his activities. Newton personally reviewed interrogation records of all captured counterfeiters, trying to find details remotely linked to William Chaloner.

While examining the report of two inmates, Cooke and White, who were on death row for counterfeiting, something stood out. The reports seemed to indicate that they were low-level criminals, but there was also mention of the official dies matter. Most significantly, both of them claimed some connection to Chaloner. Typical of such cases, they had not provided any evidence, and their claims had been dismissed.

Newton decided to meet with these criminals personally, promising them a reprieve from their sentences in exchange for detailed information on the counterfeit coin trade. Seizing this unexpected lifeline, the prisoners divulged everything they knew. Much of it was irrelevant, but Newton extracted some useful leads. The prisoners were pardoned, and their information helped expose many involved in the illicit trade.

But even so, none of the information was good enough to rope in William Chaloner, who remained at large.

Chaloner, aware of the warden's pursuit, abandoned plans to enter the mint and resumed his counterfeiting operations. Given that forging paper currency was no longer viable, he reverted to his preferred occupation.

He finalized a project to counterfeit the new machine-minted coins. He chose a secluded house in Egham, distant enough from civilization to drown out any noise. Thomas Holloway resumed managing daily operations, while Chaloner re-established secure coin distribution channels. As planned, fake 'Chaloner' crowns and half-crowns entered into circulation.

Meanwhile, the official recoinage activity had significantly accelerated. Newton's efforts eased the British economy by increasing the supply of new coins. But when Newton declared that the entire process would be completed in two years – far from the estimated decade – no one, including the king, took him seriously.

Newton outperformed everyone's expectations. The historic exercise was completed significantly under budget, refuting critics who questioned the appointment of a 'financially unwise' individual to a key position at the mint. The consensus now was that the mint had never had a better warden in its history.

Chaloner was extremely irritated by the compliments his opponent was receiving. Yet, he remained undeterred, focusing on solidifying the new counterfeiting activities, which were going well. He expanded operations by taking over several small units and assisting others in setting up coining operations throughout London. Chaloner eventually came to control the city's largest counterfeit business.

Isaac Newton did not let the euphoria of his early success distract him from his primary goal – completely eliminating criminals from the coining system. He understood this could be achieved only by apprehending William Chaloner, who was now clearly running the show. The persistent issue was the lack of concrete evidence. Although there was varying information about Chaloner's activities, no one could provide substantial proof to convict him.

Newton drew up fresh plans and personally handpicked men for the task. He trained them to infiltrate counterfeiting networks and wring out information. Also, he assured substantial rewards, including legal amnesty and monetary benefits, to anyone willing to cooperate.

As he had hoped, his men successfully infiltrated several coining gangs by exploiting weaknesses and frustrations among their members. Multiple forgery operations were dismantled as Newton ensured sufficient evidence was gathered to promptly prosecute and execute the perpetrators. Those who confessed or assisted were always rewarded as promised – an incentive publicized to attract others.

The message was clear: the warden of the mint intended to eradicate coin counterfeiting. Unfortunately, Chaloner remained out of reach.

An unexpected break came when Newton learnt that Thomas Holloway, known to be one of Chaloner's closest allies, had been arrested for debt default and sent to Newgate Prison. During questioning, Holloway alluded to William Chaloner and claimed a close friendship with the mint warden.

But instead of taking on Holloway right away, Newton first summoned another prisoner, Peers, who had also admitted to some knowledge of Chaloner, and offered him clemency in exchange for identifying Holloway as a member of Chaloner's gang. Peers agreed and corroborated Holloway's senior position in the counterfeiting ring.

Suddenly, Holloway found that the original issue of debt default had escalated into a severe charge of coining and currency fraud – punishable by death.

Newton then played the same card, offering complete amnesty if he confessed against Chaloner. Holloway found himself trapped and consequently accepted the offer. Based on Holloway's confession, Chaloner was arrested, while the former was released on his agreement to testify against Chaloner in court.

At Newgate Prison, Chaloner remained outwardly calm, maintaining that he was innocent and a victim of the warden's prejudice against him. But he was acutely aware that if Holloway testified, he would face serious consequences. Holloway was privy to all of their group's previous and current operations, including key locations and people, which Newton could use to incriminate Chaloner.

The latter's only hope was to ensure Holloway did not turn up at the trial. Chaloner used his contacts both inside and outside of Newgate to send Holloway a strong message warning him not to trust Newton and urging him to flee to Scotland, where English law was not applicable.

And so, Thomas Holloway vanished. As the main prosecution witness, everyone else's testimony, which was supposed to back up his account, also fell apart. Once more, William Chaloner was a free man.

Defiant in the face of humiliation following his arrest, Chaloner became even more determined to undermine his adversary. He wrote another petition, this time to the Parliament, expressing indignation over the way someone of his stature, after repeatedly offering to help the king and the mint, was being preyed upon, all because of the fractured ego of an ignorant, capricious warden. A hearing was scheduled, and given the backdrop of the recent failed trial, Newton found it difficult to justify humiliating a respectable man like Chaloner.

Upholding Chaloner's pleas, the court made it amply clear that it was only because of his position and significant service to the exchequer that Isaac Newton had been spared a severe reprimand.

Lotteries to Newgate

Chaloner knew he had won this round but had left behind a formidable, wounded adversary in his wake. In such circumstances, attempting a return to currency and coins would be foolhardy. Besides, he no longer had skilled men like Holloway in his employ.

However, he spotted a new opportunity – something beyond Newton's technical jurisdiction.

Facing substantial financial demands, especially during the wars, the state had experimented with various revenue-generating methods, including issuing lotteries. While these didn't substantially contribute to the exchequer, they gained popularity among small investors, prompting the government to continue these schemes even post-war.

Chaloner saw potential in printing fake lottery tickets. While most of the necessary infrastructure could be arranged, the real challenge lay in procuring high-quality printing plates for flawless execution. Without Holloway's expertise, he was forced to seek out another acquaintance from his coining days: Thomas Carter, who had some experience in these designs.

Carter agreed to assist Chaloner and introduced him to a man named Davis, who offered to help in circulating the fake tickets. Using the plates designed by Carter, Chaloner began to test print the fake lottery tickets on the same grade of paper used for the official ones. Once he was assured of the desired quality, he began to consider arrangements to sell the fakes stealthily. Davis then presented a generous offer: he was prepared to purchase the entire first batch at full price and handle their onward distribution.

Chaloner readily agreed to the proposition. But just as he was getting ready to roll out the first batch, he received word that Davis had been seen intermingling with senior government officials. Suspicions aroused, Chaloner soon had reliable information that Davis was a mole working for the Secretary of State. This was an inside operation planned by none other than the mint warden, and Davis had been promised a handsome reward to ensure Chaloner's capture with full evidence, including the fake tickets and forged printing plates. The funds offered by Davis to buy the first batch were also from the state exchequer, authorized by the secretary. Davis had also been explicitly instructed to prevent any of the fake tickets from entering circulation.

Maintaining a facade of normalcy, Chaloner began scheming. He informed Davis about plans to commence full-scale printing within a few days and collected the value of the initial lot as agreed. Then, he advanced the printing timeline, operated the presses continuously and produced more batches than planned within a short period. Chaloner had arranged trusted individuals to aggressively distribute the tickets into London's lottery markets. Soon, a significant number of counterfeit tickets saturated the circulation. Having made a decent profit, Chaloner suddenly halted operations and disappeared without a trace.

By the time Davis suspected foul play, the entire lottery operation had vanished. Understandably, the Secretary of State and everyone involved, including Newton, were incensed. Further complicating matters, they had to explain how the government funds spent on the project, as well as the supposed initial lot purchase, had ended up being wasted.

An even greater threat loomed: a large number of fake lottery tickets could well be circulating freely in the market now. Everyone in the administration knew locating these fraudulent tickets was an impossible task. A leak of this information would lead to public outrage. Under the circumstances, the high-level decision was that further inquiries and actions should be abandoned. Pleased that his scheme had succeeded, Chaloner chose to lay low for the time being.

But soon, a lottery worker, suspicious upon discovering some irregularities in a few of his tickets, reported his concerns. This escalated to the secretary, who now had no recourse than to order an investigation.

The decision was made to immediately obtain a confession from Davis and, based on his information, interrogate Chaloner and Carter. They also planned a search for the forged printing plates, which would serve as crucial evidence. Following Davis's confession, Chaloner found himself back in Newgate Prison. But he was confident none of the actions against him would yield any results. He had reliable information that even the administration shared this view. The whole exercise, it seemed, was merely a charade to convince the populace that something was being done.

Perhaps Chaloner's only oversight was underestimating Isaac Newton, a man not known for giving up easily. Despite no direct jurisdiction over the lottery matter, as soon as he heard of Chaloner's arrest, Newton decided to get involved.

Experienced in his opponent's guiles, Newton directed that Chaloner be kept under continuous high security. All movements inside the prison were to be closely monitored, and he was forbidden from meeting or writing to anyone. Distrusting the regular prison staff, Newton even had his own men placed at the prison to guard Chaloner.

Strict instructions were issued to maintain the illusion for Chaloner that the ongoing investigation and charges were only for the printing of counterfeit lottery tickets, and that the law was still attempting to prove the case of the forged plates. To strengthen this narrative, Newton personally summoned Carter and offered him mercy from the death sentence were he to testify against Chaloner in the lottery printing issue. Newton further ensured that Chaloner was informed about the meeting and the offer.

As Newton had schemed, Chaloner remained unperturbed by these developments. He was certain they would never find the printing plates he had destroyed. Without any evidence, Carter and Davis' testimonies would not hold up in court. He relished picturing the new mud on Newton's face once this was over.

What Chaloner was oblivious to was that this was precisely the impression Newton wanted to create. Nobody knew that Newton had already instructed the investigators to stop hunting for the fake plates. Instead, their attention had been now trained on Chaloner's counterfeiting past. The warden was convinced that since Chaloner had turned all his recent attention to the lottery venture, the chances of uncovering evidence from his older trails were much higher. Especially given he was personally absent from the scene.

Under Newton's direct supervision, his team worked tirelessly, employing insiders and spies to crack down on people associated with Chaloner over the years. Offers of clemency, even for capital offences, and rewards were once again liberally doled out. Gradually, many were persuaded to testify against Chaloner, backed by substantive evidence.

Newton kept the cards close to his chest, determined he would level charges only when he was certain they could withstand scrutiny. In the run-up to the trial, he used his clout to ensure that the proceedings were heard by one of the strictest judges in the country.

Everyone, including the Honourable Justice, was taken aback when in an unforeseen turn, the warden suddenly accused Chaloner of forging counterfeit currencies over several years. The focus shifted from the lottery case and, due to the gravity of the new charges, obtained a much more serious character.

Although surprised, Chaloner kept his wits about him. When the trial was reconvened, he remained confident that Newton could not prove these charges. He declined any legal aid, trusting himself to best present his arguments.

In an immediate counter-move, Newton also decided that best equipped to dismantle the defendant's arguments, he would appear in person as prosecutor for the Royal Mint. The trial commenced with heated arguments on both sides, but as Newton began to call on witness after witness to testify, Chaloner found the water steadily flowing away from his feet.

Many people with whom he had close relationships at work and in his personal life at various points in time were being called to testify against him in court. Catherine Coffey (wife of former goldsmith Patrick Coffey), Elizabeth Holloway (wife of Thomas Holloway), Thomas Taylor (the engraver who assisted with the dies) and Catherine Carter (wife of Thomas Carter), all well-informed about Chaloner's activities and with records to prove it, were among the key witnesses. In addition, Newton presented numerous others, like metal traders and smiths with whom Chaloner had worked over the years.

Everything from their interactions with Chaloner was addressed, even minor incidents matching specified dates and times, corroborating the accounts. It was as if the master counterfeiter's entire life was being laid bare for all to see. Chaloner realized Newton had expertly pulled out the right plugs, leaving him virtually unable to rebut. So, he wrote directly to Newton.

He subtly admitted a few unintentional errors and tried to justify his actions, claiming he had the mint's and kingdom's broader interests at heart. Receiving no response, he continued to write, again and again, but his communiqués remained unanswered.

In desperation, Chaloner staged a spectacle of madness. He tore his clothes and pranced around the prison like a lunatic. In this feigned state, he continued to write to Newton, pleading for a reconsideration and pardon. A portion of one of his last letters on record (in verbatim) reads as follows:

> *Most mercifull Sir*
>
> *I am going to be murthered allthough perhaps you may think not but tis true I shall be murdered the worse of all murders that is in the face of Justice and unless I am rescued by your mercifull hands ...*
>
> *And ended with the plea:*
>
> *... God allmighty knows I am murdered Therefore I humbly begg your worship will consider these Reasons and that I am convicted without Precedent and be pleased to speak to Mr Chancellor to save me from being murtherd O Dear Sir do this mercifull deed O my offending you has brought this upon me O for God's sake if not mine keep me from being murdered O dear Sir no body can save me but you. O God my God I shall be murdered unless you save me O I hope God will move your heart with mercy and pitty to do this thing for me I am*
>
> *Your near murdered humble servant*
>
> *Chaloner*

Newton chose to ignore all of Chaloner's overtures and never responded. On 4 March 1699, the court ruled that William Chaloner was guilty of multiple currency frauds and sentenced him to death by hanging. Eighteen days later, he was hanged at the gallows in Tyburn.

Following his hard-fought victory, Isaac Newton was promoted to the master of the mint – a cabinet-level position he held till his death in 1727. During this period, he also served a term as a Member of Parliament and was knighted by Queen Anne. Though he had not been a formal member of the scientific or academic fraternity since joining the mint, Newton was elected as the president of the Royal Society – the highest body of excellence in all scientific, policy and allied matters – another position he held till his death.

Curiously, the exceptional Sir Isaac Newton himself fell victim to the infamous South Sea Company investment scam, losing a sizeable portion of his savings – nearly £20,000 – when the scheme collapsed in 1720.

One can only speculate how the history of the Royal Mint and the British currency system might have unfolded had William Chaloner followed a different path.

An anonymous biography of the master counterfeiter reads: '*Thus liv'd and thus dy'd a Man who had he square'd his Talent by the Rules of Justice and integrity might have been useful to the Commonwealth: But as he follow'd only the Dictates of Vice, was as a rotten Member cut off.*'

Note:

The following may be used for understanding the British currency units of the time, though these are only approximations, as precise currency/gold standards did not exist then and were subject to frequent changes under different European rulers and regimes:

- Guinea = 1 pound = 20s (from increase in gold rates – often worth between 22 and 25 shillings)

- Pound = 20 shilling
- Pistole = 18 shilling
- Crown = 5 shilling
- Groat = 4 pennies (depending on the weight of silver, known to vary up to 8 pennies)
- Penny = 1/12th shilling (or 12 shilling = 1 penny)

2

Haridas Mundhra

The Great Investor

'Parliament must exercise vigilance and control over the biggest and most powerful financial institution it has created, the Life Insurance Corporation of India, whose misapplication of public funds we shall scrutinise today'

– FEROZE GANDHI, MP, during a speech in the Indian Parliament

From trader to tycoon

Haridas Mundhra, born as the eldest of three brothers into a small trading family in Calcutta (present-day Kolkata), showed little interest in academic studies. After completing basic education, he ventured into selling light bulbs. However, another prospect caught his attention early on.

In his spare time, young Mundhra would hurry off to the Lyons Range Building, home of the Calcutta Stock Exchange, and engross himself in the lively and intense dealings there.

Through these observations, he learnt the subtleties of share trading and decided to make it his profession. He helped small investors with their trades, receiving commissions for his services. All extra earnings went towards purchasing shares of his own. Although, these investments were generally made in smaller companies with low market prices. While he made reasonable gains on some of them, Mundhra knew this approach wouldn't get him far.

He realized that more than fundamentals, market sentiments often guided stock prices. Mundhra decided to exploit this factor to increase the value of his shares. He fabricated news about the companies he had invested in, touting access to confidential information. To his delight, the rumour-mill strategy was effective; other market traders and jobbers readily absorbed them, encouraging trades that suited Mundhra's plans. He also developed strategies to guide stock prices in desirable directions. Soon, his influence grew so impactful that his decisions began to shape the market.

Mundhra steadily moved on to larger investments and, systematically building his portfolio, emerged as one of the biggest players on the CSE. As he expanded his operations to other exchanges in the country, particularly the burgeoning Bombay Stock Exchange, he cemented his place among the wealthiest investors. As his wealth grew, so did his connections and social acceptability, which included politicians, bureaucrats and prominent businessmen. As significant amounts of money began to flow in regularly, Mundhra ventured into the tea export business through associates in England. Though unconfirmed, there were rumours that large investors like Bansilal Abhirchand of Nagpur and Vallabhswami, a renowned guru from Rajasthan, had decided to commit substantial sums (up to ₹50 lakh) to him, seeing his business aptitude. Capitalizing on the events leading up to the Second World War, Mundhra made immense profits from this venture, which he opted to retain in Britain for potential future investments abroad.

Fuelled by his vast wealth, Mundhra set his sights on acquiring ownership in a few notable Indian companies. He picked up controlling stakes in some of the best-known companies of the time, such as F&C Osler (India) Ltd, the Indian arm of a reputable British lamp manufacturer, and the large engineering concerns Richardson and Cruddas Ltd and Jessop and Co Ltd. Mundhra also acquired substantial holdings in major tea companies like Assam Tea Company and Brahmaputra Tea Co. To avoid potential legal complications, he spread the ownership of the holdings among his wife and siblings.

Not just seeing himself as a prominent stock market player, but rather as a king of acquisitions, Mundhra aimed for the largest target to date: the British India Corporation (BIC). Established in the 1920s by Sir Alexander MacRobert, who had amalgamated the businesses run by five Englishmen out of Cawnpore (present-day Kanpur), BIC traditionally engaged in goods like boots and woollen blankets and had ventured into other activities, notably sugar production and project construction, which were in demand during the Second World War. Operated under a management agency system, the ongoing wars ensured BIC's good performance in most business segments. After Indian independence in 1947, operations declined, with certain businesses like steel and construction materials being hived off. However, due to its sizeable land holding, BIC was still considered one of the country's most valuable and prestigious groups.

In his quest to acquire BIC, Mundhra found himself in a bidding war with Ramkrishna Dalmia of the Dalmia Group, one of India's biggest industrialists, known for his acquisitive approach. Mundhra utilized every resource at his disposal, including buying out British shareholders with the overseas assets he'd cleverly accumulated to outbid Dalmia and gain control of BIC. Despite paying a premium price between ₹10 and ₹12 per share, when the market value of BIC shares hovered around ₹6, Mundhra revelled in his victory. Continuing his acquisition spree, he seized control of another large managing agency operating several businesses, Turner Morrison and Co Ltd, cementing his status as one of India's leading industrialists.

Mundhra's astute takeover skills became well-known, with leading global magazines featuring him. To the business world, he was a self-made man who had climbed the ranks to join traditional, eminent Marwari houses like the Singhanias, Dalmias and even the Birlas. Naturally, he was also the subject of rumours, such as claims that he had received funding for his acquisitions from British entities, including an overseas insurance company, though none was proven. Mundhra designed layers of crossholdings within the ownership structure of his companies, all controlled by his managing agency, S. B. Industrial Development Company Ltd.

Though official reports from the period are scant, Mundhra's worth was estimated at around ₹4 crore – a whopping empire by the economic standards of the era.

Whenever these developments threatened to invite regulatory attention, Mundhra managed to convince senior officials, including the finance secretary, Haribhai M. Patel, and the RBI governor, Sir Benegal Rama Rau, that there were no grounds for concern. Even the highest authorities, like

Minister of Commerce and Industry T. T. Krishnamachari and Finance Minister H. D. Deshmukh were apprised of matters, and at some level, even Prime Minister Jawaharlal Nehru might have been briefed.

Manipulative trades

Trouble began to brew from unexpected quarters just when things were going smoothly. In business circles, most people thought that the union government would soon implement industry-friendly policies, encouraging private investments. Throughout his rampant acquisitions, Mundhra was banking on these favourable policy changes, which should have significantly boosted his share prices. But, contrary to expectations, many signals from Nehru's government appeared to be tilting towards a socialist model. To make things worse, major economic factors spurred the government toward this direction even faster.

In the aftermath of independence, many Indian businessmen had seized the opportunity to acquire industries formerly handled by Managing Agencies, a British-era corporate structure enabling a few owners to control multiple public companies, even with minor promoter holdings. However, many of these people were traditionally traders or moneylenders, with no experience in running large manufacturing entities. Consequently, they failed to see the need to spur organic growth and increase internal profitability. Instead, they expected new investments and large acquisitions to generate high returns from favourable share movements. With banks and financial institutions making funds more easily accessible, people had resorted to heavy borrowings for such investments. These trends did not auger well for the Indian industry and the country's economy, as many large factories and capital-intensive units began to fail. Banks and financial institutions were also facing the heat of increased loan defaults. All of this was threatening to increase unemployment significantly. The call to nationalize private enterprises, including banks and financial institutions, was growing louder, which the government and ruling party could not afford to ignore.

When the 1955 annual session of the Indian National Congress in Avadi passed a formal resolution signalling this direction, the message became even louder. It became clear that the government no longer favoured the erstwhile British practice of many companies being controlled under a common managing agency system and would soon introduce legislation to break this up. Predictably, the markets became jittery and stock prices fell.

Mundhra, however, knew that given the volatile nature of the markets, it would not take too long before they bounced back. But in the interim, the challenge was to ensure the large debts being used to finance the buyouts and investments were serviced on a regular basis. Unfortunately, when share prices remained low, it became impossible to liquidate the long-term positions. Many businessmen he had crossed paths with during his meteoric rise were watching like hawks to see him fail.

Mundhra decided the best course of action was to devise a strategy to address the immediate market situation. The primary issue with the market at that time was the low volume of trade. Investors and speculators were cautious, preferring to avoid risky positions during such uncertain times. Mundhra reasoned that an increase in the trading volumes of a few major companies would spark positive market sentiments, leading to an immediate market surge. He decided he would be the one to trigger this action.

Mundhra believed 'circular wash' trades would be the most effective option to jumpstart a price increase. Typically, these involve back-to-back deals for buying and selling the same number of shares at the same price, creating the illusion of high trading volumes. By executing such deals, Mundhra successfully reversed the declining market prices of his selected companies. Thereafter, he used a variety of strategies to capitalize on market sentiments, which included releasing stories about expansions and other profitable developments at these companies, which pushed up market prices even higher.

Given that prevailing stock exchange mechanisms were largely self-regulated, Mundhra used his knowledge of the systems to control both market volumes and prices. He planned the settlement of his transactions as well as the delivery of shares to suit his schemes, though he was always wary of delays and defaults. Deploying 'pump and dump' schemes, he would liquidate large positions in a flash when prices touched desired levels and buy back the same lots at the much lower prices his earlier selloffs triggered. 'Round-tripping' deals were used to create trading volumes by buying and selling the same shares repeatedly at predetermined prices. Through many such manipulative stunts, Mundhra kept the targeted stocks well under his control.

However, with the shares held in his own companies, he employed a different tactic. Despite the fact that these were also venues for his market-fixing games, Mundhra chose not to dispose of any of these shares, mostly out of fear of losing control to wily competitors. Even when the prices of his company's shares shot up (as in the case of BIC shares, which rose sharply from ₹5 to ₹14 per share after his price manipulations), he could not bring himself to liquidate any part of his holding. So, as an alternative, Mundhra decided to pledge his shares as security to banks to raise loans against them.

The proposal he submitted to the banks was to sanction him loans based on the latest market value of these shares, after adjusting a margin to cover future fluctuations. Given the acceptance Mundhra commanded and his contacts at all levels, the requests were readily accepted by the banks he approached, including Punjab National Bank (pre-nationalization), which became one of his biggest financial supporters. Predictably, Mundhra ensured that through more market manipulations, his share prices remained at the target levels he had fixed based on his need for funds. For instance, for the largest holdings in British India Corporation, Mundhra had already set a target market rate of ₹14, which would ensure that after the margin, the banks would grant him loans at a rate of ₹11 per share.

The loans sanctioned were substantial, exceeding even the original cost of acquisition of these companies. But Mundhra also knew that these temporary adjustments could not go on forever, and the markets would correct themselves once they became genuinely bullish. His estimation was that this would happen soon.

Unfortunately, the overall economic picture remained gloomy, forcing the government to incessantly grapple with several major challenges. Many of these had significant financial ramifications, and stock markets remained subdued.

In this scenario, Mundhra found it increasingly difficult to unwind many of the large market positions he had assumed.

The only way to keep the ball rolling was by executing more such deals. And most of the recent deals became merely cover-ups for earlier ones.

Creating stocks

The tightening of funds became a major issue as Mundhra continued to create such large deals. Ensuring all outstanding deals were settled on time with counter-party brokers began to pose serious concerns, and small payment defaults started to creep in.

Mundhra tried several things to bring matters under control, but the biggest hurdle now was raising more funds to stay in the game. He no longer had any shares to offer the banks as security for new loans, and all other personal sources had dried up.

Things continued to spiral out of control, landing on the radars of regulators, with complaints being filed with the company law and foreign exchange authorities. When some of these cases reached the courts, Mundhra was heavily chastised by the irate judges and directed to regularize the positions within specified timelines.

Mundhra tried to remain unfazed and worked on all possible ways to stay afloat till the winds changed, but the challenges grew. Especially when he had virtually nothing left to pledge or play around with. This was when he decided to create shares of his own.

Mundhra forged share certificates with the help of a few trusted people to create exact replicas of the originals, which he then used as collateral to obtain additional loans from banks and institutions. He became so good at it that no one suspected anything. In fact, it was only once (in 1956) that the Bombay Stock Exchange raised queries about a few of his transactions, and Mundhra quickly allayed their fears.

No one knew he was piling up a massive debt with no assets at all, even as Mundhra continued to bank on a market revival before the bubble burst to repair everything.

However, some unexpected developments in New Delhi set the cat among the pigeons. The finance minister, C. D. Deshmukh, was an eminent civil servant who had served in many prominent roles, including as the first Indian governor of the Reserve Bank of India. He was widely regarded as one of the architects of major economic reforms in the country, including the formation of the State Bank of India (SBI) and the Life Insurance Corporation of India (LIC). His abrupt decision to step down as finance minister in July 1956 over the proposed division of the Bombay State surprised the whole nation. The portfolio was handed over to the incumbent commerce and industry minister, Tiruvallur Thattai Krishnamachari (known as TTK), after Prime Minister Nehru held it for thirty-seven days.

Relationships between the Government of India and the RBI began to deteriorate soon after TTK took over as the finance minister. Following PM Nehru's strongly worded letter, the incumbent RBI governor, Benegal Rama Rau, also resigned, and a new governor, H. V. R. Iyengar, took over the central bank in March 1957.

Shortly after assuming office, the new RBI governor noticed that a large number of shares of companies were being held by banks under pledge. Even SBI, nationalized two years ago, was not immune. Inspections carried out had also raised suspicions of collusion by bank managers, especially at the Calcutta branches, in sanctioning these loans. For some reason, the matter was not pursued further at that time.

The new governor decided to order inquiries into all the loans granted by banks against the collateral of shares and learnt that such loans had skyrocketed from ₹3.30 crore in 1956 to ₹15.60 crore by mid-1957. It was also evident that many senior officials were parties to this, and all signs pointed to one person: Haridas Mundhra.

Shocked by the findings, RBI officials realized that the banking system of the country was now a ticking time bomb. But urgent actions that could force banks to hastily offload all the shares would also be detrimental. There was little doubt that it would create widespread panic, including the very real possibility of a major market crash that would be disastrous for the already troubled economy.

So, for the time being, RBI merely issued a directive that the banks ought to work out a repayment model with Mundhra, as per which shares held under the pledge could also be steadily released back to him.

But the banking industry took this unusual directive with a sense of foreboding and, citing regulatory insistence, pressed hard for repayments from Mundhra. Even those who had gone soft with him earlier (like PNB) suddenly insisted on an immediate settlement. Mundhra was also warned that they could not wait for too long, failing which forced liquidation of the shares under pledge would be the lone option.

Finding the heat suddenly raised on him, Mundhra could think of no way to arrange the large funds urgently needed in the current situation. It was soon clear that unless he did something unusual, the lenders would be constrained to find new buyers for his companies.

Surprising respite

Staring down an empty well, Mundhra decided the best option was to seek assistance from an influential person who could help and approached the business magnate G. D. Birla. However, the latter felt these issues were beyond his scope, advising Mundhra to directly approach the new finance minister. TTK was considered a businessman due to his experience running his own indenting agency, T. T. Krishnamachari & Co. (now TTK Group), in addition to his expertise in economics and finance.

Mundhra had met the minister a few times earlier when he was the commerce and industry minister. He had always found the man to take a pragmatic view of the difficulties of entrepreneurs and industrialists. TTK was also facing resistance to some of his new budget proposals, including the levy of a new expenditure tax, and Mundhra felt the minister would not want another controversy to erupt now.

Just as he hoped, the meeting proved to be very fruitful.

Mundhra was relieved to find that TTK was already aware of the major issues in the market and why he was unable to repay the large bank loans immediately. The minister also understood that if the banks pushed for a distress sale, it could have a significant impact on the already weak markets. So, after hearing Mundhra patiently, TTK assured his help.

But the decision thereafter surprised many people.

The Parliament had passed an Act nationalizing nearly 250 small insurance companies and societies to bring them under a common umbrella with effect from 1 September 1956, called the Life Insurance Corporation of India. It was conceived that LIC would work with the already nationalized SBI as a pillar for India's economic progress.

But TTK decided that LIC would buy all the shares held by banks under Mundhra's pledge and pay the market value as consideration to settle the bank loans.

The six entities identified for this buyout were Richardson Cruddas, Jessops & Company, Smith Stanistreet, Osler Lamps, Agnelo Brothers and the flagship British India Corporation. The consideration LIC would pay for the shares of these companies was determined to be a whopping sum of ₹12,686,100, which would fully repay the loans Mundhra had availed from the banks.

All normal systems and procedures for making such a large investment, including the approval of the high-level investment committee of LIC, were ignored in taking this hasty decision. Well-wishers may have defended this move from the finance minister as a positive signal to the markets in order to trigger a bull rally and justify the prices paid by LIC. But the markets did not respond to the intervention as expected, and prices remained flat.

The unusual decision greatly perturbed the RBI Governor, H. V. R. Iyengar, who was not a party to it. His anxiety mounted when rumours began to float that many of the Mundhra company shares purchased by LIC could be fake, and he decided to order another confidential inquiry into the matter.

To his horror, the governor learnt that the shares purchased by LIC to settle the bank pledges were many times more than even the share capital of the companies, which was a clear signal that many of these scrips could not be real. Further inquiries confirmed the suspicion that many of the share certificates and transfer documents deposited by Mundhra as security with the banks were fraudulent and forged.

Governor Iyengar let the information be known, though confining it to select people at higher levels in the government and administration, as he realized it would be perilous to keep the lid on such a massive scam.

Based on this information, the government decided to initiate actions at multiple levels to try and reign in the damage. Management of all Mundhra companies involved in the scam was immediately brought under a court-controlled structure, and regulators including the RBI, the income tax department and the newly formed Department of Company Affairs stepped in to take charge. Investigations were also launched into the actions of institutions, including LIC, SBI and PNB in the matter.

Given the huge sensitivity, the message from the top echelons was that everything was to be handled with the utmost confidentiality and that the finance minister should be updated on all developments regularly. The government hoped at this stage to be able to quickly regain control over the situation and avoid any major economic fallout.

However, as matters progressed, it became evident that the implications of the scam would not be limited to the stock markets and financial institutions alone.

A major issue was that many of the factories and industries owned by Mundhra employed a large number of workers, and should the units be shut down, many people would be rendered jobless. The top brass watching these developments closely were also aware that this could be extremely difficult to handle with the trade unions and the political parties backing them. A major case in point was the textile mills in Uttar Pradesh under Mundhra's BIC management, which employed more than 25,000 workers. It was known that everyone, including the state's chief minister, was anxiously looking up to the union government to revive business operations and ensure that people would not lose their jobs.

Whether things could have been brought under control without anyone hearing about it, one will never know – for the news ultimately leaked out.

Ram Subhag Singh, a Member of Parliament, heard rumours about some suspicious transactions involving Mundhra. So he decided to mention the matter during the question hour in the Parliament. In his response, the finance minister admitted that the government, too, had heard these rumours, but he affirmed that the regulatory reviews and inspections had proved it all wrong.

This seemed perfectly satisfactory to the questioning member and to most others there. However, one MP present during the discussion suddenly realized that something seemed to be fishy.

Lawmaker strikes

Some say that the esteemed MP noticed the finance minister's legs shaking under the table while responding, which sparked his curiosity. Whatever the actual trigger was, the MP felt there might be a significant matter worth delving into and soon saw signs that his premonitions might be correct. In his inimitable style, he made sure to gather all pertinent facts and information before seeking to bring the issue back to the Parliament floor.

This MP was none other than Feroze Gandhi. Even as the prime minister's son-in-law, he was known for his fiercely independent stance if he found merit in an issue. Gandhi had a reputation for thorough study before presenting issues. Though generally of a gentle persona, his well-presented speeches could often make things very challenging for those targeted. Even senior members of the Treasury bench had encountered his wrath when, in 1955, he levelled strong allegations against misuse of public institutions for the benefit of certain prominent businessmen. He demonstrated how these organizations, including insurance companies, were exploited for illegal personal gains, such as for funding new acquisitions. This led to men like Ram Krishna Dalmia and Sachin Devkekar of the Times of India Group facing judicial reviews. They were later convicted and imprisoned. To a large extent, the nationalization of LIC was itself a fallout of the scam Feroz Gandhi brought to public attention.

So, when the MP questioned LIC's purchase of shares in the Mundhra-owned companies from banks, at least some people sensed trouble was on the horizon. Feroze Gandhi's Parliament-floor speech on 16 December 1957 is still considered an embodiment of autonomous, politically unaffiliated thought.

The best efforts of Finance Minister TTK and Finance Secretary H. M. Patel failed to address Gandhi's questions. Especially when the MP backed all his queries with further details, leaving many critical points unanswered.

Aware he was losing ground, Mundhra resorted to various tactics, like frantic backdoor parleys with Parliament members, in hopes of influencing Feroze Gandhi to back off.

But no effort prevailed.

The media latched on to the proceedings, putting

everyone in the administrative machinery, up to Prime Minister Nehru, under pressure to explain why life insurance premiums collected from nearly 5.5 million policyholders in the trust of a government entity, had been so hastily redirected to futile investments in violation of prescribed protocols.

Left with few other choices, the government felt compelled to commission an independent judicial review. Honourable M. C. Chagla, the retired Chief Justice of the Bombay high court, was appointed to lead the commission in January 1958.

Marking independent India's first truly transparent scrutiny, the Chagla Commission initiated an investigation. Numerous individuals, including senior officials from the finance ministry, LIC and leading market operators, were summoned. Every hearing of the committee – spanning over twenty-four days – was open to the public and attracted large audiences. Feroze Gandhi also appeared in person to submit his findings. Members of the high-level LIC investment committee, bypassed in the investment decision, were summoned. They testified that if the matter had been presented to them, they would have objected to any dealings involving Haridas Mundhra, as he was already facing share forgery charges from the BSE.

The commission rejected the arguments of the finance secretary, who suggested that Mundhra could dump these shares in the markets out of fear, leading to a massive collapse.

Finally, it was ruled that LIC had been deliberately defrauded in making these investments.

Patel, together with the LIC Chairman G. R. Kamat and Managing Director L. S. Vaidyanathan, were identified as the main perpetrators. Even though the finance minister was not explicitly implicated, strong comments emphasizing his involvement were made, as seen in Justice Chagla's statement:

> *In my opinion, in any case, it is clear that constitutionally, the minister is responsible for the action taken by his secretary with regard to this transaction. It is clear that a minister must take the responsibility for actions done by his subordinates. He cannot take shelter behind them, nor can he disown their action.*

Following the scathing remarks of the commission, T. T. Krishnamachari resigned as the finance minister in February 1958; however, Prime Minister Nehru, presumably upset at the downfall of a trusted colleague, wrote to comfort him: '*Despite the clear finding of the Commission so far as you are concerned, I am most convinced that your part in this matter was the smallest and that you did not even know what was done.*'

The findings of the Chagla Commission were presented to the Parliament and adopted as a resolution in February 1958. Subsequently, the government appointed a three-member commission headed by Justice Vivian Bose as a Board of Enquiry in May 1958 to further examine the specific charges against the finance secretary and senior LIC officials.

The Vivian Bose Commission largely ratified the findings of the Chagla Commission, including the abuse of authority by the named senior officials. Interestingly, this commission went a step further, alleging that the government's actions to assist Mundhra through LIC seemed to be quid pro quo for two substantial donations Mundhra made before the share purchase: a sum of ₹1.50 lakh donated to the Uttar Pradesh Congress and another ₹1 lakh to the party's central fund.

Besides the monetary contributions, Mundhra had also promised to reopen the Kanpur Mills, which employed a significant workforce, since any closure could herald trouble for the party in the upcoming Uttar Pradesh elections.

The commission recommended the immediate removal of the finance secretary and retirement of the senior LIC officials involved in the scam.

However, when the Union Public Service Commission was directed to advise the government on suitable action against the erring officials, they chose to conduct their own assessment of the events. This analysis exonerated the finance secretary and managing director of LIC, while only 'censuring' the chairman. Despite formal dissent from one UPSC member (J. Sivashunmugam Pillai), the government quickly accepted this decision.

Haridas Mundhra was apprehended from his luxury suite at the Claridges Hotel in New Delhi. After a trial, he was sentenced to twenty-two years in prison.

Once the second term of the Congress-led government ended, TTK was re-elected to the Parliament in the 1962 elections. Nehru offered to reinstate him as a cabinet minister, though not in the finance portfolio. TTK accepted and served initially as a cabinet minister without any portfolio before he was appointed as the Minister for Economic and Defence Cooperation. In 1964, he was once again reappointed as the finance minister, a position he held for another two years until his retirement.

TTK passed away later in 1974, and Haridas Mundhra, the man who brought him down, passed away in 2018. LIC, the victim, carries on.

3

Hugh Cameron

The Artful Manager

> 'The Litigation with regard to the Royal British Bank proceeds apace. Chancery and bankruptcy are still struggling for the oyster, while the unfortunate shareholders and creditors will be rewarded with the respective shells – one in the shape of heavy contributions, the other with diminished dividends.'
>
> – *Bankers' Magazine*, vol. 16, 1856

Founding a new bank

In 1847, John Menzies returned to London after serving a fulfilling career at the Edinburgh General Register House, the home of the Scottish national archives. Initially planning to enjoy a peaceful retirement, he found himself struggling to contribute something meaningful to London. As he explored opportunities, the banking system caught his attention.

From his time in Scotland, Menzies was aware of the success of share and security-based lending businesses.

But he noticed that the model wasn't widely replicated in England.

Upon discussing his ideas with some friends, Menzies realized that a finance company modelled after the Scottish approach could be highly successful in London. Unsure of the next steps, his friends advised him to seek the counsel of prominent lawyer Edward Mullins. Mullins was a successful entrepreneur in London, with sizeable investments in several business ventures. Arranging a meeting with Mullins was not easy, but a common friend helped facilitate this.

In Mullins' opulent law office on Great James Street, Menzies presented his business ideas. Menzies was pleased to find that Mullins was already well informed about all developments in the stock markets, including that the London Stock Exchange was planning a major expansion soon to accommodate increasing investor interest. Consequently, Menzies was able to quickly convince Mullins about the viability of his new project; and in turn Menzies graciously offered to introduce him to several of his esteemed friends and business associates who could help.

Unfortunately, their ambitious plans were interrupted by an unexpected shift in Britain's economy. The low interest rates at the time had encouraged many to borrow heavily from banks for investing in securities, particularly in the new railway companies promising high returns. But by the end of 1847, many of these companies had failed, sparking a crisis in the stock markets. This was followed by massive crop failures in both England and Ireland, leading to significant food shortages, especially of corn. As commodity prices spiralled out of control, immediate imports from the US and elsewhere became the only option to alleviate the crisis.

The economy was in a free fall, and with the passing of the Bank Charter Act, 1844, which mandated all new currency issuance to be backed by either gold or government securities, any intervention by the Bank of England as the traditional 'lender of last resort' was no longer an option to manage the crisis. Recovery took time, eventually necessitating the repeal of the law itself.

During this tumultuous period, other pressing issues preoccupied Mullins and he lost interest in the finance company project. Menzies recognized that in this economic climate, a lender focused on securities would not have the appeal it previously had.

But it was imperative to do something. Nearly a year later, Menzies approached Mullins again, this time with a new proposal: setting up a joint-stock bank in England.

The benchmark was once again Scottish establishments like Union Bank of Scotland and Clydesdale Bank, which operated under joint-stock models. In this structure, bank ownership was not confined to a small group of promoters as per the usual practice, instead allowing a broad range of stockholders to invest and withdraw at will. These Scottish banks aggressively mobilized public deposits by offering attractive returns. By opening new branches in various locations, they ensured an ever-expanding customer outreach.

Managed by independent directors and professionals, these banks had moved away from the conventional models of small-scale lending and bill discounting models. Instead, they offered many innovative products, such as overdraft and cash credit facilities tailored for specific customers and requirements, which gained popularity among the business and trading communities.

Thanks to the growth propelled by the Industrial Revolution, these banks were able to successfully deploy their large pool of funds in key sectors like iron, construction and railways, generating excellent profits. Though they started with small operations, these banks quickly grew to take on even larger players like the Bank of Scotland.

Menzies told Mullins that even though the British Parliament had also passed enabling laws like the Joint Stock Companies Act and the Joint Stock Bank Act in 1844 to encourage a similar model, English banks were still wary of venturing away from their traditional systems. A few banks, like Marylebone Bank, had tested this model only to fail swiftly due to internal issues.

'Since none of our banks are stepping forward, some of the Scottish banks are now foraying into England too,' Menzies told the much-captivated Mullins. 'I know that Clydesdale is opening many new branches here soon, adding to the three recently opened up north.'

Menzies pitched that a venture like this, based in London, had high chances of success. But it required the backing of influential figures who could build investor and public confidence.

Mullins was convinced Menzies was onto a promising venture and once again offered his support. However, when they started meeting with affluent and influential individuals to present the project and secure their support, the response was disappointing. Many believed that such a bank wouldn't have potential beyond the metropolitan areas. Others, like the reputed Alderman Farebrother, felt that the present banking system in London was sufficient. Some of the more informed individuals thought that a joint-stock arrangement, which exposed promoters to unlimited liability, wasn't an appealing model.

Mullins and Menzies were on the verge of losing hope when they had a chance meeting with a man named Edward Moxhay.

A well-networked person in London, Edward Moxhay owned a prominent building in London called the Hall of Commerce, which had been formerly rented out to the Bank of England. The bank had recently exited the lease to cut costs, and despite the prime location and perfect furnishings, Moxhay struggled to find new tenants. When a mutual friend introduced Moxhay to Mullins and Menzies, they agreed that the proposed new bank, if things went according to plan, would rent the Hall of Commerce. A relieved Moxhay also offered that until the bank was ready to occupy the large premises, one of his smaller offices at Gresham Chambers could be used temporarily free of charge. He also promised to support the project by promoting it among his friends and acquaintances.

Moxhay introduced Mullins and Menzies to John MacGregor, a highly respected figure in London. MacGregor, an MP for Glasgow, had held several key positions, including the Secretary of the Board of Trade. This allowed him to interact with many notable individuals in business and commerce.

Delighted with this connection, Mullins and Menzies presented their project to MacGregor. After listening to their pitch, MacGregor agreed to join the bank's board as a promoter–director and readily accepted the chairman's role. John Thomas King, who ran an established printing business, also agreed to serve as a director with the informal understanding that his business would handle all the bank's future printing jobs.

Having MacGregor on the board greatly facilitated the project's promotion. Several influential businessmen and prominent professionals agreed to join the board as directors, thanks to MacGregor's connections. Humphrey Brown, the MP for Tewkesbury and MacGregor's good friend, as well as John Moxon, a retired stock exchange member, and Arthur Anderson, an MP for Orkney, agreed to be trustees for the bank.

Mullins was appointed as solicitor, while Menzies became the first secretary. James Godfrey Elster, who enjoyed substantial goodwill among wealthy investors, was selected as the manager.

After completing the preliminaries, they received permission to launch the bank as the British Bank. According to the law, the business could only commence after the required capital was paid up and the charter of incorporation was issued, which allowed the word 'royal' to be added as a prefix. This necessitated immediate issuance of a prospectus, followed by aggressive marketing efforts to enlist capital subscribers.

It was at this juncture that Hugh Innes Cameron, destined to play a significant role in the downfall of this ambitious venture, entered the picture.

Headwinds

John MacGregor knew Cameron from his days as the political and legal agent of the influential real estate investor, Sir James Matheson Bart. Learning that Cameron was formerly associated with the National Bank at Dingwall and knowledgeable in banking matters, MacGregor invited Cameron to attend some of the bank meetings. He requested that the latter take a close look at the draft prospectus before it was circulated among prospective investors. Cameron vetted the document thoroughly, even making comparisons with other banks that had recently gone public, like the English and Scotch Bank. His knowledge of banking, especially the insights into the Scottish systems, impressed the directors so much that they began to press him to join the bank, though Cameron did not accept the offer.

In February 1849, the British Bank issued its prospectus with a capital of £500,000, inviting investments in 5,000 shares of £100 each. A sum of £50 was to be paid up initially, while the balance would be called for later.

But before things took off, news began to circulate that an earlier project promoted by the same chairman, John MacGregor, had failed badly, leaving many investors with losses. Despite strong denials and assurances from the chairman, some of the prominent directors also felt unsure about continuing their association and decided to quit the bank. Though Menzies and Mullins tried their best to restore the sinking public confidence, even putting out several advertisements, nothing seemed to work.

Desperate, the board reached out to Cameron, who agreed to help salvage the situation. But now he insisted on being given an official role and requested that the board appoint him as the manager of the bank. This led to some friction, especially when Menzies felt obligated to honour the earlier commitment to appoint James Godfrey Elster as the first manager. Eventually, MacGregor stepped in to break the deadlock, arguing that Cameron could help the bank as the manager and convinced the board to approve the decision.

One of Cameron's first recommendations after assuming charge was for the board to reduce the capital of the bank from £500,000 to £100,000. This way, only £50,000 would be required to obtain the charter and start operations. Overriding objections from Menzies that the reduced capital was inadequate for a bank of this size, MacGregor helped Cameron push through this decision as well.

Once firmly in the saddle, Cameron began to steadily exert his influence on all key matters. Relying on the backing of the chairman, he did everything possible to establish his superior position while constantly trying to bring down the role of the two original founders. It helped Cameron's cause even more when Mullins and Menzies failed to handle certain critical situations effectively during the capital-raising efforts. One noteworthy incident occurred when the duo planned a large event to promote the project to new investors. The event was widely publicized, but only a small number of people attended, leaving everyone at the bank extremely embarrassed. This led to unpleasant spats with the directors, and later, it was only through the efforts of Cameron that they managed to reconvene and conduct the meeting successfully.

Mullins was astute enough to realize that the balance of power was shifting and began to soften his stance in favour of Cameron on many issues. But Menzies, who had a stronger sense of ownership in the project he had conceived, was adamantly opposed, leading to even more friction with Cameron.

The reduced capital proposed by Cameron was fully subscribed, and in September 1849, the bank received the Royal Charter, allowing them to change the name to Royal British Bank and commence operations.

But, even amidst the buzz surrounding the launch of activities, some of the directors began to feel a sense of disquiet about the project's real state of affairs. Alderman

Richard Hartley Kennedy, who was also the deputy chairman of the Oriental Bank, was one of the prominent persons who shared this feeling and, at a board meeting, insisted on the urgent presentation of up-to-date accounts.

That afternoon, Mullins barged into Menzies's office, sweating profusely.

'Mr. Kennedy has called for the detailed accounts,' he worriedly told Menzies, who failed to see what the concern was about when all the shareholder receipts and expenses had been accounted for fully.

'I've drawn some personal expenses from the company ... time and again ... in all, about £130,' Mullins sheepishly admitted to his friend. 'I'll put in a cheque immediately, but need a little time to have it cleared,' he pleaded, and Menzies decided to close his eyes, making sure that the presentation of the accounts went through satisfactorily.

Cameron was dissatisfied that, as Secretary, Menzies retained a lot of statutory authority, which he had recently demonstrated when an agenda for raising Cameron's remuneration came before the board. Asserting that his present remuneration was not commensurate with his experience and contributions to the bank, Cameron had submitted a request for an increase in salary, including a share of the bank's profits. Menzies objected to the proposal, and Cameron knew that as long as the secretary did not agree, such a proposal could not be passed by the board, even with the chairman's intervention. He also realized that as long as Menzies was around, many of his larger schemes would not fructify and decided that it was imperative to evict him from the bank at the earliest. But as the true founder of the bank, evicting Menzies would not be an easy task, especially when the secretary had the full backing of Mullins, the solicitor of the bank.

Cameron was still contemplating his options when he started noticing a shift in Mullins' attitude towards him. Known to support Menzies in all matters, of late though, Cameron began to observe a change in the way Mullins dealt with many of the secretary's objections. Because he knew Mullins was inherently gullible and susceptible to financial enticements, Cameron decided to test his theory.

He planned a business trip, ostensibly to solicit new investments from the northern parts, including New Castle and Scotland, and requested Mullins to accompany him. During the journey, Cameron gently sowed suspicions in Mullins' mind about the overpowering role of Menzies in the management. Cameron's pitch was that besides the present position of solicitor, Mullins ought to be secretary as well, thus ensuring they would both effectively run the bank henceforth. He also made generous financial offers to entice Mullins, like large reimbursements from the bank for fictitious travel and other expenses. By the time they returned to London, Cameron had won Mullins over, and it was mutually agreed that Menzies would be ousted.

Finding no monetary or other lapses to use against the secretary, Cameron and Mullins began to create several troublesome situations, which the unsuspecting Menzies suddenly found quite vexatious. Whenever matters threatened to escalate, Cameron and Mullins used their combined influence with the board, including with MacGregor, to make their crafty schemes work.

As the tides turned against Menzies, people seemed to fully forget even his role in setting up the bank, and all his protests fell on deaf ears. When the board summarily rejected his representation to explain things from his point of view, Menzies knew he had to put in his papers. As an acknowledgement of the founder's contribution to the Royal British Bank, the management decided to pay him a parting compensation of £400.

Shortly after Menzies exited, Mullins was requested to take charge as the secretary as well, and one of his first acts was to propose changes in the powers, responsibilities and remuneration of the manager.

All of Cameron's demands, including a seven-year term, were approved, together with the remuneration of £1,250 in the first year, £1,500 in the second, £1,750 in the third and £2,000 thereafter, as sought by him. The board even granted a suo moto increase in housing allowance from £200 to £250, as they felt his request was 'too low'. Apart from this, Cameron was also granted an incentive of 3 per cent on profits, to be later raised to 4 per cent. Nobody questioned why such an exorbitant remuneration was warranted at this early stage of the bank's activities when even the operations were yet to begin.

Keeping Mullins ingratiated with the extra payments and benefits, Cameron began to exert a free hand in all the key bank affairs. Chairman MacGregor was also mostly on his side, which cemented things even more when Cameron was given an unexpected opportunity.

The grip tightens

Thomas Bridges, a respectable builder who shared a close friendship with MacGregor, was promised a contract to furnish some of the new bank branches. On this understanding, he agreed to MacGregor's request to take twenty shares in the bank and handed over £200 towards the initial amount owed on the shares to him. However, unbeknownst to anyone in the bank, the chairman, who was in desperate need of funds, decided to temporarily appropriate the money for his own use.

The matter came to Cameron's attention when he ran into a dispute with Bridges and decided to cancel the contract, prompting the infuriated builder to claim repayment of the share money he had paid the chairman.

Realizing MacGregor's precarious condition, the crafty manager immediately offered to assist him by sanctioning a personal loan from the bank to repay Bridges. Cameron accomplished this by discounting an accommodation cheque issued in favour of MacGregor. Thereafter, he played on the chairman's financial weaknesses by offering him further support using bank funds, including £400 towards his qualification shares to continue as a director and an assistance of £400 against a cheque drawn by the former secretary (Mullins') brother, who was promised a senior position at the bank as consideration. The manager took care of all these documentation requirements in person. Each time Cameron helped MacGregor regularize these commitments, he was delighted with the firm hold he had on the chairman now.

On his part, though, MacGregor never felt he was being done any favours. Sensing that a slippery person like Cameron was likely to have some questionable past dealings, the savvy politician commissioned sources of his own to dig deeper into the man. As expected, what he discovered did not disappoint him.

MacGregor learnt that Hughes Cameron, who started as a law professional before moving into banking, had a long history of involvement in financial scandals. From early days, he had mastered presenting himself as an erudite and religious gentleman, capable of winning over the trust of influential personalities. His close relationships with eminent businessmen like Sir James Matheson and senior officials such as Joseph Parkes (Taxing Masters of the Court of Chancery) were the biggest testimony of these talents. Through confidential sources MacGregor learnt that at most workplaces, Cameron was known to be willing to resort to devious actions for his own gain.

Not too long ago, while serving as a parliamentary agent in partnership with George Bain and Theodore Martin (solicitors licensed by the British Parliament to present or oppose private bills), it was courtesy of his connections that Cameron had managed to evade arrest for serious charges of cheating. So, MacGregor felt that, in reality, he was doing Cameron a favour by suppressing this information and decided to let things be, at least as long as it benefitted him.

Apart from MacGregor, Cameron steadily gained the confidence of other important directors, such as the businessmen Edward Esdaile, Richard Kennedy, William Owen and John Stapleton. Others, like Humphrey Brown and John Gwynne, who ran the large Bushmills Ironworks in Ireland, were also provided quick financial support whenever they needed to stay quiet. Cameron slowly ousted all those who threatened his authority, including some of the first directors who were opposed to his autocratic ways.

Now firmly in control, Cameron began to award large contracts to and execute significant deals on behalf of the bank with his chosen collaborators. Despite his original promise to Edward Moxhay to operate the bank from his Hall of Commerce, Cameron decided to lease another building at Tokenhouse Yard as the main office. He also contracted an Edinburgh-based contracting firm with no prior experience in London to entirely refurbish the new bank. Traditional printing associate John Thomas King was abruptly replaced without notice, and the contract was awarded to a new printer – Wilson and Co. Many loyal early contributors were denied their due remunerations, including the commissions promised to those who secured initial share investments. Cameron also appointed his son-in-law, Henry Macleod, to a senior post at the bank with an exorbitant salary.

Wielding his significant power with the unwavering support of Secretary Mullins and Chairman John MacGregor, Cameron evaded any questioning of his actions. The official minutes always displayed such deeds as being in the bank's best interest. Only a few insiders were aware of Cameron's personal profit from these arrangements and that no deal could be entered on behalf of the bank without fulfilling his lofty demands.

Simultaneously, on the operational front, Cameron was able to smartly cultivate the impression that the Royal British Bank was flourishing. The interest rates on deposits were attractive, and funds had started to flow in from both large and small account holders, which Cameron and his team showcased as public faith in the bank. In August 1855, the bank was admitted to the Bankers' Clearing House, and new branches were regularly opened to propel business growth.

Cameron's true game began with managing and utilizing these funds. Claiming to innovate, these funds were represented in records as higher-return loans and investments to yield substantial profits. In reality, Cameron was redirecting large portions of these funds to directors close to him and other interested parties. Violating banking norms, large funds were invested in speculative ventures, though he was well aware of the greater risk of losing money compared to the projected fanciful returns.

Cameron devised parallel bookkeeping systems, including separate accounts for direct management and tracking of actual transactions while cleverly falsifying the official numbers to look bright and rosy. He also assembled a trustworthy team around him, comprising staff and accountants, who could handle all compliance requirements, like audits.

Cameron and Mullins went to great lengths to ensure the mandatory requirements were strictly adhered to, such as organizing regular meetings of the directors where monthly operations and official numbers were discussed. They also held annual shareholder meetings where comprehensive audited results were presented, leaving no complaints about transparency and no questions unanswered.

With the financial results showing good profits, Cameron persuaded the board to pay dividends between 4 and 6 per cent to all shareholders. He also obtained a sanction to increase the capital to £300,000, while advising the board to wait a little longer for share values to increase before venturing into the market.

Everyone – the employees, directors, investors and the public at large – believed the Royal British Bank was performing well and growing rapidly. Positive market reactions bolstered the bank's progress, leading to a steep climb in share prices.

Cameron painted a near-perfect panorama for everyone to see. Except for a few people close to him, no one suspected the orchestrated diversions, fraudulent transactions and account manipulations.

The reality, though, was soon to be revealed. The first rumbling emerged in April 1856. As joint-stock companies increasingly surfaced in Britain, intense discussions were going on in business and government circles about these ownership structures, especially in the context of unlimited shareholder liability. There was also a growing anticipation that, led by Robert Lowe, vice-president of the Board of Trade, a new law would be introduced in the Parliament to limit such liability to the value of their investment.

Amidst this, a new trade magazine called the *Joint Stock Companies' Journal* was launched in early 1856, focusing on the functioning of large joint-stock companies and banks in Britain and began to publish a series of 'investigative' articles.

By default, the Royal British Bank, which had no parallels among joint-stock banks in Britain, became one of the primary subjects of their analysis. The magazine deployed astute journalists with sources who could provide insider information, leading to explosive news about the new bank. Although they initially refrained from naming the bank, it soon led to a barrage of allegations against the Royal British Bank with stories of suspicious accounting and legal infractions.

At a hastily convened board meeting, some directors expressed dissatisfaction with the detrimental publicity and demanded swift investigation. But Cameron and Mullins, backed by MacGregor, dismissed it as petty libel spread by resentful competitors and disgruntled former associates. They persuaded the board to maintain their complete faith in the management.

Righting the wrongs

As the journal continued to expose dubious loans to directors and risky commitments to speculative businesses, other business publications jumped on the bandwagon.

Stories about substantial losses from failed investments, like significant mining interests in Wales that potentially threatened even the bank's insolvency, began circulating. The market reacted to these reports, leading to a drop in share values from £50 to £45 in July 1856.

Sensing the need for urgent repair, the board called an extraordinary general meeting of shareholders to clarify the situation. Even though a favourable resolution was passed at the meeting, public faith continued to spiral downwards and, by September 1856, the shares plummeted to a new low of £27.

The latest crash in market value induced panic among small depositors as well, triggering a wave of requests for urgent withdrawals. As people thronged all the bank's offices and branches, demanding immediate redemption of their deposits, it quickly escalated into a massive run no one could control.

The Royal British Bank, depleting all available funds, had no choice but to close its operations at 11 a.m. on 3 September 1856 and declare bankruptcy, leaving depositors stranded outside the doors.

There were public demands for an immediate inspection of the bank's affairs, overseen by a depositor-appointed committee. Yet the directors rejected the request, choosing instead to hire an independent accountant to verify and report on the state of financial affairs to the board.

The verification was conducted by a senior accountant named Coleman, and his detailed report was presented a few weeks later. Over a four-hour-long presentation, he highlighted the following key findings:

- Apart from the official books of accounts that were audited, several other records having a bearing on the bank's operations, including a personal ledger kept in the secret custody of Cameron, were found in his chambers at Threadneedle Street.

- Many unofficial entries and corrections in the financial statements were made in the personal handwriting of Cameron.
- Although a sum of £50,000 was shown as the subscribed capital to obtain the charter, a large portion of this was already spent on preliminary and other expenses like travelling and administrative expenses for setting up the bank.
- The real capital available when the bank commenced business in November 1849 was only £18,000.
- Large amounts had been spent on fitting and furnishing the new bank premises.
- Expenses spent out of the initial capital were incorrectly reported by deferring recognition to present these as utilization from later deposits.
- If the expenses were reported properly, the bank would not have met the capital criteria to receive its Banking Charter and could not have commenced business.
- Large overdrafts and loans recommended by directors were sanctioned by Cameron for speculative and illegal purposes as under:

Cefn Gwyne Mine: a large mining venture in Wales	£1,00,000
Langley Colliery Fields	£6000
Mr Tarte, Builder	£10,000
Mr Dent, plumber	£5000
A reputed Northern Baronet	£10,000
James Baring of the Chartered Australian Land, Mining, & Refining Company	£2000

On Security of the Islington Market Company	£14,000
On forged warrants connected with the estate of Joseph Windle Cole	Considerable sum
On Oliver's house at Liverpool	£13,000
On Westminster Improvement Bonds	£4000

- Most of these businesses and projects were fraudulent and failed quickly, making any possibility of recovery remote.
- The bank had not made any profits at all since inception, and the financial results were consistently falsified by the management.
- Although the entire capital of the bank was lost and bad debts were prevalent, Cameron presented successive accounts in August 1855, February 1856 and August 1856, reporting high profits and distributing dividends.
- Thomas Chandler, one of the shareholders appointed to audit the bank's accounts, was actually a medical surgeon with some interests in a brick-making business and lacked any accounting qualifications required for the position.
- The 'auditor' had merely accepted the doctored accounts read out to him by one of the bank's accountants, Thomas Craufurd, without conducting independent verifications of any kind.
- If accounts had been presented correctly, the shareholders would not have received any dividends.
- All dividends paid during the earlier years, averaging 4–6 per cent per annum, originated either from the company's capital or depositor's funds, both of which were illegal.

- Additionally, personal advances were granted to some directors and key personnel for unspecified purposes:

Humphrey Brown, MP, Director	£70,000
Hugh Innes Cameron, Manager	£30,000
John Gwynne, Director	£14,000
John MacGregor, MP Chairman	£7,000
Edward Mullins, Secretary and Solicitor	£7,000
Thomas Chandler, Auditor	£2,000
Total	**£130,000**

- Several violations in the terms of the charter of incorporation and other laws were noted, including unjust retention of the board seats by some of the directors beyond their term.
- Even while the share value was falling sharply, the board had actively planned to raise more funds from the market at a fictitious premium of £5 per share.
- Several personal expenses of the directors, key personnel, and relatives (such as Henry Macleod) were paid using the bank funds.
- In conclusion: the total liabilities of the bank were estimated at £539,131, against which assets considered good and recoverable were valued at only £288,644, resulting in a huge shortfall.

Based on these findings, proceedings were initiated in the Court of Bankruptcy, and warrants were issued for the arrest of the key directors and the manager. The primary charge was that the accused had conspired to cheat individuals who became the customers of the bank.

The trial overseen by Lord Campbell, the chief justice of the Court of Queen's Bench, commenced in 1858, drawing so much media and public attention that the prince of Wales arrived in person to sit with the chief justice on the opening day. Numerous rounds of intense and lengthy arguments ensued. But throughout the proceedings spanning thirteen days, most people following the case closely were left feeling that undue leniency was being shown to the people accused of this fraud, especially Cameron.

Even in summing up the matter for jury consideration, the honourable chief justice seemed to soften the issue, stating, '*Cameron had borne a high character, he was a sanguine man, and hoped that the bank would become a valuable establishment; it would be for the jury to say whether, being disappointed in that hope, he had not resorted to unworthy means, and become a party in a scheme for deceiving the shareholders.*'

Not surprisingly, though found guilty by the jury, the main accused, including Cameron, were acquitted of the charge that they had established and run the bank with the intent to defraud the public. Their only fault was performing certain fraudulent acts, purportedly to maximize the bank's profits. The jury also noted that given the lack of a specific law to handle this kind of violation and, considering this was the first offence of those accused, they deserved lenient sentences.

Cameron, along with Humphrey Brown and Edward Esdaile, found to be most involved in the alleged transactions, were sentenced to a one-year imprisonment at the Queen's Prison. Directors Richard Kennedy and William Owen received sentences of nine and six months respectively, while another director, John Stapleton, was fined one shilling for failure to report his suspicions. Henry Macleod, Cameron's son-in-law, was sentenced to three months. John MacGregor, who had run away to Boulogne in France even while the trial was in progress, died there in 1857 before the sentencing.

Due to the lack of clarity on whether shareholders were personally liable in such scenarios, the proceedings to compensate the depositors took much longer. One argument was that as a joint-stock company with unlimited liability, the shareholders were obligated to make up the losses to the depositors. An equally strong counter was that merely two hundred and seventy shareholders, excluding the directors and those directly involved in the fraud, could not be expected to compensate more than 6,000 depositors. Moreover, many of the shareholders were small traders, clerks, widows and servants, who themselves had suffered losses. Even the state, expected to facilitate a settlement, was unable to take a firm stance.

Ultimately, recoveries from the personal resources of the directors and key managerial personnel were scant, as most of them were already heavily in debt elsewhere. Even Cameron, who had the largest remuneration from the bank, was found to carry a large personal debt of £5,000 to MP Alexander Matheson.

Through a lengthy settlement process overseen by the court, several compromise arrangements were made and broken. Finally, only fractional sums were paid out and, by that point, several impatient depositors had already sold off their entitlements to financiers at large discounts. More than four years after the bank's failure, depositors received an aggregate settlement of £406,500 against their total dues of £542,000, resulting in a massive loss of £135,500. In the final settlement structure, the small depositors were hit much harder, with many not even receiving 10 per cent of their dues.

In the wake of the Royal British Bank's collapse, other notable banks, such as the London and Eastern Bank, the Northumberland and Durham District Bank and the Western Bank of Scotland, also faced similar fates in this period.

Experts flagged the lack of proper legislation over joint-stock banks, inadequate control systems and ineffective audit mechanisms as the key causes of these failures. These catastrophes, however, became the triggers for major legislative reforms in the corporate governance systems in Britain.

Note:

For better appreciation, the equivalent loss to depositors of the Royal British Bank in current money value is about £18.50 million ($25 million) or ₹190 crore.

4

Chia Teck Leng

The King of Gamblers

> 'Sometimes, the simplest solution or scheme is obvious only to a genius. The fact that his massive defalcations and movements of funds remained undetected for more than four years must surely attest to the correctness of the Prosecution's assertion that this was the work of a criminal genius.'
>
> – HONOURABLE JUSTICE TAY YONG KWANG of the Singapore High Court, in the matter of *Public Prosecutor vs Chia Teck Leng*

The early life of Chia Teck Leng was quite typical – born in October 1959 into a middle-class Singaporean family, he performed well in school and eventually gained admission into the esteemed National University of Singapore, graduating with merit in accounting. Chia launched his professional career at Arthur Andersen, one of the 'Big Five' accounting and consulting firms of the era. Over the years, he climbed the corporate ladder to the finance controller position at Swire Pacific Offshore Services, a large marine services firm. The steady ascent brought all the attendant benefits, such as a premium car and a well-furnished condominium in an upmarket locality, but generally, his lifestyle remained simple. He found his life partner along the way – a teacher at a Singapore school – and they settled into a quiet, happy life with their two boys. Recognized for his simplicity and friendliness, sincerity and integrity were the cornerstones of his personal and professional lives.

Chia Teck Leng was deemed a genuinely respectable gentleman in every sense. But his transformation started sometime in 1994. It was standard practice for his company to host events on luxurious cruise lines. During one such event, Chia was drawn to the bright lights and loud music of the onboard casino. Initially hesitant, the attractive hostess encouraged him to play. Reluctantly, he indulged and surprisingly, ended up earning more than he had anticipated.

Returning to his regular routine, Chia was pulled by the temptation of the casino. This attraction spread to other gambling centres. Loss didn't deter him, with the gambler's optimism luring him back to the tables. Unbeknownst to him, he had developed a casino addiction.

Chia's initial modest bets on roulette, baccarat or blackjack tables rapidly escalated as he continuously raised the stakes. But he dismissed his exceeding expenditures as insignificant at the gambling table, choosing to remain ignorant of the extent of the bets placed by the high rollers he admired.

Learning that gambling was also about bringing method to good luck, Chia began to integrate some strategies into his routines. One of these was to frequent casinos where he consistently won. The Stars Cruise's on-board casinos, from which he usually left with sizeable winnings, were a particular favourite.

'*That casino targeted the mass market, and the overall stakes were relatively low. Nevertheless, the experience was exhilarating for one so new to it. Like an inexperienced teenager succumbing to the lure of a newly discovered vice, I was soon hooked. Whether by coincidence or good fortune, I could never tell, but I was then a consistent winner. As the stake of my bets increased in proportion to the frequency of my trips to the casinos, so did my bank balance,*' he would later write.

The casino management decided to recognize his patronage by sanctioning him a special line of credit – an entitlement reserved for their most exclusive customers. The limit approved initially was $75,000, but as Chia's stakes increased, so did his line of credit. His reputation earned him similar privileges at other casinos, enabling him to gamble beyond his means.

However, the casinos eventually hit their credit limit and politely declined further hikes. Unfazed, Chia was determined not to let financial constraints hinder his gambling and began to fund his game plans with external borrowings. He quickly exhausted all personal sources, soon relying on the large credit card limits and personal overdrafts granted by banks due to his position as a senior corporate executive. Planning to finance his habits only temporarily with borrowed funds, he intended to settle his debt with his winnings. But the lure of casino tables had no beginning or end. Soon, Chia was scouring all possible sources for large loans.

Even when his personal debt levels crossed $100,000, Chia remained unconcerned. He was riding a winning horse, confident that such setbacks were temporary. These losses would reverse sooner than later – even before each evening ended. The most powerful validation came when the wind suddenly shifted, and his winnings soared past the magical million-dollar mark in a single day.

Chia also derived comfort from the gambler's mathematical logic, particularly the concept of a low 'house advantage'. This principle suggested that the number of times the casino could beat players was minimal. Even if it fluctuated between casinos and the games one played, the general house-win rate estimated by experts was only between 2.5 and 5 per cent. This meant the chances of a player winning at the table ranged as high as 95 to 97.5 per cent – a certainty Chia believed in more than most life aspects.

In his perspective, as long as he had large sums of money at his disposal, there was little to worry about. But amidst these joys, he encountered a major hurdle. He yearned to lavish his newfound wealth on high-end luxuries. The way his old world was structured, though, any drastic changes would certainly raise eyebrows.

With few other options than to continue life as a simple, loyal employee and a doting family man, Chia decided to create another parallel world for himself – one where he could immerse himself in all the rich pleasures he desired and could now afford. He successfully kept these two lives separate, even keeping his wife oblivious of his alternate persona.

Conceit and fallacy

One August evening in 1988, the winds suddenly changed again. Chia lost nearly $750,000 or three-fourths of his total earnings, within hours at the betting table. Torn by the faith that this, too, was temporary, he quickly lost the balance as well.

Almost in a trice, Chia seemed to have lost everything – other than the huge debts he had run up. A significant concern was the amounts owed to casinos and junket operators, notorious for their aggressive debt collection tactics. To appease the creditors, he partially repaid them using his monthly income from Swire Pacific Offshore Services, but it was insufficient to cover the vast debt. With consistent repayment delays converting into defaults and the mounting threats leading him to desperate thoughts, Chia realized he could no longer manage the crisis in this manner.

The only solution he could come up with now was to return to gambling and make some quick money. But he no longer had the time to accumulate a robust surplus, resorting to instant pursuit of larger stakes.

This meant leaving his usual mid-tier casinos, which catered to the moderately wealthy or high-income tourists, where betting and credit limits were moderate. Certainly not in the ballpark of what Chia was now imagining.

He knew that the only way to target sizeable winnings was to play at the really big casinos, frequented by the wealthiest and most serious gamblers. Such casinos typically fell into one of the two broad categories: those located at exotic vacation spots around the world and the exclusive clubs open only to members or special invitees. These establishments typically provided myriad amenities to their affluent clients, and there were seldom monetary or credit limits.

Chia targeted casinos in Australia, the United Kingdom, Hong Kong, Malaysia, Cambodia and the Philippines. But one thing was clear. Even if he managed to gain entry, it would still take a lot of money to sustain play in these high-stakes casinos – something he didn't possess.

All amounts diverted from his salary immediately

vanished into his towering debt. With no prospects of new loans and struggling to manage his existing ones, he started to explore better-paying jobs.

Upon discovering that Asia Pacific Breweries Singapore (APBS), a subsidiary of a global brewery conglomerate, was looking for a finance head, Chia applied and started the position in January 1999. Listed on the Singapore Stock Exchange, APBS was a highly reputable company with strong financial stability, and everyone, including the banks in Singapore, was keen to do business with them. As the chief financial officer, Chia was now responsible for overseeing the company's accounts, holding final approval over all monetary transactions and banking matters.

The pay was good but significantly fell short of meeting his large commitments. As repayments continued to mount and his ambitious gambling plans stagnated, Chia turned desperate, looking for ways to raise additional funds.

It was then that he spotted the opportunity to manipulate the company's bank accounts. APBS primarily conducted business with four banks in Singapore, from which Chia selected Skandinaviska Enskilda Banken (SEB), a Nordic bank. He began by learning how to duplicate the signatures of ABPS's top hierarchy, including the chief executive, Koh Poh Tiong, the director Ton Blum and the managing director of Fraser and Neave Tan Yam Pin, who controlled a large stake in APBS. Utilizing the senior officials' original signatures available in the company's financial records, he practised them until he could create impeccable reproductions. Along with this, he forged company letterheads, the official seal and other relevant documents.

Using these documents, he created a board resolution that authorized him as the CFO to open and solely operate a new bank account on behalf of the company with SEB. Chia also set up a personal account of his own, though with a different bank, as part of his scheme.

Once these accounts were established, Chia submitted a falsified board request to SEB seeking a large business loan for the company. He instructed that the loan was to be credited to the new company account opened with the bank. APBS being a very important client, SEB quickly sanctioned the new loan and credited the money to the 'new company account' as well. And using his sole access rights, Chia moved the funds from the SEB account to his own. Backed by this money, he gained entries to a couple of premium casinos and began to try his hand at much larger stakes than he had ever played before.

This was the first instance of Chia funding his gambling interests by defrauding the company's bankers, though, as always, he purportedly intended to use this only as a temporary measure until he had made back his money. But luck was no longer on his side and he lost the money with equal haste.

Like most fraudsters, Chia found ways to rationalize his actions, seeing his current predicament as a temporary setback and justifying his decision to seek additional illicit financial aid.

So, he made another loan request to SEB, and when these funds also evaporated quickly, Chia decided to carry his scam to the other banks as well. Soon he had swindled large sums from Sakura Bank Limited (later Sumitomo Mitsui Banking Corporation), Fuji Bank Limited (later Mizuho Corporate Bank Ltd) and the German bank Bayerische Hypound Vereinsbank Aktiengesellschaft (HVB), besides, of course, SEB. Everything was done so convincingly that none of these banks suspected anything. The bank managers were thrilled with the sudden chance to grow their business through more loans to a prized client like APBS. Chia enjoyed their increased respect, while ensuring a smooth transfer of additional funds to the SEB account he managed for onward transfers to his chosen casinos.

As the volume of transactions and transferred amounts grew, Chia set up multiple bank accounts around the world, including in Switzerland and Australia. He devised intricate layers of complex transactions to obscure the real source of funds and covered up all the trails in the company accounts. To avoid raising red flags with the bankers, he ensured there were no defaults in servicing any of their loans. He accomplished this by obtaining new loans to service the previous ones and rotating different banks for concealment. This way, all the bank loans remained current in the books of the company with no overdue payments, leaving the management and auditors none the wiser.

With a practically endless supply of money, Chia worked his way into some of the world's most prestigious private casinos, such as the exclusive London Ritz and the Crown in Australia. He gradually increased his bets, even to the point where a single bet of $100,000 meant little to him. Over four years, starting from 1999, Chia's reputation as a formidable high roller skyrocketed. Casinos worldwide courted him, offering luring indulgences, including personal charter flights and opulent suites, to have him play at their establishments.

All along, Chia cleverly maintained his parallel lives without causing any suspicion. He even earned a major promotion as Group Finance Head of the parent company, Asia Pacific Breweries Ltd, on a handsome annual remuneration of $300,000. Among the senior most executives of the entire group, he was handling worldwide operations of the group now. Family and all those close to him were extremely proud, obviously unaware of the other side of affairs. It was while expertly juggling these contrasting roles that Chia had a unique experience in 2002.

Downfall

Chia was now at a stage where winning or losing a few million no longer bothered him, confident that he could secure any sums required as loans from the company's banks. The minor stakes at the mass-market casinos he had started from seemed a distant past, though he occasionally revisited them for sheer nostalgia.

One humid April evening, he decided to visit one such casino on a luxury cruise. Quickly, Chia was assigned a smart young croupier, Li Jin, to help him at the tables. That evening proved particularly fortunate for him as he left with winnings amounting to $1 million.

From thereon, Chia started to perceive Li as his lucky charm and persuaded her to quit her casino job and accompany him on his gambling ventures. The attractive and well-educated woman quickly went from being his close confidante to his mistress. Chia even arranged a fake alias and passport for Li to facilitate her overseas travels with him. Chia bought expensive cars, exquisite apartments and costly jewellery and gifts, and together with Li, enjoyed life among the best possible luxuries.

Meanwhile, unexpected developments taking shape elsewhere, would soon reach him. Back in the 1980s, while Singapore emerged as a global finance centre, authorities recognized the need for a specialized department to handle white-collar crimes. The Commercial Crime Department (CCD), established in 1984 (later renamed Commercial Affairs Department or the CAD) was vested with expansive investigative powers to address the issue of frauds and allied crimes. Soon CAD developed into an extremely efficient unit led by talented officers who reported directly to the Ministry of Home Affairs.

One of its key focus areas was to combat financial and commercial crimes in Singapore, and their officers worked closely with banks, financial institutions, corporations, telecommunication companies and government agencies to achieve this. They also established numerous channels to gather information, which included data-sharing arrangements with investigative agencies around the world.

In early 2003, CAD started receiving information about suspicious international transactions involving the banks of Asia Pacific Breweries, with initial inquiries suggesting the involvement of the group's senior finance head. When it was discovered that the main suspect was one of the world's largest gamblers, the investigations intensified. It was revealed that vast amounts were funnelled to the finance head's personal accounts from the company's banks under the pretence of official loans.

On 2 September 2003, Chia was detained at his house for further questioning. Initially, he faced two charges of cheating and defrauding SEB of $3 million through forgery. Li Jin was also arrested as an accomplice in the scam.

Over the following months, investigators uncovered more details about Chia's dealings, raising many more charges.

Unlike many others in his position, Chia chose to cooperate with the investigators and voluntarily confessed to the charges brought against him.

Eventually, he was charged on forty-six counts, including four criminal violations and two counts of money laundering through gambling casinos. He was also accused of assisting his mistress in obtaining fake IDs and passports, which she used frequently for foreign travel.

When Chia's trial began in 2004, less than a year after his arrest, it was by far the largest commercial fraud case Singapore had ever witnessed. Chia's lawyers argued that their client, while guilty, was a first-time offender who had never conspired to cheat gullible individuals. On the contrary, he had generously supported large charities, such as relief for the floods in Cambodia. His lawyers pointed to the lack of proper due diligence and internal control failures on part of the banks that allowed for such a situation to have arisen. Further, they emphasized Chia's full cooperation throughout the inquiry and investigation, arguing that he had not prolonged matters by disputing charges. A sentimental appeal was also made via a letter from Chia's sons to the court, declaring that, although ashamed of their father's professional conduct, they wished to see their father freed earlier: '*We also hope that you will grant us our dearest wish to see our father as a free man again earlier as lessening his sentence, is not only making it easier on him, but a lot easier on us, the people who are truly innocent in this case. Thank you very much.*'

Unfortunately for Chia, none of these arguments swayed the Honourable Justice Tay Yong Kwang's ruling: '*I am touched by the tender words of the two teenage sons of the accused. The accused may have lost everything else, but he still has the immeasurably valuable gift of love from his two sons. Their young hands pen words that only mature mouths speak. To the two young men, whom I shall not address by name in this judgment out of respect for their privacy, I assure you the court appreciates your anguish and anxiety. Indeed, you should continue loving your father as his guilt is confined to the charges and none of them accuses him of being a bad dad. The court's sentence will probably disappoint you but that is not because the court does not believe you.*'

The final verdict clarified that Chia was not being penalized for gambling, as this was itself not an illegal activity in Singapore, but for the financial crimes that were '*directed to strike at the heart of banking and commerce*' and considered '*enough to feed many people for life*', warranting harsh punishment. The judge explicitly stated that his ruling in such a case, which had captured the world's attention too, had a role in reassuring the global business and investing community that Singapore, as a strong financial centre, would not take white-collar crimes lightly.

On 2 April 2004, Chia, forty-four years old, was sentenced to serve a prison term of forty-two years – the longest jail term awarded in Singapore for a commercial crime.

The authorities initially pegged the value of money defrauded by Chia across the banks in Singapore at $117 million. But when efforts were launched to recover whatever was possible from his assets and personal sources, officials managed to collect only about $35 million, leaving nearly $82 million untraceable. Later, in 2013, the quantum of assessed fraud increased further when sums swindled through casinos in Australia and other foreign locations were fully traced. Even though officials detected additional funds parked in overseas accounts or invested in Benami entities, especially under Li Jin's name, nearly $62 million was finally put down as lost due to Chia's gambling. After investigation, authorities managed to recover around an additional $35 million. The recovered assets comprised funds from multiple bank accounts, as well as those belonging to some family members and Chia's girlfriend, along with personal assets, such as expensive condominiums and jewellery.

Chia did not contest the asset settlement, but both his wife and girlfriend made claims that the assets weren't a consequence of his gambling and should be released. While most of these claims were rejected, significant gaps remained in settling the bank dues.

The four defrauded banks also initiated legal actions against Asia Pacific Breweries. However, Fuji Bank Suo Moto later withdrew its appeal and the other banks' suits were dismissed. The apex court rebuked the banks for pursuing a lucrative business opportunity without due diligence.

A few years into his jail term, Chia sought permission to write an article about the workings of casinos. His thirteen-page article, 'Taming the Casino Dragon', revealed many of the subtleties of these establishments, emphasizing it was neither the charges nor the commissions levied by them for playing there that kept this business going.

Instead, he said, it was the powerful, hidden devil called the 'house advantage', which every gambling aficionado trusts but can never permanently escape. In other words, while flattering, the 'house' always deceives.

Chia continues to serve his sentence at the Singapore Changi Prison to date.

5

Hegestratos

The First Fraudster

> 'Now between this man Zenothemis and myself there has been no contract or agreement in writing, as he himself acknowledges in his complaint. He states that he made a loan to Hegestratus, a shipowner, and that after the latter was lost at sea, we appropriated the cargo. This is his charge in the complaint. The same speech will suffice to prove to you that his action is not maintainable, and to make you see the whole of his plot and his rascality.'
>
> – DEMOSTHENES, renowned Greek logographer and advocate in ancient Athens, in the case against Zenothemis

Merchant friends

Once upon a time, around 300 BCE, two Greek merchants named Hegestratos and Zenothemis ran a modest shipping business in Athens. They put in all their money and borrowed heavily to buy an old ship, which they plied between various ports to transport goods. Hegestratos, better at customer relations, would get orders, while Zenothemis handled procurement, sorting and packing.

Despite their dedicated efforts, the orders were usually small, rarely exceeding a few *staters* (56.32 kilograms) of wheat or barley. Occasionally, they transported olives or grapes, but the orders were seldom large enough to secure a significant profit. The need to operate the vessel without a full load further reduced their margins. Claims from unsatisfied customers, whether for quality issues, delivery delays or other reasons, always resulted in direct losses.

The modest income barely provided daily sustenance and certainly did not allow for luxuries. Their financial struggles were a constant source of family discontent.

One day, Hegestratos learnt from a common friend that a prominent merchant in Athens, Protos, was looking for someone to supply and transport an extensive maize load. Although sceptical of his chances, Hegestratos decided to seize the opportunity.

Fortunately, luck was on their side, and Hegestratos managed to secure the order – several *talantons* (150 kilograms) of maize to be sourced from Syracuse, Sicily and then shipped to Athens. This was by far their biggest contract, and they knew substantial profits awaited if the order was properly executed. Protos generously agreed to defray their travel expenses separately, allowing them to immediately journey to Syracuse to finalize the purchase arrangements.

Actively exploring all options for sourcing maize, Zenothemis met some of the leading granary owners and negotiated a favourable rate. The only issue was that the merchants were unwilling to offer any credit, meaning the buyers would have to raise the funds required to finance the stocks. Borrowings were their lone option, but even with this added cost, it seemed like they could make a good profit.

While Zenothemis was finalizing the deal with the merchants, Hegestratos was hard at work on the shipping and financing arrangements, which were often the trickiest parts of such deals.

A major issue faced by traders at the time was that ships would frequently get damaged during the perilous voyage, often sinking at sea. Given the condition of their old ship, the partners knew this was a very realistic risk for them. More so when the vessel would be laden to capacity with the large load of maize to be shipped. There was little doubt that with the large debt they would assume, such a catastrophe would finish them off forever.

'Should we take on such a huge risk?' the worried Zenothemis repeatedly asked his partner.

But Hegestratos, an expert at such matters, had a plan in mind. 'Bottomry and respondentia contracts,' he said with a broad smile. Bottomry was a form of specialized financial arrangement that enabled vessel owners to borrow funds against the collateral security of their own ship. The borrowing would cover the costs of shipping as well as the repair of the vessel in case the ship ran into damage.

'The lender will offer almost the full value of the ship as a loan under this arrangement, and the ship owner will have to repay it with interest only after completing the voyage,' he clarified.

Respondentia was an extension of the bottomry arrangement, where, in addition to the ship, the cargo would also be offered as security to avail of a higher loan. Like the bottomry arrangement, the loan on the cargo, together with interest thereon, would also have to be repaid only when the cargo was delivered at the destination port.

Zenothemis was not sure how borrowing more funds would be the best option for them. At least not until his partner shared something vital about the arrangement.

'A big advantage,' Hegestratos now said, 'is that if a major calamity happens, resulting in the loss of the ship and cargo, the lender will forego the entire loan and interest, making it like comprehensive insurance as well.'

There was, of course, a further cost for this, which the lender charged in the form of an added maritime interest.

'Obviously, they factor in the occasional loss from a vessel going down while fixing these rates,' Hegestratos said, clarifying why this was much higher than the rates charged on normal loans.

They did their math and agreed that they stood to make fair gains, even with the higher maritime interest. In any case, the risk of the vessel sinking with the entire cargo was too severe to contemplate, deciding to move ahead.

Before returning to Athens, they established the conditions of the respondentia loan with a lender and sailed back with maize samples for Protos's approval. Zenothemis was content with the progress and the anticipated profit. But Hegestratos remained restless. Unable to shake off the thought of how much margin they were losing due to the elevated finance costs, he started exploring alternatives.

Then an idea dawned upon him – one that could potentially lead them to substantial wealth. Yet it was so outrageous that he chose to keep it from Zenothemis at this stage.

Treacherous plans

As soon as they reached Athens, Hegestratos met with Protos alone. He presented the Syracuse maize samples and made an additional proposal.

'We can procure a much better grade than what you have now seen ... at the same rates too,' he offered, 'but we need a special favour from you.'

Hegestratos suggested that considering the substantial financing costs, accessing higher quality maize would only be feasible if Protos provided an advance for the entire load. He knew that Protos was a rich man and convinced him that if the full payment was made upfront, the higher-quality maize procured at the same rates would bring in significantly higher returns. And the initial advance could also be recouped in a very short period. He deliberately avoided any mention of the financing arrangements to cover the risk to the ship and cargo.

Zenothemis was pleased that Hegestratos had managed to get a full advance for the materials from Protos. But knowing how much costlier the other maize variety would be, he failed to understand how they could honour such a commitment. Even with the savings in interest, they would not make any profits if higher grades were to be supplied at the earlier rates. Nevertheless, he decided to trust Hegestratos's judgement.

It was only when they were en route to Syracuse to close the deal that Hegestratos disclosed his actual plan.

In Syracuse, they would still procure the same grade of grains originally decided, now fully paid for using the advance from Protos. Records would show that this maize was loaded onto their ship. But in reality, they would dispose of the goods in Sicily itself – ideally in small lots to negotiate the best possible margins and avoid drawing attention.

Thereafter, using the fraudulent shipping documents, the bottomry and respondentia contracts would be executed, with the moneylender covering both the assessed value of the ship and the value of maize supposedly on board. Hegestratos had already made several cosmetic changes to make their ship look much better than its real condition and hoped to secure the best possible valuation from the lenders. Once the loan was received and stocks were disposed of fully, they would sail back from Syracuse.

'The next stage is the most crucial part of our plan,' Hegestratos explained to his utterly bewildered partner as they approached the Sicilian coast.

Hegestratos would deliberately damage the ship's keel so badly that the vessel would sink halfway through the voyage. Given the state of the ship, Hegestratos was confident that a few strong blows with a large axe would be enough to bring it down quickly. Meanwhile, Zenothemis would release the small safety boat kept on board and wait for the duo to row away as soon as the vessel began to sink.

'Sad ... that except for us, the whole crew will have to go down with the ship,' Hegestratos said, though without any tinge of remorse.

Once the ship supposedly carrying a full cargo sank, the bottomry and respondentia contracts would come into play, forcing lenders to waive the loan and its accrued interests. Hegestratos affirmed that since Protos had fully paid for the grains, they were legally his property, making any loss during the voyage his liability.

'The poor ship owners have no further liability,' he joked.

With his calculations, they stood to make a huge killing on multiple accounts, including the foregone loan and the proceeds of the grain sale. It was potentially more than enough for both of them to retire and lead comfortable lives.

Initially taken aback by the plan, specifically the sacrifice of the entire crew at sea, Zenothemis eventually concurred with Hegestratos' perspective of their joint best interests.

Once in Syracuse, they started executing their plan. They swiftly coordinated with grain merchants to supply the agreed-upon grains in smaller quantities and recruited an agent to secure optimal selling rates.

The bottomry and respondentia contracts were implemented as planned, and both of them were pleased with the notably higher ship valuation assigned by the lenders. Zenothemis initially baulked at the raised interest, but Hegestratos reassured him that these were merely hypothetical, as they would fulfil their plan and need not repay anything.

Hegestratos personally made out all the papers necessary to show that the ship was laden with the full cargo of maize. He made sure that no one, other than them, knew about the plan. The ship's crew, who were wondering why they were sailing back empty, were told that the original arrangement had not materialized due to unexpected circumstances. Thus, the ship set sail on the return voyage to Athens.

The journey was peaceful, and when they were almost halfway, Hegestratos decided that it was time to put their plan into action. He had ordered a surprise party to keep the crew distracted, while Zenothemis would stealthily launch the safety boat to row away.

'Let there be enough drink, music, and dancing,' Hegestratos ordered.

This was also to make sure that the axe-falls at the bottom of the ship would not be heard on the upper deck. Satisfied that everything was going well, Hegestratos quietly slipped away to the bottom of the vessel, armed with a heavy, sharp axe.

Plans go awry

The unexpected announcement of a party was met with enthusiasm and light-hearted excitement as the entire crew gathered on the upper deck. But, just as Zenothemis was beginning to head away to the safety boat to release it, the ship's captain arrived on the deck. He was in a chatty mood, insisting that at least he be told why this sudden surprise party was being held. Even as the other crew members continued joining them, he kept on talking, which made it impossible for Zenothemis to break away to unfasten the safety boat.

Suddenly, the captain paused.

'Do you hear something unusual?' he asked.

Zenothemis could clearly hear distinct thumping sounds from below but knew he needed to play it cool.

'No,' he shook his head, pretending to strain his ears to pick out any irregular sounds.

The captain soon heard the sounds again – it was as if something was knocking on the bottom of the boat, and the sounds were growing louder.

'We can hear something, Captain,' the crew on the deck confirmed.

There couldn't be any denial now that something unusual was happening at the bottom of the vessel.

Without wasting time, the captain rushed down, quickly barking out orders that some members of the crew were to accompany him to the lower parts, while others were to secure safety positions. He also instructed some people to stay on the upper deck with the ship owner and assist him in an emergency. Zenothemis, left with no other choice, had to play along, abruptly terminating his plans to unfasten the safety boat.

The noise amplified as the captain descended, but he couldn't discern what was causing the disturbance. But when he finally reached the lowest level, he reeled back in surprise.

By the dim light of an oil lantern, he saw Hegestratos standing at the keel.

'Sir!' the captain voiced his astonishment.

Hegestratos was similarly stunned by the sudden intrusion. But he was also a man of quick wit.

Swiftly, he hid the axe behind his back and tried to maintain his appearance of calm, asking, 'Why are all of you here?'

'We thought we heard something from down below, sir,' the captain replied.

Seizing the opportunity, Hegestratos responded, 'Exactly! I was resting in my cabin when I thought I noticed the noise. I didn't want to disturb anyone and decided to inspect it myself. But it must've been rats. Probably fighting badly. Everything seems fine. Let's return to the deck. I hear Zenothemis has organized a grand party for us.'

Hegestratos made as though to move away but did not stir from where he stood as he was still hiding the axe.

The captain cast a sweeping glance around the keel, seemingly satisfied that nothing required his attention. But even as he turned back towards the ladder, one of the crew members suddenly exclaimed, 'Sir ... do you have an axe behind your back?'

Hegestratos hadn't noticed a crewman conducting his own inspection who now stood behind him, pointing at the axe.

Maintaining his composure, Hegestratos quickly replied, 'I wasn't sure what the noise was. So, I brought this with me. Just in case ...'

The captain stopped in his tracks now. The thuds he'd heard had reminded him of a swinging axe. Most importantly, why would the shipowner try to hide the axe in this manner? Something didn't seem right.

He briskly walked up to Hegestratos and noticed that the part of the keel on which the shipowner stood looked freshly chipped. Also, Hegestratos was now feverishly trying to cover up the marks with his boots.

Sensing he was about to escape, the captain lunged at the shipowner. But Hegestratos stepped aside quickly and, before anyone in the group realized what was going on, the agile shipowner dashed towards the ladder. Amidst the ensuing chaos, he thought he could get to the open deck and swim out to the safety boats, which, he assumed, Zenothemis would have launched by now.

What greeted Zenothemis and the waiting crew on the deck was a perspiring, distraught Hegestratos bursting onto the deck in haste. Unaware of his partner's presence on deck, before anyone could speak, Hegestratos had leapt overboard. To the bewildered spectators under the dim moonlight, he seemed to be swimming increasingly further from the ship, as if seeking something. Only Zenothemis understood that Hegestratos was frantically searching for the yet-to-be-launched safety boat. Soon, he seemed to lose direction, flailing in desperation.

Hegestratos could swim, but not well enough to navigate the sea for too long, which had become too rough for even the crew members to make a rescue dive. And as soon as he realized something was wrong and there was no safety boat in sight, he began to panic.

As the captain and rest of the crew reached the upper deck, all they saw was a pair of hands waving madly before they submerged. Left with few options, Zenothemis confessed their whole plan, albeit by twisting the story to emphasize his resistance to the plan and repeated attempts to prevent his partner from carrying on with it. Whether the captain and crew believed him or not, Zenothemis was arrested upon their arrival in Athens.

The primary charges against him concerned cheating Protos by diverting his money to buy and sell grains fraudulently in Syracuse. He was tried in Athens and imprisoned for a long time.

During the trial, Demosthenes, one of the most respected statesmen and a prolific orator of the time, acted as the logographer – an ancient Greek system of preparing speeches for use in trials – and advocate. His speeches lambasted Hegestratos and Zenothemis's malevolent scheme.

In his own words (translated):

> *I will tell you, men of the jury, though Heaven knows it gives me pain to do so; but I must. There exists in the Peiraeus (Athen's port) a gang of scoundrels closely leagued with one another.*

Seafarers of the time would have said that the spirit of Hegestratos haunted the seas for many more years, as several greedy merchants tried to emulate him using bottomry contracts to cheat lenders by deliberately sinking their ships and cargo, often with the crew on board. Thankfully, these practices ceased in the shipping trade later.

6

Jeanne de Valois

The Friendly Imposter

> 'The Diamond Necklace, which was the fatal spring of all my misfortunes, the source of all my miseries, has afforded matter of public speculation to almost every rank of persons, in almost every kingdom in Europe.'
>
> – COMTESSE DE LA MOTTE, in her memoirs

Dubious royalty

In the mid-sixteenth century, Henry II, King of France, conferred the title of 'Count Saint-Rémy' on an illegitimate son born to his favourite mistress, Nicole de Savigny. It was nearly two centuries later that Jeanne de Valois was born into this lineage.

By then, the family had fallen into abject poverty, and the girl's father, Jacques de Valois, had become among the best-known drunkards in their little commune of Fontette by the Aube River. Though steeped in financial distress, Jacques was adamant that the family should maintain their 'noble' status and chose to style himself 'Baron de Saint-Rémy' after their ancestor.

His death, followed in quick succession by her mother's, left Jeanne and her two siblings to fend for themselves. Many times, even begging for daily food. Only when a few kind-hearted benefactors, led by a clergyman, took pity on them and relocated them to a decent living place near Paris did things improve.

While their brother was granted a commission at the military academy, Jeanne and her sister, Marie-Anne, were enrolled at a residential school there. The arrangement was that the girls would join the church after school. But when they emerged as educated young ladies, their views had evolved and the two of them now wished for a life outside of religion. The change of heart did not go down well with their caretakers, and the girls decided it was best to move away.

Courtesy of their training as manteau (dress)-makers, they secured placements with a noble family at Bar-sur-Aube known as the Surmounts, and under the loving care of Madame de Boulainvilliers, life became comfortable.

But after a little while, Jeanne became enamoured with her employers' affluent lifestyles, including their elite social status. Recalling her father's claims to the family title, she decided to self-style herself as 'de Valois-Saint Rémy' and was soon flaunting her 'nobility'.

Using her personal charms, she managed to catch the attention of a young gentleman of the family named Marc-Antoine Nicolas de la Motte, who served as an officer of the gendarmerie. The proud Surmount family was dismayed when the couple abruptly announced that Jeanne was many months pregnant with Nicolas's child, forced to consent to the marriage due to a lack of honourable alternatives. She gave birth to twins a month after the wedding, but the children did not survive long.

To Jeanne's shock, she found out later in the marriage that her husband would not receive a noble title or a share of the family fortune. But determined not to be swayed by the setbacks, she resolved to create the life she wanted to live on her own. During this time, her brother Jacques died in harness in the military, and Mary-Anne, who had rediscovered spirituality, decided to join the church as their sponsoring patrons had willed.

Cobbling together whatever they had, Nicholas and Jeanne decided to move to Paris, where they assumed the sobriquets of Comte and Comtesse de La Motte Valois and started a new life. Jeanne forgot everything in their past and immersed herself in the pleasures of the great city, making sure to catch the attention of the elite Parisian society.

Before she had realized it, all the funds they had travelled with depleted quickly.

Not one to be cowed down, Jeanne remained resolute to find new ways of making money. By now she'd understood that Nicholas was not smart enough to support her plans. With the relationship deteriorating, she decided to use her physical appeal to seek better partners.

One such person she befriended was Nicholas' fellow officer in the gendarmerie force, a charming man named Rétaux de Villette, with whom she began a relationship. Her selection was further reinforced when she found out that de Villette was adept at using innovative schemes to lure gullible targets, especially rich ladies. Upon realizing that de Villette could also forge handwriting and signatures with ease, Jeanne decided this was the right relationship for her.

In all likelihood, de Villette had not intended to be in a long-term relationship with Jeanne, but after discovering that she had a razor-sharp mind and many novel money-making ideas, their bond grew deeper.

Nicholas, though still the official husband, saw that it would benefit him to turn a blind eye to his wife's personal affairs and decided to join her and de Villette in their schemes to defraud credulous victims.

Things went well for the trio, who made a good living off of their small scams. But soon, Jeanne realized that this wasn't enough either. It was obvious to her that with their abilities, they should look for bigger opportunities. While hunting for potential targets, Jeanne's gaze fell on none less than the queen of France, Marie Antoinette herself.

Jeanne used her connections to gain entry into the Versailles Palace Gardens after learning that the queen granted short audiences to select members of the public. She returned several times after that, each time closely observing the queen. She also interacted with other visitors to learn everything she could about Marie Antoinette.

Jeanne learnt that Marie, born as Archduchess of Austria to the Holy Roman Emperor and Archduke of Austria, Francis I, and Queen Maria Theresa, had been betrothed to the grandson of King Louis XV (of the French ancien régime) as part of a peace treaty between France and Austria following the Seven Years' War. Her arrival in France as a fourteen-year-old girl was not received favourably by many members of the royal court, in particular those opposed to Austria. But over time, she had solidified her position, eventually evicting all of her opponents, including her father-in-law's powerful mistress, Madame du Barry. Many such heads were rolled, but by the time Marie had finished exacting her vengeance, she had lost interest in state matters, instead turning to a life of great luxury and merriment. Her expensive tastes in fashion, personal chateaus and fondness for gambling were all fodder for the local rumour mill. As were her choices in friends, including questionable male companions like Count Axel von Fersen, who had recently returned from service in America. Marie was well-known for her acerbic tongue, especially in the wake of criticism. It was still common gossip that during the Flour War, which drove up food prices and triggered shortages a few years ago, she had scornfully advised 'those who couldn't afford flour to make bread, to eat cake instead'. Everything affirmed the queen's temperamental self, which had also caused many people to dislike her, even within the royal court.

Jeanne had also observed that there was a select group of confidants who generally surrounded the queen. From what she had heard, they wielded considerable influence over Marie Antoinette. Most of them were women of the elite, like Marie-Louise and Princesse de Lamballe, or titled gentlemen like Baron de Besenval, Duc de Coigny and Count Valentin Esterházy. But encouragingly, this group also included a few from simpler backgrounds. Among these was a former governess of the royal children, who was later conferred the title of Duchesse de Polignac and presented a sprawling chateau within the palace grounds as her residence. Though considered rare by her supercilious standards, the queen was believed to nurse a soft spot for ladies of high birth who were not financially endowed.

So, Jeanne decided that this was the best way to gain entry into the queen's inner circle. As Comtesse de la Motte Valois, she tapped into every possible network so that someone with court connections would secure her at least a brief audience with the queen. When it was revealed that Queen Marie was pregnant again and would cut back on all public appearances, she pushed even harder.

Ensnaring a queen

Jeanne did not know that Queen Marie had an elaborate system in place to verify the antecedents of those she met directly. More so given the recent increase in her critics and opponents.

So, even though the name of Comtesse de la Motte Valois was formally mentioned in front of the queen, reports on the comtesse were not satisfactory. Many details pointed to a shady and suspicious past, and Jeanne was denied permission to meet the queen.

The response disappointed her considerably, but once again, Jeanne did not let it linger for long and soon came up with another idea. She decided that even if she had failed to actually befriend the queen, her financial plans might still work if she could create the public impression that Marie Antoinette was close to her.

Jeanne began by visiting the queen's private palace at the Chateau of Petit Trianon every day. Though she did not have permission to enter, she made sure her visits were noticed by the people who worked there, especially the guards and queen's regular staff. When questioned, she feigned an air of guilt and said she could not reveal why she was going to meet the queen daily. While pleading not to press any further, she made sure to pique their interests by insisting that the entire matter of her visits was to be kept strictly confidential in the queen's personal interests.

As she had hoped, the moment she turned her back, rumours began to circulate, and soon elaborate stories were being spun about the noble lady known as the Comtesse de la Motte Valois's clandestine meetings with the queen. Nicholas and Rétaux did their part to spice things up, adding a sexual twist to ensure that Queen Marie's latest female liaison was widely publicized in Paris.

Jeanne had been aware of the rumours surrounding the queen's suspected relations earlier too, involving both men and women. The royal court had been ignoring it to avoid drawing more public attention.

So, Jeanne was confident that this gossip would also not invite official attention and proceeded boldly with her plans. Once she was certain the news of her closeness with the queen had spread widely enough, Jeanne began to unravel her financial schemes. This proved much easier than she had anticipated. All she had to do was assure people that she would use her friendship with the queen to seek royal intervention in their problems. Jeanne convinced them that their issues would be immediately escalated to the queen, though formalities at the court might take a little longer for a complete resolution. Inevitably, Jeanne made sure to extract good sums from the grateful, though always in the name of donations for the charities she claimed to support.

Led by Jeanne, Nicholas and Retaux were delighted by the quick success of the scheme and the money they were now making.

This was when Jeanne met Cardinal de Rohan. It was while attending a public event as the Comtesse de la Motte Valois that she first saw de Rohan, one of the most powerful figures in the kingdom. She noticed something sensual in the way the cardinal kept staring at her that evening and decided it was worth investigating further. Her hunch was affirmed, when she learnt more about him.

Cardinal de Rohan was a member of the reputed de Rohan family, which had long occupied the position of Bishop of Strasbourg. Many of his ancestors had held prominent titles, making them one of France's most influential families. After his uncle passed away in 1779, de Rohan was elevated to bishop, which also conferred a status equivalent to a prince of the Holy Roman empire. While living in Paris, the cardinal also served in many important administrative roles, working closely with the king and senior members of the royal court.

But what gripped Jeanne's attention were the chatters that despite his exalted status as a holy man of the cloth, the cardinal was also passionate about worldly pleasures. The rumours claimed that apart from seeking bribes for bestowing his favours, carnal pleasures were a significant weakness too.

Given that she had already caught his eye, Jeanne became increasingly convinced that the cardinal was a worthwhile target.

But like the queen, he moved only among the highest echelons, and Jeanne was unsure how to approach him. Then she learnt of another intriguing individual who could prove useful in her mission.

This was Count Alessandro di Cagliostro, who was held in high esteem by the royal family for his mystical healing skills, known to share a particularly close friendship with the cardinal.

After learning that Cagliostro granted personal audiences to those seeking his healing services, especially those willing to pay a good fee, Jeanne sought a meeting with him. Claiming to be the queen's close friend, Comtesse de La Motte Valois, she requested complete confidentiality, which Cagliostro readily obliged. Assuming the air of a confused lady in need of counsel, she used her gentle charm to gain Cagliostro's trust before requesting an introduction to the cardinal.

Though Jeanne quickly realized Cagliostro was also a fraud, she listened patiently as he told her about his travels, how he learnt from famous people across the world and how he met de Rohan while in Lyon to advance his Masonic interests. Cagliostro's entry into the royal court was facilitated by the cardinal, using which he claimed to have quickly established a close bond with the royal family by summoning the king's departed forefathers to an official dinner. After a few more meetings with her, Cagliostro was only too happy to formally introduce the queen's closest friend to the cardinal. But in Cardinal de Rohan, Jeanne discovered a very different personality from what she had imagined.

Cardinal in line

Courtesy of his family riches, de Rohan had never found anything wanting, and the affluence was reflected in all aspects of his lifestyle. But it surprised Jeanne that under this persona, there was also an extremely tender man with an almost childlike yearning for emotional support. She soon learnt that the biggest cause of his vexation was that despite his high position, he did not enjoy the real confidence of the royal family. There was, however, a good reason for this.

During the reign of former King Louis XV, de Rohan was close to everyone in the royal court, particularly the dominant faction led by the secretary for war and foreign affairs, Duc d'Aiguillon. This affinity ensured that de Rohan also enjoyed the backing of the king's all-powerful mistress, Madame du Barry, who oversaw many aspects of the royal court, including foreign relations. This group was vehemently opposed to the idea of France entering into any understanding with Austria after the Seven Years' War and continued to express their dissent when the wedding between the heir to the French throne and Marie, the daughter of the Austrian monarch, was solemnized. Forced to accept the alliance, Duc d'Aiguillon decided that somebody loyal to him and Madame du Barry should be delegated to Austria as the French Ambassador, and de Rohan was assigned this important mission.

De Rohan enjoyed all the pleasures Vienna had to offer, though he was always conscientious about his role. After settling in, he realized that the best option was to cleverly balance his position and began to devise a plan that would earn the Austrian queen's trust while also pleasing his masters back home. When de Rohan learnt that Queen Maria Theresa was fed up with her daughter Marie's extravagant lifestyle in France, he hired spies to spread slander about her daughter's misdeeds to the Austrian queen.

He reasoned that if he could exploit the queen's discomfort about her daughter, he would please the duke back home and simultaneously unfold a personal plan of his own. So, while poisoning Queen Maria Theresa's mind, de Rohan secretly travelled to France to meet the young Princess Marie Antoinette where he revealed how poorly her mother thought of her, while telling others about the princess' improper conduct. This annoyed the young Marie considerably, and she instructed de Rohan to act as her confidant in Austria and keep a close eye on her mother's words and actions. At some point, he also began to think that the young Marie had fallen in love with him and, in turn, started to foster strong feelings for her.

Unbeknownst to de Rohan, reports about his devious game reached Wenzel Anton, the prince of Kaunitz-Rietberg, who advised the Austrian court on international affairs, and soon reached the ears of Queen Maria Theresa. The furious Austrian queen immediately took umbrage to de Rohan's actions in Vienna, including his lavish lifestyle, and conveyed her feelings to her daughter in France.

Given the influence de Rohan enjoyed with the ruling regime, the princess decided not to take any hasty action. But as soon as King Louis XV died and her husband ascended the French throne, the new queen began to wield her axe. While ridding the court quickly of all those who were close to the old administration and opposed to the Austrian alliance, including Madame du Barry and Duc d'Aiguillon, she ensured de Rohan was also ordered to return immediately from his deputation to Vienna. Only because of his high family status and religious responsibilities was he allowed to remain in the royal court. Though, at all stages, Marie made sure he would receive nothing more than his conventional family rights.

So, contrary to all expectations, de Rohan had returned to a very different royal court at the Versailles palace. Not only were all his former friends and allies gone, but he was now in the company of those who disliked, if not hated, him. Forced to seek help from outsiders like the king of Poland to be nominated as a cardinal, nothing changed even after he assumed the important seat of Bishop of Strasbourg.

Most painfully, the very woman he deeply loved, Queen Marie herself, was at the top of the list of his adversaries.

Jeanne had heard some of these stories from Cagliostro, but the details came directly from the cardinal, who was becoming increasingly at ease in the company of the comtesse. There was nothing de Rohan did not share with his charming and compassionate friend as their friendship grew and the meetings became more frequent. Soon after, Parisian society learnt that the queen's friend, Comtesse de la Motte Valois, had also become the new mistress of Cardinal de Rohan.

Jeanne knew better than to deny this, as she began to plan how to profit from the connection. She knew that the cardinal's greatest desire was to win back Marie Antoinette's favour and regain a place of respect in the court. She also knew that a good part of the affection de Rohan was showering on her was in the bona fide belief that the comtesse was a close acquaintance of the queen.

Jeanne set out to spin a new web of deceit around the cardinal. She began by implying subtly that she could persuade her close friend, the queen, to at least hear what the cardinal had to say. De Rohan was naturally overjoyed with the offer and agreed to do anything in return if Jeanne could truly accomplish the impossible.

Jeanne began to play the role of an intermediary between the cardinal and Queen Marie, taking care not to raise any suspicions. She told him that while she was initially furious and refused to even mention his name, Queen Marie had gradually come around to listening to the cardinal's sincere apologies and fervent pleas. Jeanne created the impression that the ice between the cardinal and the queen was thawing fast, assuring that Marie, too, had always harboured soft feelings for him. Regrettably, she had fallen prey to some people who poisoned her mind against him at some point.

However, the clouds had now cleared and she knew the truth.

Soon, Jeanne told the besotted cardinal that the queen had openly declared her deepest affection for him and wished to establish regular communication through letters. De Rohan unleashed the most romantic prose and verses known to him and was on cloud nine when Jeanne handed over an immediate response from his dear beloved, responding in the same vein.

What Jeanne had done was to rely on the forging skills of Rétaux de Villette to create the queen's reply. As the letters became a regular affair, she let the ink flow liberally to convince the love-blinded Cardinal that Marie was confiding in him now. The poor man's joys heightened further when Queen Marie confirmed that the cardinal was officially pardoned and would soon be appointed as one of the most prominent ministers in the royal court. The only minor difficulty Jeanne encountered at times was to thwart the love-torn cardinal's frequent appeals to set up a personal meeting with his paramour. She achieved this by citing the enormous risk of attempting such a secret meeting.

Once she was certain that the cardinal had well and truly fallen into her net, Jeanne slyly introduced her own personal agenda through Marie's letters.

Marie now sought the cardinal's assistance in streamlining some of the official regulations that made it difficult for the queen to directly contribute to some of the charities and social causes she supported. She wrote that if the cardinal was willing to support this proposal, the funding arrangements could be coordinated by her trusted friend, Comtesse de la Motte Valois. Just as Jeanne foresaw, the cardinal backed the idea without any hesitation, and thereafter, whenever the queen made him a monetary request, the enamoured gentleman would hand over to Jeanne many times more than what was requested.

Jeanne, who was overjoyed with how things had turned out, kept the scheme going, taking care not to raise the cardinal's suspicions by making too many demands.

Then, one day, she had two unexpected visitors – the renowned Parisian jewellers Charles Auguste Boehmer and Paul Bassange, who desired to meet Comtesse de la Motte Valois with a strange request.

More than a decade ago, the former king, Louis XV, had summoned these brilliant jewellers to his court to give them a rare command. The order was to create a diamond necklace like no other, which he intended to give to his beloved mistress Madame du Barry. No expense was to be spared, and a royal commission was formally established, authorizing the state to fund the entire cost of this necklace without limit.

Acting on this, the excited jewellers began to work on the design of the masterpiece, which was completed after many rounds of revision and approval. They then travelled to many places to personally select the best possible diamonds available in the world, collecting 647 of the finest stones, close to 2,800 carats. But just as they were in the final stages of setting the necklace, King Louis XV contracted smallpox and suddenly passed away. Soon after his ascension, the new king and his consort exiled many senior members of the former court, including Madame du Barry.

The jewellers were understandably troubled by this development. Especially when they were carrying a huge liability of 2 million livres towards the diamonds purchased for making the invaluable necklace. Backed by the royal commission, all the diamonds had been procured on the guarantee of the earlier king's order, which unfortunately stood nullified following his death. But they also trusted that even if it was technically a matter of discretion, in such circumstances, the successor to the throne would honour the earlier liability, and the jewellers rushed to the new king with their request.

King Louis XVI, however, felt that this decision ought to be left to his wife and agreed to buy it for her if Queen Marie Antoinette so desired.

The jewellers approached the young queen to present the grand necklace, pinning all hopes on her well-known fondness for expensive ornaments. But they were in for a huge shock.

Love's doings

When the eminent jewellers proudly presented their masterpiece before her, Queen Marie refused to show the slightest interest in the necklace. She summarily dismissed them from her presence, claiming that the ornament was far too expensive.

The jewellers tried many more times to persuade the queen to change her mind, including during the grand celebrations marking the birth of her first son. But she refused to budge, advising them to sell it elsewhere.

The jewellers, now frantic, tried their best to sell the necklace to someone else, but given the huge price, found no takers.

In desperation, they went back to the queen, and this time, the much-respected senior jeweller Charles Auguste Boehmer literally fell at her feet, pleading that they would have to kill themselves unless she reconsidered. But Marie remained uninterested, even remarking that the price of the fancy necklace could buy seventy-four naval ships, which France needed more desperately. She sent them away with the advice that instead of trying to sell the necklace as a whole, they ought to break it up into individual stones and sell them instead.

Only later did the jewellers learn the real reason behind the queen's sudden show of austerity.

Marie Antoinette still harboured a deep hatred for Madame du Barry, the person for whom the necklace was created. Now it was her wish that the necklace be destroyed.

Jeanne heard the tale patiently, but she wondered why the two renowned jewellers wanted to share all this with her. A little later, though, she understood she was meant to intervene.

'Only recently,' Boehmer said, 'did we hear that the queen listens to her dearest new friend, the noble lady, Comtesse de la Motte Valois, above everyone else.

They were hopeful that the comtesse could make the queen reconsider her decision. Naturally, they were willing to provide excellent rewards in exchange for her assistance.

Jeanne's immediate impulse was to refuse the proposal, especially when it directly involved the king and queen. But when she found that the cardinal was fully ignorant of the developments around the fabulous necklace, Jeanne began to wonder if there was a great money-making opportunity hidden in this episode. So, she told the relieved jewellers she would try to push their cause with the queen.

Soon, she was working on the finer details of a scheme, also briefing Rétaux and Nicholas about the parts each of them had to play in this grand con. She informed de Rohan that the queen wanted her to relay a special message about a rare necklace Marie had set her mind on. Ever since Marie had heard about this rare ornament, she wanted to own it very badly. But the queen feared that making such a costly purchase, particularly when the nation's finances were reeling, could invite a lot of criticism. Given the need for secrecy, Marie had devised an alternate plan.

Jeanne convinced de Rohan that as the only person Marie trusted to handle such a matter, she wanted him to finalize the purchase on her behalf. The queen was certain that, backed by her personal guarantee, the jewellers would accept settlements in the form of post-dated payment notes issued by the cardinal. In turn, Marie would arrange for the funds to be remitted privately to the cardinal before the payment notes fell due.

But this time, the cardinal hesitated. Jeanne knew that while love had temporarily blinded him, the cardinal was no fool and could be tempted to use this request to try to meet the queen in person. It was not as if the cardinal did not have access to the palace if he wanted to, and Jeanne dreaded to think about what the queen's reaction would be if he actually met her to discuss the necklace.

As it became clear that a simple letter from the queen would not suffice this time, Jeanne decided that if only an illusion of a quick tete-a-tete with Queen Marie could be created, the deal could be sealed. She commissioned Nicholas and Rétaux with the urgent task of finding someone who could pass for Queen Marie, at least under dim lights. And to her delight, they managed to identify a prostitute named Nicole le Guay d'Oliva, who, apart from having a passable resemblance to the queen, was also used to undertaking her professional activities as a noble lady under the fake title of Baroness d'Olivia. It also didn't hurt that the lady was familiar with the royal gardens, having served prominent clients there. Jeanne personally trained d'Olivia on how to conduct herself and speak like Marie, recalling everything she had learnt about the queen from her previous visits. Ensuring that everything was in order, Jeanne expressed Marie's desire for a personal meeting, sending the cardinal over the moon.

On a beautiful spring night, with the light all but gone down fully, the clandestine meeting between Cardinal de Rohan and 'Queen Marie Antoinette' took place at one of the most scenic parts of the Versailles Palace gardens, called the Grove of Venus. Though with her head covered to avoid any risk of exposure, the sight of his beautiful ladylove in flowing white muslin robes mesmerized de Rohan completely. And even if it was a short meeting, the poor man left the garden clutching the rose gifted by her to his heart, shivering violently with excitement. He had barely managed to utter his concurrence to Marie's request to buy the necklace for her.

Just as Jeanne hoped, the smitten cardinal had fallen completely for the scheme, so she quickly handed over another letter in which Marie conveyed her desire to wear the necklace at one of the palace's forthcoming celebrations.

De Rohan immediately began negotiations with the thankful jewellers, who generously struck down the final price to 1.6 million livres. It was agreed that the payment would be made in four equal instalments through the cardinal's payment notes, backed by the queen's confirmation. As instructed by Marie, the cardinal would personally receive the necklace from the jewellers at his palace, from where it would be delivered to the queen by a trusted messenger.

Jeanne created all the necessary documents, including the fake guarantee issued by Queen Marie in favour of the jewellers and the unsuspecting cardinal duly issued his payment notes. The jewellers handed over the necklace to the cardinal at his palace, from where Rétaux – posing as the queen's official messenger – took delivery. Nicholas and Rétaux immediately broke the necklace, ripping out each stone, with Nicholas fleeing to England to sell each diamond individually. The plan was for Jeanne and Rétaux to finish up any outstanding business in Paris and join Nicholas as soon as possible. They would then retire to a luxurious lifestyle far from the reach of French law. The plan was executed precisely thanks to Jeanne's skill and precision. But things were not about to end there.

Jeanne knew that trying to end the relationship with de Rohan abruptly would invite suspicion, and the cardinal was certainly powerful enough to come after her with vengeance. She now decided that it was best to wait till the diamonds were sold and they had enough money to escape.

Increasingly, Jeanne became convinced that if she played her cards well, she could even conceal her own role in this episode. For now, she decided that it was best to let the cardinal remain in his dreamy state until she was ready to strike.

So, the joyous cardinal continued to live in his mythical world, regularly exchanging letters laced with passionate and amorous sentiments with his love, Marie.

What necklace?

Days went by, and many festive occasions came and went. Every time, the cardinal would eagerly go to the palace, hoping to see the queen wearing the precious necklace he had bought for her. But it never happened, and he began to lose patience. Jeanne, however, kept mollifying him with doting assurances that the queen was still waiting for the right moment. She believed that in a few more months, she would be able to finish everything in Paris as planned and flee.

But certain things that Jeanne had not anticipated in her plan were taking place. Boehmer and Bassange did not merely see themselves as businessmen, priding themselves on being brilliant artisans. Though they were overjoyed to recover their money, it bothered them that even months after the sale, the queen had never exhibited their masterpiece in public. But the last thing they also wanted was to upset the queen any further over the necklace, so they waited patiently.

The initial shock came when the first instalment agreed upon with the cardinal fell due for payment. The jewellers sent the payment note for encashment, never doubting anything for a moment. But since the queen had not transferred the funds to him and de Rohan did not want to take any risks, he refused their payment.

De Rohan assumed that, in the midst of her busy schedule, Marie had forgotten about the commitment. He told the jewellers to wait a little longer because sending her a reminder on this account would be a major embarrassment.

The gentlemen waited, confident they had the queen's personal guarantee.

But as de Rohan continued making the same plea, their fears grew and Boehmer decided to send a very respectful and humble reminder directly to the queen. Beginning with his concern that the necklace was not to her liking, as she had not yet worn it publicly, he concluded with a request that she make the pending payment at her earliest convenience.

When the letter reached Queen Marie Antoinette, she was irate that this was yet another attempt by the jewellers to sell her the necklace, ordering the letter to be burned without any response.

Boehmer, who knew one of the queen's aides named Madame Campan well, was furious when he learnt from her how rudely his letter had been handled. In a fit of rage, he remarked that the queen had broken her promise after purchasing such a valuable necklace. Madame Campan was familiar enough with the queen's wardrobe to know that there was no such grand necklace as claimed, and she insisted that Boehmer clarify his grave accusation.

Suspicions provoked, Boehmer broke the promise of confidentiality given to the cardinal and told Madame Campan everything that had happened, including how de Rohan had mediated the purchase of the necklace with the queen's close friend, the comtesse, and how the cardinal had issued his payment notes backed by a confirmation from Her Majesty. Noticing the lady's astonishment, Boehmer emphasized that he and his partner had personally handed over the necklace at the cardinal's residence for collection.

Whatever doubts Madame Campan nursed about Boehmer spinning a fantasy tale ended when the latter showed her the signed assurances from the queen confirming the instalment payments as agreed. Although he did not express it explicitly, Boehmer expressed his strong suspicion that the queen was having an affair with the cardinal, mediated by the comtesse. When the queen's aide informed her of the shocking news, Marie decided to immediately inform her husband.

King Louis XVI issued urgent orders to summon Cardinal de Rohan and requested that the queen also be present. Given the possibility of official documents being misused, the official keeper of seals was also directed to be in attendance.

Cardinal de Rohan was in the midst of religious duties when he received the urgent summons and rushed to the palace in pontifical robes, though he had no idea why he had been called there. His confusion was heightened by the queen's presence.

'I demand to know where the necklace is right now,' His Majesty finally said.

A thoroughly bewildered cardinal replied that it was with the queen, which she promptly denied. De Rohan's immediate thought was that, as the necklace deal had become exposed, she was trying to hide the truth. But after a little while, he realized there could be more to the affair than he believed and decided that the best option was to come fully clean.

He shared everything, including how the queen's dearest friend, Comtesse de la Motte Valois, brought Marie and him together, relayed their passionate letters to each other, and even arranged a secret rendezvous in the palace garden leading to the purchase of the necklace. De Rohan insisted that he had proof of everything, even Marie's request to purchase the necklace on her behalf under personal guarantees.

Marie Antoinette furiously rebutted these allegations,

saying that she knew no one by the name of Comtesse Jeanne de la Motte Valois and that she had never written to or met the cardinal anywhere. She reiterated that she had always disliked and detested him, ever since his days in Austria and that nothing had changed.

The outraged cardinal sought permission to have his secretary bring all the correspondence from Queen Marie to him, claiming that a parallel search of her private chambers would reveal his letters to her too.

Marie readily agreed to any search, though the king felt that this should wait until the letters purportedly sent by her were first produced.

The cardinal's secretary brought the correspondence, and there was plenty of it. But as soon as the keeper of seals examined the letters, he announced that the signatures were not those of the queen. One of the capital mistakes Jeanne, or rather Rétaux de Villette, who had created all the forged letters, had committed was signing the letters as 'Marie-Antoinette de France'. Possibly from her lack of proper noble bearings, Jeanne was also unaware that French royals always signed in their baptismal names, and Queen Marie always issued her letters as 'Maria Antonia Josepha Johanna' only. One can only imagine that the wiser cardinal also missed noticing this amidst the letter's other passionate contents.

When he realized that it was not the queen who had written the letters, the king's rage grew. There was already so much libel about his wife, and even if he had chosen to ignore it earlier, King Louis XVI was severely affected by the slander since the birth of their son. And it angered him terribly to hear the cardinal openly profess his feelings for the queen. It also seemed unacceptable that a man of such high nobility and royal position had not spotted such a basic flaw in the queen's forged signatures.

King Louis XVI was soon convinced that the entire episode, including the alleged role of Comtesse Jeanne de la Motte, was the work of de Rohan himself. He was certain that this was an attempt to retaliate against the royal couple for ignoring him in court.

Given the gravity of the situation, the king issued an immediate ruling that Cardinal de Rohan had purposefully committed treason with the help of lowly fraudsters as aides and was to be arrested immediately.

Martyr

Before she knew what had transpired, Jeanne was also taken into custody. So, too, were Rétaux, the sex worker Nicole d'Oliva and the mystic healer Count Cagliostro. Only Nicholas remained free, as he was away in England trying to sell the diamonds.

All the accused, including the cardinal and the women, were sent to Bastille Prison, and it seemed forgone that the terrible guillotine would fall on their heads very soon. But things took a very different turn after that.

The fiscal affairs of France were deteriorating fast, and King Louis XVI was facing difficulties addressing the key issues of economic slowdown, population explosion and rising unemployment. The problems were worsened by successive harsh winters, causing huge crop failures and soaring food prices. He decided to impose more taxes in order to finance administrative expenses and royal affairs, pushing people to new lows of poverty and starvation.

At the same time, none of these ground realities appeared to have affected the extravagant lifestyle of the royals, especially Queen Marie Antoinette. The mood on the streets was one of frustration, which quickly turned into rage as anger against those in power grew stronger by the day. In response, the administration decided to deal with the public outrage using force, and hundreds of protestors were taken into custody each day. As the fortress-turned-prison of Bastille filled with marchers and dissenters, it started to become a symbol of grave injustice to ordinary people as well. Once people heard of the diamond necklace scandal, the judgement on the street was immediately in favour of the accused housed in Bastille.

Cardinal de Rohan was a revered man, and the royal court's dislike for him was known. People believed that the episode was a stunt orchestrated by the evil Queen Marie Antoinette to grab the priceless necklace by framing him.

Jeanne and her fellow accused also received plenty of public empathy as mere commoners who had tried to somehow eke out a living in these tough times. The consensus emerged that a terrible injustice had been meted out by the fiendish administration, and people began to strum up stories of the brutal torture they were being subjected to at Bastille. Leading up to the trial, the affair continued to generate tremendous interest, while revulsion for the royal family mounted rapidly. Queen Marie, perceived as the symbol of the nation's troubles, was now the major target of everyone's anger.

The trial in the necklace matter commenced before Parlement de Paris at the royal palace in May 1786 and drew so much attention that the proceedings were under constant public scrutiny. Under the circumstances, members of the court hearing the case also faced immense pressure in trying to be fair in the public's eye, while upholding the king's will.

There was also the issue of Cardinal de Rohan's exalted holy status, and his close relations with many European sovereigns, to be kept in mind.

After lengthy hearings, the court eventually decided that Cardinal de Rohan, who had acted in the bona fide belief that he was discharging the queen's royal instructions and was innocent in the necklace scandal, should be released from Bastille. But to save the king's face, the court also ruled that it was solely up to His Highness to pardon or punish de Rohan for trying to establish a personal relationship with the married queen, including attempting to meet her in a secret night rendezvous.

The very least King Louis XVI could do to comfort his bitterly outraged queen was to banish de Rohan from the royal court and order him to pay a large penalty to the state for his misdeeds.

The cardinal's friend, Cagliostro, was found innocent because he was unaware of these schemes, as was the sex worker, Nicole d'Oliva, who did not know she had become a pawn in a larger fraud.

Rétaux de Villette was found guilty of having forged the letters using the queen's name and banished. Though not present, Nicolas de la Motte was also found guilty and sentenced to serve as a slave in a rowing galley.

The harshest punishment was reserved for Jeanne.

After concluding she was the real brain behind the scheme, the court ordered her to be publicly stripped, whipped and physically marked as a thief with a branding iron before being sent to a special prison for women in Salpêtrière.

Even those members of the public who may have thought the court's order was fair were completely changed when they witnessed the terrible execution of Jeanne's sentence in public. Her loud wails of distress and pain as she was violently charred by the steaming branding rod elicited the strongest possible sentiments of anger and resentment among all those present. In many ways, it became a catalyst for the historical events that followed.

Jeanne spent close to two years at the Salpêtrière Prison before she chalked up a plan to escape. Cutting her hair short and dressing up as a boy, she managed to fox the prison guards and flee to England.

Sadly, neither Rétaux nor Nicholas could be found there as she hoped, and she was forced to live a frugal life with few resources. Forced into debt, she tried to publish her memoirs, hoping that the story of the diamond necklace would catch the attention of some readers, but nothing significant came of it.

From the occasional news she heard, Jeanne knew that back in France, the 'Commoners', who were officially identified as the Third Estate in the Estates General Assembly had raised a strong rebellion against the First (Clergy) and Second (Noble) Estates, eventually overruling King Louis XVI's authority to constitute a separate National Assembly. A little later, around mid-1789, violence broke out in Paris. The terrible Bastille Prison had been stormed by revolutionaries, symbolizing a mass movement determined to throw out the royals.

Jeanne heard that for the first time, the guillotines at Bastille were busy decapitating royal heads instead of the commoners. As she continued to hear inspiring news about the French Revolution fully ousting the monarchy and installing a people's government, Jeanne felt that this might be a good time to return home. But she knew that if her debtors in London caught wind of her plans, they would make things difficult for her. So, she decided to keep everything secret.

Unfortunately, word of her proposed plans leaked out somehow, and one morning in 1791, a slew of debtors unexpectedly began to knock on her door. When she refused to open, they threatened to break in and resort to violent recovery methods. In a panic, Jeanne decided that the best way to escape was through the apartment window, even if it was a little high. She made the bold leap, but slipped and fell on the street, cracking her skull.

The young lady, who travestied so successfully in Paris as the Comtesse Jeanne de la Motte, died in London without knowing that the name of Jeanne de Valois-Saint-Rémy and the story of the diamond necklace were among the triggers of the terrible revolution that eventually brought down the guillotine on the heads of France's last monarch, King Louis XVI, and his beloved wife, Queen Marie Antoinette.

But in all likelihood, Cardinal de Rohan, who returned to religious duties after the revolution and enjoyed great acceptance for his anti-monarchy views until he died in 1803, might have known.

7

Kenneth Lay

The Energy Chief

'Have you been anxiously awaiting the day, Mr. Lay, when you could finally tell your side of the story concerning the fall of Enron?' the eminent criminal defence and federal crimes attorney George Mccall Secrest, Jr., asked.

'Let me answer that in two ways, Mr Secrest,' the accused replied. 'I mean, number one, I doubt anybody awaits anxiously the day when they can get on the stand in a federal district court where they're accused of federal crimes. But number two, yes, I've been very anxious to tell what I believe is the truth about what happened at Enron, I've even tried from time to time certainly in speeches and various venues, but certainly, the information that's been pouring in from all other side has overwhelmed that. But yes, I am very, very anxious and am trying to do whatever I can to get the truth out about what really happened at Enron.'

'Mr Lay, that day has arrived. Let's get started,' said the attorney.

Self-made

In the small, unincorporated community of Tyrone, along the supplemental route of Missouri H. in Texas, events of historical importance were rare. People still talked about the decades-old post office being moved out in the early 1960s as one of its most significant events.

Omer Lay, a member of this community, was the son of Andrew Jackson Lay and Mathilda Ellen Owen. Though the Lays once ran a successful general-purpose goods business, the store eventually failed, leading Omer to grow up in poverty. The Lay family, deeply religious, were active members of the local Baptist church. After trying various odd jobs, Omer turned to the way of faith and became a Baptist preacher, which, if little else, brought daily bread to the family table. He married the equally religious Ruth Ester Rees, and the family continued to lead a simple and frugal life. They firmly believed that even if it meant seeking the help of a kind relative from time to time, they would never resort to any wrongdoing.

When the family decided to relocate to Columbia, Missouri, in search of better opportunities, they enrolled their son, Kenneth Lay, born in 1942, at David H. Hickman High School. Thankfully, the boy did well academically, earning admission to the University of Missouri. There, supplementing his scholarship with income from odd jobs, he graduated with honours in arts and completed a master's in economics.

Influenced by one of his professors, Dr Pinkney C. Walker, Lay developed an early interest in the economics of oil and gas. After college, he joined Humble Oil and Refining, one of the oldest companies in Texas, owned by Standard Oil, a New Jersey oil major. At the time, the company was in the process of a merger with its parent. Although he left before the formation of the unified Exxon Corporation, Lay's role as an economist in the corporate planning department furnished him with significant insights into the American oil industry.

Shifting roles, he enrolled as an officer candidate in the US Navy, serving for three years and rising to the rank of lieutenant. Posted to the Office of Navy Comptroller and Financial Analyst at the Pentagon, he honed his financial skills while working closely with several key members of the US defence and general administration. He also completed a doctorate in economics from the University of Houston during this period along with teaching night classes at George Washington University.

When his former mentor, Dr Pinkney C. Walker, became Commissioner of the Federal Power Commission (FPC), which regulated the interstate electric utilities and natural gas industry, Lay felt a calling to return to the energy sector. An offer came from Dr Walker himself for Lay to join him at the FPC.

This position brought him closer to prominent figures in the energy sector, including industrialists and government officials. Throughout the two-year stint, Lay gained considerable exposure to the operational aspects of the highly regulated sector. He learnt that ever since the landmark Supreme Court ruling in *Phillips Petroleum Co. vs Wisconsin* in 1954, the Federal Energy Regulatory Commission and other authorities had been trying to find acceptable mechanisms for pricing oil and natural gas. The challenge was to avoid giving undue advantage to either interstate or intrastate suppliers while striking the right balance between producers and pipeline operators.

However, none of the wellhead-pricing policies rolled out by the government to fix the value of products had worked satisfactorily. The general sentiment within the industry was that even if low rates augmented demand, it became unviable for gas producers to operate profitably, especially given the large investments needed for new exploration. These confusing policies also led to large volumes of sales taking place through spot market mechanisms, where the transactions were driven solely by short-term demand and supply positions, wreaking further havoc on the market prices. The sudden embargo announced by OPEC nations, led by Saudi Arabia, on countries backing Israel in the Yom Kippur War, including the US, was threatening to worsen matters, with many of the consuming states staring at major power outages affecting schools and households.

The entire administration was under pressure to find solutions swiftly, and young Lay was sure many changes would have to be brought in soon to deregulate and free up the energy sector. He was enjoying the policymaking role and even received a quick promotion as Deputy Undersecretary of Energy, reporting directly to the Secretary of Interior. But after a while, Lay began to feel that this was also an opportune time to return to the industry.

In 1974, he joined Florida Gas Transmission, a large company operating natural gas pipelines and allied activities across the US. Within two years of joining as the vice-president, he was elevated to president, heading the company during its acquisition by the much larger Continental Resources Group. This also meant that he was now the youngest person in the country to lead a large energy major, and soon established himself as a notable business leader across all prominent trade and social circles.

As Lay had expected, the government began to introduce major reforms, such as bringing together multiple regulatory authorities under a common Department of Energy headed by a prominent secretary and passing the Natural Gas Policy Act of 1978, which granted more autonomy to energy companies. The industry saw these as steps in the right direction, and energy majors responded by committing large investments to expand their operations.

Despite directing an operation with diverse interests in exploration, production, transmission, gas processing, infrastructure management and real estate, Lay now wanted to move on to something even bigger.

His aspiration lay in Houston, considered the energy hub of the US. He made a pitch through a senior friend named Jack Bowen, who had earlier moved from Florida Gas to head Transco, an even larger energy conglomerate. Soon Lay received an offer to join the Houston headquarters of Transco as the president and chief operating officer.

Transco was struggling to handle the new policy environment, especially the price volatility, and the new COO's immediate task was to ramp up operations. Linda Harold, Lay's private secretary at Florida Gas, also moved with him, and they were married a little later.

Working with the experienced Jack Bowen, Lay introduced many innovative schemes, like the industry's first spot-market scheme. Even while their peers were grappling with the market chaos, Transco's stock prices rose significantly, and Ken Lay's leadership skills became an even bigger talking point across the oil and natural gas sectors.

Lay's move from Transco was, however, unplanned.

Houston Natural Gas (HNG) was a large energy company that had been in operation since 1925. They had also been facing issues due to the recent policy changes. Profitability and employee morale were at a very low ebb and their biggest concern was a lack of efficient leadership to manoeuvre the company through difficult times.

Another behemoth in the energy sector, Coastal Corporation, was eyeing HNG for a potential takeover. Oscar Wyatt, the founder and chairman of Coastal approached his good friend Jack Bowen, requesting Transco's support in negotiating the deal. Bowen, who had a soft corner for his old friend, backed the move and nominated Kenneth Lay to join the HNG board as a Transco nominee to oversee the process.

Lay did such an outstanding job of seeing the deal through that once the takeover was completed and the search for a new CEO of HNG began, he was an obvious choice for the position.

Though Lay had not thought about quitting Transco, the opportunity to head HNG as president and CEO was too good to throw away. The remuneration and personal benefits were also much more lucrative. So, with Jack Bowen's blessing, Lay relocated to HNG, which was also in Houston and not far from his former Transco office.

Lay made many changes at HNG. Significantly, he decided to dispose of all non-oil and gas assets carried by the company and turn the focus fully on their core oil businesses. Clear that acquiring companies which had synergy with HNG's operations was the way forward, Lay pushed for the takeover of two major pipeline companies, including his former company, Florida Gas.

The arrival at HNG signalled the beginning of the greater things to follow in Kenneth Lay's life, even if it would eventually lead to his downfall.

Bigger is better

One day, Lay received an unexpected request from his friend Sam Segnar, the CEO of the Omaha-based energy company InterNorth, who was facing a curious predicament. Much like HNG, InterNorth aspired to follow the acquisition route to expand its presence in natural gas and other businesses, including plastics. But unbeknownst to Segnar, a major venture capitalist, Irwin Jacobs, had picked up around one-third of InterNorth's shareholdings from the market, positioning the company as the target for a takeover.

Segnar, convinced that Jacobs did not have any long-term interest in the company, sought Lay's help to stave off the hostile bid. He proposed that given the synergy in the operations of both companies, InterNorth could acquire HNG through a 'friendly' merger, creating America's second-largest pipeline company – an entity too large for Jacobs to acquire. Recognizing the potential for a beneficial agreement amidst Segnar's distress, Lay consented to the plan but negotiated meticulously before finalizing the arrangement.

When the merger took place in May 1985, creating an entity called HNG/InterNorth headquartered in Omaha, the price of $2.3 billion paid by InterNorth at $70 per share of HNG was much higher than the prevailing market value of $45. Although this meant that the merged entity would have to assume a large debt, Lay knew that as a significant beneficiary, he had no reason to complain. He also influenced the new entity's corporate structure to ensure that he had greater control over the reconstituted board of the merged company. As planned, the merged entity blocked Jacobs from all takeover bids, and Lay also forced the hunter to exit his stake in full. Segnar continued as CEO, but within a few months, Lay quietly pushed the board to vote him out and took over as the new CEO in November 1985. In February 1986, he was elected Chairman.

Despite opposition from a few former directors, Lay shifted the company headquarters back to Houston and decided that it needed a new name now. After spending nearly $100,000 on consultants, the name 'Enteron' was identified, but when its similarity to the human intestine was indicated, he decided to modify it.

And Enron was born.

Lay worked tirelessly on his mission to turn Enron into the largest pipeline company in the US. There were many significant challenges to deal with, including the Peruvian government's decision to nationalize energy assets, resulting in a crash in oil prices from $30 per barrel to $10.

Traditionally, the production of natural gas and its pipeline transportation were operated as distinct businesses, with producers entering into long-term contracts with pipeline companies on 'take or pay' commitments that would insulate both sides from demand–supply volatility and price fluctuations. But the regulatory changes introduced in the mid-1980s changed these dynamics by giving producers the option to choose the most competitive pipeline operator without any long-term obligations.

Lay was also optimistic that the company could take advantage of the newly deregulated environment and become profitable. He knew that the way towards a quantum jump for companies like Enron was to become larger and more efficient in capturing the market. He began to run the twin engines of ensuring internal pipeline capacity expansion while constantly looking at new projects and aggressive mergers. The plans included consolidation of all gas pipeline activities under an entity called Enron Gas Pipeline Operating Company, expanding exploration activities under a dedicated division called Enron Oil and Gas and adding new power plants and cogeneration units that focused on electric power. Soon, Enron became the first nationwide interstate natural gas pipeline operator. Under Lay's stewardship, many more new divisions and ventures continued to open as Enron spread its wings rapidly.

Despite this, Lay remained concerned about surfing in the near future.

In its first year of operations (1985), Enron reported losses of $79 million. By the end of 1986, even though there was still an operating loss, the accountants managed to find large write-backs from earlier tax recoveries and turned it into a profit of $556 million. The jugglery did not, however, impress the investors or analysts, prompting Moody's to downgrade the rating to 'below investment' or, in less polite words, to 'junk' grade.

Lay knew that many of the plans he was rolling out needed time to bear fruit, whereas market expectations were always high and investors as a class were unwilling to be patient. Besides, there were also some genuine financial issues at hand, particularly the large debt burden from the merger. Even a slight default in repayment would be catastrophic.

He was still trying to figure out how to convert future plans into immediately reportable numbers when the Internal Audit department approached him with an unexpected problem. They had preliminary suspicions that there were financial anomalies at Enron Oil Trading (EOT), based in Valhalla, New York.

EOT was a specialized division engaged in oil trading, a business vertical that had gained prominence more recently. Long-term contracts in crude had been popular for a while, but only as a mechanism to hedge the risk of price volatility based on the physical delivery of agreed volumes. In the new market-driven policy environment, oil had assumed the character of a financial asset, and companies began to execute deals based on price fluctuations that did not necessarily involve physical deliveries. This was a tricky business that was managed through complex contracts like 'twinning' arrangements, which involved the sale and buy-back of identical lots of the commodity contracted with the same counterparty, allowing the parties to book the net profit or loss on such deals without having to take physical delivery. If undertaken correctly, the deals could generate huge profits, but they could also turn into steep losses. Most importantly, it needed smart people with trading skills to effectively manage operations.

Lay had decided that the small oil trades hitherto carried on by some employees of the erstwhile InterNorth were not good enough to leverage this opportunity. So, he created a dedicated division run by specialists to undertake this activity at a much larger scale. Given the nature of the business, which required traders to strike deals quickly whenever price movements were right, Lay granted the veteran commodity traders, Lois Borget, the president of the division, and Thomas Mastroeni, the treasurer, sweeping powers to take on such trades freely. On his part, he remained happy as long as they made money for the company on an overall basis.

To Lay's great delight, EOT reported increasing profits, even when most other divisions were losing money. In 1985, when all of Enron was in the red, EOT brought in profits of $10 million to help cut down the overall loss, and when the number shot up to $28 million in 1986, Lay was convinced the team should go on without interference from other management levels.

However, the preliminary findings of an internal audit in early 1987 worried him. The audit found that a bank account opened under EOT's name, operated by Borget and Mastroeni at the Eastern Savings Bank, was not being reported to the accounts division at the company headquarters. Several deals aggregating millions of dollars had been routed through this account. Most significantly, around $2 million had been transferred from it to Mastroeni's personal account at the same bank. Upon further investigation, major irregularities were found in the accounting of large contracts executed by the two senior traders with three other companies on a 'twinning' basis.

The standard accounting practice for such deals was to only record the net profit or loss. But the audit noted that while the sales limb of the contract was accounted for in the company books at the end of 1986, the corresponding purchase was deferred to the beginning of the next financial year. This signalled a clear accounting mismatch on account of the entire profits being booked in 1986 and reversed only later in the following year. The sums involved were material and Lay knew that if the preliminary findings were proven correct, reported incomes for 1986 had been significantly overstated. The audit also raised suspicions that Borget and Mastroeni had kept these deals hidden by tampering with the company's bank accounts. They had deleted certain transactions and opened their personal bank accounts to park the income from these contracts.

When Lay met the two senior gentlemen, they defended themselves earnestly. They claimed they had merely acceded to requests from Enron's accounting department to report profits from the EOT division in order to help cut down the company's aggregate losses. Deleting some of the transactions from the company's bank statements and routing it through a personal bank account outside the books, they argued, was only a conduit they had chosen to comply with these requests.

By this time, Lay was suspicious and ordered a full investigation.

To his shock, the investigation revealed massive frauds orchestrated by the two trusted dealers. Riding their assessment of future oil prices, they had executed deals that were many times their authorized limits, unwinding them later to keep the profits. These transactions were routed through their separate personal bank accounts, and the duo kept everything concealed from the accounts department, even drawing large bonuses based on the fudged profits.

Borget and Mastroeni were dismissed and, during the legal proceedings, admitted to the offences, including the creation of shell companies to facilitate fictitious trades. The entire episode was obviously stressful, but with the dismissals, Lay felt the issue was fully behind them now.

Or so he thought.

Giant in trouble

When the financial impact of the fraudulent transactions was fully assessed, it was found that the exposure from these deals had exceeded one billion dollars.

Lay wasted little time in making decisions. The first was to immediately shut down EOT as a separate division. He then commissioned Mike Muckleroy, a former commodity trader who now headed another Enron division to minimize the potential hit on the company's reported numbers. To Lay's great relief, Mike used his knowledge of commodity transactions and the confusing accounting norms to bring down the loss to a much more manageable range of $142 million to $190 million. The smart accountants at Enron found ways to spread the loss over multiple financial years, with only $85 million being charged off in 1987. These adjustments reduced the write-off below the regulatory materiality limits, allowing Enron to close the matter without reporting the one-time loss separately to the exchange.

The share price fell temporarily, but under the circumstances, this was the least of Lay's worries. He returned to rolling out more initiatives that would ramp up Enron's core businesses.

One of the major decisions was to move into unregulated markets, which could generate higher profits than from controlled activities. Enron also entered the newly deregulated UK energy market, signalling its transformation into a multinational energy corporation.

One of Lay's key priorities was to ensure Enron always presented a portrait of strict corporate governance and ethical business practices. The company had a high-profile Board of Directors, stacked with independent experts, and several committees, including the audit committee, functioned robustly. Many secretaries, policy advisors and ambassadors were known to have sizeable personal holdings in the company's equity shares, as Enron was known for winning awards and accolades for its high compliance standards.

Lay had also made sure he was compensated well. As Enron grew, he drew larger salaries, allowances and bonuses, apart from share participation and generous perks, such as the exclusive use of the company's Lear jets.

While setting himself up as one of the most well-known voices on issues related to the oil and energy sector, Lay built close friendships with many prominent people, including the Bush family, publicly stating that, '*I've been a strong financial and political supporter of, first, President Bush Sr. when he was running for president, and even when he ran for president a time or two and failed.*' Later, he supposedly declined an offer from the president to serve as the US Energy Secretary.

But Lay did not overtly associate with any political party, making significant contributions to Bill Clinton's campaign as well. Many people who supported Enron's causes are believed to have benefitted from Lay's interventions. One example is Tom Ridge, the former governor of Pennsylvania who was appointed Secretary of Homeland Security.

In a largely government-controlled industry, Lay was able to wield his influence to obtain many vital sanctions and relaxations for Enron from key regulators, such as the Federal Energy Regulatory Commission (FERC), the Securities Exchange Commission (SEC) and the Commodity Futures Trading Commission (CFTC). He even managed to sway important decisions at the Pentagon, like awarding large energy supply contracts to private firms.

Soon, it was not about Ken Lay lobbying for concessions but about him controlling critical policy matters themselves. Many key decisions in the energy sector, such as the passing of the Natural Gas Decontrol Act and the introduction of tax concessions for new well explorations, were rumoured to be tailor-made for Enron's requirements.

Given the growing pressure of his position, and the constant pressure to match earnings expectations, Lay began to keep his eyes open for a good second in command.

In 1991, he met Jeffrey Skilling.

Skilling was a Harvard MBA graduate who had worked closely with Enron as a senior consultant at McKinsey & Company. He also shared Lay's vision of taking Enron into uncharted market spaces and shared several ideas to achieve this successfully. Impressed by the young man, Lay invited Skilling to join the company at a senior management level.

Just as he had hoped, Skilling worked closely with Lay to lead Enron on a meteoric rise, even through a period of considerable policy change and deregulation. Among the many new initiatives was the creation of a structured marketplace for natural gas, which, unlike oil, had never existed before. Lay backed Skilling in running the 'Gas Bank', a novel venture which operated like a massive supermarket for natural gas. Under the gas bank scheme, Enron would buy gas from multiple suppliers and make the quantities available for sale to a wide network of customers at contracted prices. This would ensure a guaranteed mechanism for supply of natural gas at predictable prices. But when gas suppliers seemed hesitant to catch on to the new idea, Enron tweaked the scheme by allowing suppliers to directly supply gas to customers at contracted prices, though Enron would guarantee the prices to cover all fluctuations. This effectively served as the forerunner for an active futures market in which energy derivatives (contracts with energy products as underlying) became tradeable by market players at a future date and price.

Lay nominated Skilling as the CEO of Enron Gas Services, which was later merged into Enron Capital and Trade Resources after becoming the company's largest business segment. What started as a small natural gas wholesale business with around seventy employees grew to employ more than 5,000 people.

Under Skilling's leadership, Enron forayed into many new areas, including financing oil and gas producers, trading in futures and options on the commodity exchanges and dealing in swaps and other derivatives. When Richard Kinder, one of Lay's old friends from the early days of Enron, quit as President and Chief Operating Officer to start his own pipeline company in 1996, Lay knew exactly who could fill this position.

In 1997, Jeffrey Skilling replaced Kinder, now next only to Kenneth Lay in the organizational hierarchy.

With Jeff Skilling's rise, many things changed at Enron, most significantly the end of the culture of working among friends. Skilling believed in highly organized structures characterized by formal appraisals, bonuses, promotions and spot-firing. Large divisions were broken into smaller units, which were driven to compete against each other for larger profits, turning the company into a high-pressure cooker where numbers superseded everything else.

Lay had few complaints about these changes because he knew Skilling was focused on delivering results.

Lay also authorized Skilling to hire Andrew Fastow, an MBA with banking and finance experience, to head the accounting team, who was elevated as Chief Financial Officer within a few years.

Several major expansions occurred during the 1990s, led by the new management team, including the decision to enter the electricity business in California. Lay's decision to promote natural gas-powered electricity as a cleaner option delivered the extra push for the company. Enron set up a nationwide power and natural gas retail marketing company, The New Power Co, jointly with IBM and AOL Time Warner to serve households and small businesses. Through major acquisitions, Enron also expanded into many other new business segments, like operating water plants and paper plants.

By the end of the nineties, the internet explosion led Lay and the team to decide that even if it wasn't their core business, Enron should have a significant presence in this new sector. A division was set up to provide high-speed optic fibre connectivity, which, apart from offering physical infrastructure, would also trade in optic-fibre bandwidth. Through Enron Broadband Service, the company entered into long-term contracts (in some cases, going up to twenty years) for providing digital and telecom services, including on-demand video entertainment. Enron Online was established to provide e-services, specifically online energy trading, and massive investments were made through Enron Broadband in building high-speed networks for this project. Enron also partnered with many large players, like Blockbuster Video, a major video rental chain.

Under Enron International headed by the intrepid Rebecca Mark, large projects were initiated outside America too. Massive power plant projects were undertaken in many parts of the world, including Australia, Europe and Asia, with the largest being the $3 billion Dabhol project proposed as a public–private joint venture in India.

Despite this, Lay, Skilling and the rest of the management remained uncomfortable that most of these new projects would take time to reflect in the company's reported numbers, and that immediate market expectations could not be assuaged by mere assurances. .

Only in the books

With results expectations driving the top management to desperation, Lay and Skilling decided they needed to find a way to keep everyone happy and authorized Fastow to do whatever was possible. Enron's problems were triggered when the finance team responded by unleashing a spate of accounting jugglery to inflate the numbers.

Inflating Revenue

Revenues were shored up by various accounting adjustments. Back-to-back sale contracts were recorded at the gross values of both sales and purchases separately, though, in reality, the company only realized the net income from such transactions. Transactions which ought to have been treated as financial liabilities were recognized as revenue. Several deals were fabricated to recognize book profits, including a fictitious sale of Nigerian power-driven barges valued at $12 million to Merrill Lynch in 1999, for which Fastow roped in some Merrill employees also as abettors. The company also used the new online, media and telecom divisions to recognize large revenues based on unrealistic revenue estimates.

Booking future or uncertain profits

Enron began to recognize the future income, expected to accrue over the tenure of trading contracts on a 'mark-to-market' basis (MTM), based on the management estimates of the present value of future cash flows. This was carried out as soon as the contracts were signed. No consideration was given to the possibility that many energy contracts would not generate income as projected due to price fluctuations and other factors. Whenever losses occurred, the accounts team hid them by recording estimated profits from additional contracts. Several innovative accounting adjustments using complex trading instruments and derivatives were adopted, many of which had no precedence and fell outside the purview of the generally accepted accounting norms that had been notified by regulators and accounting standards boards. The commodity trading division, where the accounting rules were ambiguous, was a major area identified for fictitious adjustments.

Deferring write-offs

Enron adopted the accounting practice of 'snowballing' as a regular policy, which allowed them to defer writing-off incurred and sunk costs on cancelled projects by creating documents to show that these projects had not been finally abandoned yet.

Suppressing impairment losses

Impairment losses on many troubled ventures were concealed, including the broadband venture, which alone had incurred losses of around $1.2 billion, and Wessex Water with losses of $700 million.

SPE accounting

But the most significant accounting jugglery Enron engaged in was the use of special-purpose vehicles to shift Enron's massive debt liability out of the company's books. Entities having different legal structures, like Asset LLCs, LLPs, securitization and investment trusts were established to operate as special purpose entities, including in various tax havens. In reality, the company controlled these entities, but on the surface, there was nothing to show any relationship with either Enron or any of the key managerial personnel attracting the provisions of control or significant influence. Many complex adjustments were made using hundreds of such SPEs to thoroughly cook the Enron books.

The general modus operandi employed was for Enron (or their official subsidiaries) to transfer some of their assets to such a special purpose entity. These would be treated as having been sold in the Enron books and capitalized as assets of the SPE. In reality, many of these represented badly impaired assets (including those on which future profits were earlier recognized by Enron on MTM basis). Rightfully, Enron should have recognized the losses on these assets. But instead, these were treated as ones transferred to the SPEs at inflated 'fair market' values. This enabled Enron to book both significant revenues and profits on the sale of the assets.

Further, under the prevailing regulations at the time, SPEs engaging in such transactions (commonly known as asset securitizations) were required to issue only 3 per cent of the value of the assets acquired by way of equity to the sellers and could raise up to 97 per cent of the value as loans to settle the difference. Enron used this route liberally to raise substantial loans in the SPEs against the inflated value of its own bad assets transferred. The company made 'Total Return Swap' agreements with lending institutions, guaranteeing that if the SPE's assets did not generate adequate returns, Enron would repay the loans. This guarantee further allowed the company to effectively retain control of the transferred assets without having to record them in its books or recognize losses on them. The loan proceeds were then returned to it as payment for the assets transferred. Enron capitalized SPEs and raised loans using complex instruments such as derivative financial instruments, restricted stock and stock acquisition rights, in addition to traditional business assets. Since none of the SPEs had any direct relationship with Enron (or its official subsidiaries), the accounting regulations of the time also did not require any sort of consolidation of the SPE accounts either. And Enron managed to keep all these huge loans only in the books of the SPEs without appearing as debts on its balance sheet. Many large lenders and institutions, including the Canadian Imperial Bank of Commerce and JP Morgan Chase & Co lent millions to the SPEs under these arrangements, as it became an excellent conduit for Enron to raise loans without having to carry it in the company books. Everyone who was aware of this practice knew that if these loans had also rightfully been considered as liabilities, the company's credit rating would have fallen to shreds. No one, especially Enron's investors, understood the situation.

Under Fastow's careful eye, the company established hundreds of such SPEs to move out large portions of their debt liabilities and steadily routed many questionable transactions, like ineffective hedges, on which the company should have recognized losses. Booking fictitious profits on the asset sales, they effectively exploited the lacunae in the accounting regulations (known as FAS 140 accounting) to keep huge debts and losses out of the company's books. Only some minimal disclosures were made in the periodic results, which were conveniently buried under oodles of data in the published financial statements.

As Fastow's astute accounting team found ways to sweep numerous matters under the carpet, Lay took comfort in the fact that they could disguise all the issues until their circumstances improved, and Enron could absorb these losses. Through the 1990s, they adopted several complex and tricky accounting practices to keep investors in the dark about the real financial position of the company. Fastow also managed to control the high-profile auditor firm, Arthur Andersen, by offering a huge audit fee of $25 million and consulting charges of $27 million (average). At times, he used veiled threats like involving one of the other Big 5 firms, such as Ernst & Young or PricewaterhouseCoopers, to conduct certain assignments for high fees, which obviously rattled the auditors.

Almost as if to validate what Enron was doing, the SEC confirmed the technical correctness of the accounting policies being adopted, even issuing guidance for other energy companies to follow these pioneering practices.

There were only a few rare complaints from whistleblowers such as James Alexander, an executive at Enron Global Power, and Sherron Watkins, an employee who had heard of some irregularities from a friend at Arthur Andersen; Lay however, chose to dismiss all these immediately as malicious acts of the odd disgruntled employees.

Even as the company was losing billions of dollars and accumulating huge debts, Lay, Skilling and Fastow made sure everything looked rosy on paper. Internal numbers showed massive spurts and Enron's revenues leapt from $13 billion in 1996 to over $100 billion in 2000, putting them in the top ten companies on the *Fortune* Global 500 list. Debt levels appeared to be well under control as profits soared and the stock tickers buzzed louder by the day.

Stock prices climbed from $20–25 per share in 1998 to the $40 range within a year after Enron reported significant growth in 1999 and continued to spiral up to $90 when quarterly numbers reported in 2000 shattered all the street forecasts. Over the fifteen years under Ken Lay, Enron's market capitalization had grown from around $2 billion in 1985 to $60 billion, and the company was named the most innovative in America by *Fortune* in their 'Most Admired Companies' survey.

In Lay's own words, '*And even allowing for dilution from new shares issued and used for purchases and whatever, the shareholder that would have left his or her investment in that company for that 15 years would have had about a 15-fold increase in their return, which is two to three times what would be realized in just investing in the Standard and Poor 500.*'

No eyebrows were raised when employee compensation, especially for the top-level executives, also broke all ceilings. Only those in the close coterie knew that besides the huge pay packets, many members of the senior management team were also freely using insider information to make millions through their own trades in Enron stocks.

Around this time, the *Wall Street Journal* carried an educative article in their September 2000 issue about the mark-to-market accounting practices being followed in the energy sector. James Steven Chanos, an investment manager, was among those who read it closely. As someone known in market circles as a short seller who sold select stocks in advance in order to repurchase them later at a lower price, Chanos was always on the hunt for shares whose prices could fall sharply. Reading through the article, which explained how large companies like Enron recognized large revenues and profits based on estimates, Chanos suspected that this could be yet another bubble about to burst. His own analysis of the financial reports and exchange filings submitted by Enron showed major inconsistencies. On discovering that the company was operating at a fund cost of around 9 per cent while their real earning rate was only about 7 per cent, he knew from previous experience that trouble loomed on the horizon.

In November 2000, Chanos decided to short the Enron stock by entering into large advance sale contracts, signalling to the market that he anticipated a near-term fall in prices.

The company, however, was quick to maintain that it stood firmly by its accounting practices. Thankfully, most people seemed to accept Enron's claims, rubbishing this as another speculative attempt by a short seller, especially when stock prices were on a roll and financial guidance for the following year also appeared strong.

But then the March issue of *Fortune* carried an article written by former investment banker and well-known journalist Bethany McLean, repeating the question of whether Enron shares were overpriced. Originally influenced by Chanos's views, McLean had conducted detailed inquiries her own and in successive articles, continued to level serious charges about the financial affairs at Enron, including the inconsistent cash flows and the possibility of large debts remaining unreported.

As markets and investors began to get incited by these back-to-back articles, Enron found itself in the public glare again.

But Lay, Skilling and Fastow were able to subdue the noise this time too, spinning more tales to maintain the facade with the press and investors. When reputed fund manager Richard Grubman commented at a press conference that Enron was the only financial institution that couldn't produce a balance sheet or cash flow statement with their earnings, Jeff Skilling promptly retorted, '*Thank you very much; we appreciate that ... asshole.*'

In the midst of this, in February 2001, Lay decided to elevate Jeff Skilling to the position of CEO of the entire group, while also announcing his decision to continue in a more relaxed role as the chairman.

When Enron reported first-quarter profits of $536 million in April 2001, and the July 2001 results also outdid expectations, all market concerns seemed to have blown over. There was renewed optimism that the share prices, which had tumbled to the $45–50 range after the recent negative publicity, would start to soar again.

Lay, on the other hand, knew that the company was far from being in a comfortable position.

The whole country, particularly the western areas, was struggling with highly volatile energy prices, and many key divisions, like Enron Energy Services in California, were facing major operating issues. Serious political and financial challenges threatened to derail the massive Dabhol Power

Project, which was being set up as a joint venture between Enron and the government-owned Maharashtra Power Development Corporation in India. Many new projects, including a high-profile collaboration with IBM and AOL Time Warner, had failed to take off as planned.

The main concern remained that the company was presently in no position to take any financial hits for such large losses. Overseas assets had already been inflated by around $5 billion, and nearly $7 billion of losses had been concealed under one head or the other. Lay knew that if things were reviewed now, it could destroy their numbers, though he remained optimistic that the company could regularize these anomalies over the next few years.

When stars fall out

Then, on 14 August 2001, Jeff Skilling suddenly announced his decision to quit as the CEO. While he insisted that it was a personal decision unrelated to Enron, market players were quick to note that just before announcing the decision, Skilling had liquidated a sizeable portion of his shareholding in the company at the prevailing high prices, pocketing nearly $33 million.

Predictably, share prices fell sharply after this sensational development.

Lay immediately reassumed charge as CEO and assured everyone that there was no cause for concern at Enron. '*[If] there is anything material and we're not reporting it, we'll be breaking the law. We don't break the law,*' he affirmed, confident that his timely intervention would bring matters under control.

But the entire economy was in a slump, with large dot-com bubbles bursting everywhere and many businesses failing.

To re-energize activities, Lay introduced new faces into many key managerial positions and worked on new plans, like disposing of Enron's 65 per cent stake in the failed Dabhol Plant. Lay kept his fingers crossed that the market would view these as positive steps and arrest the downslide in prices since Skilling's sudden departure.

But sentiments had deteriorated to the point where, no matter what Lay tried, Enron was unable to restore the same levels of confidence among investors, analysts and the media. On the contrary, the noise was growing so loud that no meaningful information could be drawn from Enron's complex financial statements and stock market filings. Stock prices continued to plummet, dropping below $15.

By September 2001, though, after the horrifying attacks on the Twin Towers in New York, the world had lost interest in this case.

Banking on the unexpected relief, Lay made a quick decision. In October 2001, Enron announced that it would restate its financial statements for the years 1997 to 2000. The stated reason was the need to make certain accounting corrections arising from unexpected developments affecting the global economy. Enron claimed these were genuine business losses from certain large investments that had failed despite their best efforts. To defend his position, Lay also criticized some of the government's recent policies, including the unscientific deregulation of the energy industry, which he claimed caused large operating losses for Enron too.

The restatement wiped out $615 million (nearly 25 per cent) of the profits reported for earlier periods. Together with an increase in liabilities of $630 million, shareholder equity at the end of 2000 had eroded by around $1.2 billion. Nevertheless, Lay and the Enron top brass continued to hope that things would settle down now.

But once the intense attention around 9/11 events decreased, Lay and his team found that even after the restatement, most analysts and investors were not convinced by Enron's numbers. Share prices continued falling, soon dropping to single digits.

The Board of Directors, which was also facing considerable public embarrassment from the restatements and the plummeting market prices, decided to intervene. And CFO Andrew Fastow was summoned for detailed quizzing.

Before the board, Fastow admitted to having chaperoned certain questionable accounting adjustments. He also conceded to making personal gains of nearly $30 million, mainly from transactions with the controversial SPVs that he managed.

Lay, however, prevailed on the board to back his trusted confidant, even making a public announcement that they continued to repose full faith in Fastow as the CFO, stressing that '*aggressive accounting does not mean illegal accounting*'.

But things had already gone too far, especially once Fastow's admission of guilt became public knowledge. Debt levels had crossed all critical thresholds, and Lay was aware that though the liquidity crisis was well hidden, the company had very little cash on hand. Relations with the bankers who financed the company also took a turn for the worse when they refused to continue dealing with a publicly tainted CFO. Enron could not afford any friction with them, so, against his best wishes, Lay was eventually compelled to bring the axe down on Fastow.

Jeff McMahon, a senior executive at the company, was asked to take over as CFO, with the urgent commission of bringing down the massive debt levels. But matters worsened when credit rating agencies, including Moody's and Fitch, indicated a downgrade in the company's debt and commercial paper ratings. The actual downgrade occurred a few weeks later, choking the fund position fully. With this action, most financial experts began to publicly agree that Enron could already be bankrupt.

As stock prices continued to slide downward to new lows of $7 and threatened to move further southwards, Lay and his team knew they were staring at a major disaster. Almost as a last resort, Lay approached Dynegy, a large energy player partly owned by the Chevron group, to take over Enron. For the first time in his illustrious career, Lay played second fiddle, as negotiations were largely conducted on Dynegy's terms. The only thing Lay insisted on was a personal compensation of $60 million to hand over Enron's control to them. An in-principle understanding was struck, which included financial support from Dynegy to discharge Enron's massive liabilities and Lay began to hope that the worst was over.

However, before the deal could be concluded, Enron was required by accounting regulations to restate its earlier financials for the years 1997 to 2000. These adjustments resulted in many more significant changes, mostly on account of having to recognize more losses from previously unaccounted-for SPV transactions. On 16 October, Enron reported a whopping loss of $618 million for the third quarter of 2001.

A week later, the SEC announced an investigation into the accounting and financial affairs of the company. Fortunately for Lay, the jolt from the second restatement did not cause Dynegy to withdraw from their offer, though they insisted on returning to the table to modify the terms. Lay could only helplessly agree when Dynegy slashed their initial offer by almost half after the fresh rounds of negotiations.

Despite their best efforts, Lay and his team were unable to reduce the company's debt significantly, which now far exceeded available cash. The credit rating agencies, who had shown some leniency when the deal with Dynegy seemed to be imminent, decided they could no longer wait, especially after the second restatement. By the end of November 2001, they announced a reduction in Enron's debt rating to junk.

Much like the proverbial last nail, the SEC also announced the completion of its investigations, reporting on major accounting irregularities and frauds that remained unresolved. Fingers were also pointed at Arthur Andersen, and its removal as the company's auditors was seen as a mere formality.

The latest developments effectively dumped any remaining expectations that Enron's numbers might continue to be reliable.

Stock prices fell below $1, and Dynegy announced their decision to back out of the deal.

Amidst credible news that Enron's total liabilities were now close to $23 billion, Enron began the official process of filing for bankruptcy on 30 November 2001. Proceedings began in Europe, before moving to the United States.

In December 2001, multiple agencies, including the FBI, Justice Department, Labor Department and SEC, launched investigations, along with several Congressional hearings.

All aspects of the company's operations, including the roles of key players such as Kenneth Lay, Jeffrey Skilling and

Andrew Fastow, came under detailed scrutiny. Radars were also trained on the role of Arthur Andersen.

With the media from all over the world keeping a close watch on the company, rumours, claims and speculations also flew around freely. Throughout the high-profile proceedings, investigators faced many challenges, including dealing with demands from highly placed sources. Former Vice-chairman Clifford Baxter's death by suicide after agreeing to testify before the Congressional committee caused another flurry of suspicions and raised the heat further.

On 23 January 2002, Ken Lay resigned as the CEO and chairman of Enron through a public announcement. He stated that he had even refused to accept the $60 million severance compensation offered to him by the Enron board. A few days later, his young wife Linda also appeared on a TV show in tears, claiming their family was bankrupt due to the unexpected Enron collapse.

Only one way forward

The investigations into the company affairs took nearly three and a half years, reporting extensive evidence of how financial information was forged through a series of falsified transactions and fraudulent accounting practices. Revenues for the period from 1996 to 2000 were artificially ballooned from realistic levels of $13 billion to over $100 billion. Large portions of the company's $30 billion debt were concealed. Nearly 3,500 dummy entities were set up across various offshore havens to route fictitious deals. Through special-purpose entities under names like Chewco, Whitewing, LJM Cayman, Swap Sub and Raptors, massive losses from failed investments like CalPERS and Rhythms were hidden. Between 1999 and mid-2001, senior executives and directors of the company sold 17.3 million shares worth $1.1 billion. Investigators also revealed that Lay had tried to use all contacts at his disposal, including at President George W. Bush's office, especially when the rating agencies had tightened the noose.

Among the senior executives at Enron, Lay, Skilling and Fastow were found to have derived the most significant personal benefits from these frauds. The graph of Kenneth Lay's remuneration showed that from levels of $1.5 million in 1990, his pay had risen to more than $5 million by 1999. Several additional payments, including lavish perquisites and allowances, were also made, apart from many 'special rewards' granted by the board whenever Enron's reported numbers or stock prices crossed expectations. Over the three years between 1999 and 2001, officially touted as Enron's best years, Lay had received an aggregate remuneration of nearly $200 million.

He had also executed several large-value transactions in the shares of Enron. During 2001 alone, Lay sold 1.77 million shares for approximately $70 million, which were passed off as a share buyback by the company. As late as September 2001, when he was actually selling his own Enron stocks aggressively, Lay had personally assured the company employees that their accounting practices were legal and appropriate, encouraging them to continue investing in the company's shares. Everything in his lifestyle reflected the wealth he had amassed from the company. The family travelled only in the Enron fleet of jets, owning more than twenty huge mansions and estates in the Texas and Colorado areas.

On 8 July 2004, Lay surrendered before the FBI and, though he was indicted on various grounds of fraud and manipulation, chose to plead innocent.

During the proceedings, Lay (and Skilling) made many arguments, attempting to shift the blame on executives like Fastow and his assistants like Ben Glisan Jr., the former Enron treasurer, and Michael Kopper, who had supposedly been entrusted with all financial and accounting matters. This was the opening statement of the senior trial lawyer, Dan Petrocelli, in defence of Lay:

> *There is a man, by the way, who did steal a nickel, stole more than a nickel, stole about $25 million plus worth of nickel; and that was Andrew Fastow; and he was helped by a man named Ben Glisan, who we're going to see, and a man named Michael Kopper, who I hope we're going to see. And these three men – you didn't hear much about them – they ripped Enron off. They stole from Enron. They violated Enron's trust. Enron was the victim of their fraud. And the evidence is going to be what Andrew Fastow stole and what Ben Glisan stole and Michael Kopper stole was hidden from Jeff Skilling, was hidden from Ken Lay, was hidden from the board of directors; and it didn't even surface until the very end, indeed, after the bankruptcy. And I want to make something clear. I am not saying that Andrew Fastow's crimes against Enron brought Enron down. I mean, he stole big money. He stole $25 million. As big as that is, that's not big enough to bring Enron down, Enron was a hundred billion dollar corporation. So Andrew Fastow did not bring Enron down. He sure did not help though.*

Lay submitted that though he had made a lot of money, he had also lost a lot of it. He denied committing any tax or investment fraud, claiming that he had supported several public causes and large charities. He also argued that he and

Skilling had not tried to set up any hidden bank accounts in tax havens and escape from facing trial, as they knew they were innocent.

When accused of using unfair practices like creating artificial power shortages to push up market-determined prices in the California electricity supply project, Lay was particularly critical, saying that '*indeed, a market like California is not good for Enron ... but the most important thing is, Enron did not cause the California crisis.*'

During the trial, the authorities cut amnesty deals with many of the involved individuals. Finally, sixteen people who were either current or former employees of the company pleaded guilty. Five outsiders, including some Merrill Lynch employees who had assisted Fastow in falsifying transactions, also admitted to their roles. Fastow himself testified against Lay and Skilling, along with seven others who had been direct accomplices to the two top men.

Skilling, in a March 2001 interview, famously said, '*We are the good guys. We are on the side of angels.*' He was sentenced to twenty-four years in prison, which was later reduced to fourteen years on subsequent appeals. He was released in February 2019 after serving twelve years.

Fastow was sentenced to ten years, while his wife, who assisted in his schemes, received a one-year sentence. Many key executives were found guilty of abetting the fraud and received differing sentences, while some, like Kopper, were pardoned as part of the deal for having cooperated with the proceedings.

The auditor, Arthur Andersen, was also charged on multiple counts, including shredding large amounts of evidence. A penalty of $7 million was imposed on it, and the SEC announced a ban on the firm from rendering any future services. Though the ban was later overturned by the Supreme Court, nothing remained of the once-Big 5 firm by then, having already shuttered operations the world over.

As per estimates, investors lost nearly $74 billion, particularly during the seemingly miraculous rally that saw share prices soar past the $90 mark in early 2000 before crashing by the end of the year. Enron owed nearly $67 billion in debt, and though the real estate and other valuable assets of the company were auctioned or otherwise disposed of, creditors lost heavily.

Over 20,000 employees lost their jobs, though some partial settlements were later made based on class-action suits. Overall, there was an air of distressing losses and damages, and the fallout of the Enron scandal was felt across most economies in the world. The case led to a slew of new amendments in the regulatory, financial and corporate governance frameworks, including the introduction of the Sarbanes-Oxley Act (SOX), 2002, to regulate publicly listed entities in the US.

Kenneth Lay was found guilty of six counts of securities and wire fraud. But he continued to keep a brave face, saying, '*I don't fear jail because I know I'm not guilty. I know I did nothing wrong. I did nothing criminal, and I also believe my God will get me through this.*'

The popular legal view was that he would receive a sentence of up to forty-five years.

Before the final sentencing, Lay suffered a massive heart attack at his home in Colorado and passed away on 5 July 2006.

Because the death of the defendant automatically ends all ongoing appellate proceedings under US law, the conviction against Lay was formally overturned on 17 October 2006.

Nevertheless, the US Department of Justice assured that legal action would continue to secure remedies for those who had suffered losses.

Following a private funeral in Aspen, a grand memorial service was held for Kenneth Lay at the First United Methodist Church in Houston. The event was attended by a galaxy of personalities, such as former President George H. W. Bush, to bid goodbye to one of the most highly rated business leaders the world has seen.

'*Have you pursued the American dream*?' Lay was asked during the trial, to which he replied: '*I guess, at least, certainly early on, I never thought of it in those terms, but certainly other people have characterized it that way, that I've not only pursued the American dream, I've achieved it. I suppose we could say the last few years, I've also achieved the American nightmare.*'

8

Oscar Hartzell

The Dream Merchant

'So far as His Majesty's Government is aware, there is no unsettled or unappropriated estate in existence which formerly belonged to Sir Francis Drake or to any member of his family.'

– SIR J. GILMOUR, Home Secretary, UK, on the decision to deport Hartzell

Sudie hears a tale

In the year 1910, 360 years after the lifetime of Sir Francis Drake, the illustrious admiral who rose from humble origins to command the royal fleet of Queen Elizabeth I, Sudie Whitaker, a young American widow, first heard tales of his adventures. She listened with rapt attention to stories of the sixteenth-century seafarer, such as his famed victories against the Spanish Armada and the Portuguese fleet. After amassing large treasures during his voyages across the world, Sir Francis Drake had died at sea somewhere off Panama.

Following rumours that he and Queen Elizabeth I had an illegitimate son, the British government was said to have quietly buried everything related to the succession of his huge estate.

This popular tale stuck in Sudie's mind, and she soon began to smell a good money-making proposition from it. She roped in her trusted friend Milo Lewis, who was a lawyer, and together, the two of them made up a story they could sell.

After learning that the Late Sir Francis Drake once owned a large house near Devon in England called Buckland Abbey, they chose Plymouth as the site of where the supposed estate was located. They then created convincing documents, including title deeds and maps showing locations and boundaries, to prove their claims.

The plan was to tell people that ever since Sudie had heard about Sir Drake's estate, she had wondered if one of her distant cousins named George Drake might be connected to the family. With great efforts, she would claim to have traced back his family tree to establish that he was indeed the great-grand relative of the original buccaneer. Meaning that as a surviving heir, George Drake had a rightful claim now to his ancestor's estate.

Sudie and Milo then used public information like telephone lists to compile a list of some people with the surname 'Drake' whom they planned to pass off as supposed relatives and thus legal heirs too of the admiral. They created documents, including title deeds and maps showing the locations and boundaries of the supposed estate and a power of attorney purportedly executed by the identified legal heirs authorizing Sudie to act as their official representative in all estate-related matters.

Once the papers were ready, Sudie and Milo launched their money-making scheme.

They would approach suitable targets with the story of the massive estate, telling them that given the complexities involved in disposing of such a large estate, the legal heirs had decided to launch a scheme that would allow individual investors also to buy small, undivided shares in the large estate. This would allow even small investors to participate in the scheme at reduced market prices, earning them large returns when the estate was sold later. Sudie, backed by Milo, even lent the investment scheme an element of generosity, emphasizing how many small American investors could now partake in this windfall.

Their claim was that a 'tiny' investment of $50 would fetch a guaranteed amount of not less than $100,000 upon the sale of the estate.

Backed by the documents and assurances of the lawyer accompanying her, nobody they called on had any doubts about the scheme or Sudie's role as the authorized person in this matter.

Many people were lured into investing in the 'lucrative' scheme, who, in turn, became the best brand ambassadors. So much so that as soon as someone made an investment, Sudie and Milo would be swamped with requests from friends and relatives of such people to also join. Even those with frugal savings formed groups to buy at least one share jointly. Meanwhile, Sudie and Milo remained wary of the dangers of overstaying at any location and were constantly on the move. It was while travelling across towns and villages that they reached the small Hartzell farm in Iowa.

Oscar also hears the tale

The Hartzells had always made an honest living on their farm in Monmouth, in western Illinois, United States, steadily acquiring nearly 400 acres of farmland over time. Sixteen-year-old Oscar Hartzell also joined the family farm after completing his formal schooling. A few years later, he met and married Daisy Rees, a pretty girl from nearby Gerlaw, and together they continued to work on the farm. After a while, though, Oscar began to feel discontented and decided to seek a bigger challenge.

He relocated from Monmouth to Madison County, where he started a business of buying and selling land, particularly farmland, which promised high returns. He was doing well until he received news of an unexpected tragedy at home – his father's death after a riding accident.

When the family estate was partitioned, Oscar decided to invest his share in a new ranch. This venture progressed well too until another misfortune hit. This time, in the form of an epidemic, affecting all his livestock. The losses were huge, and unable to salvage the situation, Oscar was forced to shut down the ranch to reach a compromise with the creditors.

Since another attempt at the farming business was risky, Oscar decided to return to real estate. This time, he chose De Moines, which was close to his home in Madison County, charting a plan to invest in properties that would appreciate quickly. Relying heavily on borrowed funds, he chose to make investments in small land parcels that could be sold to those in the low- or mid-income groups. Once again, things did not go as planned, especially when real estate became one of the first sectors to be hit by the impending financial depression. When demand for new housing fell sharply, it was typically the lower and mid-income segments of the market that bore the brunt of the damage. Oscar was soon staring at an inventory of properties that could not be marketed, while carrying the large debts he had run up. The only way out was to declare bankruptcy.

Depressed and financially shattered due to repeated business failures, Oscar decided to seek a regular job. He was able to secure a position as an officer in the local police force, with a modest, albeit assured, salary. The work was unlike anything he had done before but he was soon enjoying the varied challenges and experiences it offered. After gaining acceptance from both seniors and colleagues, he was swiftly promoted to deputy sheriff. A little later, when the post of sheriff became vacant and elections were announced, Oscar's name started to seriously do the rounds. Though some of his well-wishing seniors advised him that it was still early in his official career, he let his current popularity influence him and decided to throw his hat into the ring. It turned out to be a tough and bitterly fought election, and despite his best efforts and campaigning hard, Oscar lost. To make matters worse, the money spent on the campaign had exceeded all his estimates, and Oscar was in the red yet again. Having lost face in the police department, he became depressed and decided to quit and return to his mother, who now lived on a small farm in Iowa with his brother, Canfield.

His family welcomed him back warmly, but Oscar's gloomy mood lingered for much longer. Things had just begun to return to normalcy when they were surprised by two unexpected visitors at the farm one afternoon.

Sudie Whitaker and Milo Lewis had selected Oscar's mother as a potential target for their estate scheme. Pretending to be delighted that Mrs Hartzell had already heard about the wonderful scheme from some of her church and village friends, they took the family through their well-rehearsed storytelling drill. Just as they'd hoped, Mrs Hartzell quickly consented to invest her entire savings of $6,000 with them. Sudie promised the woman that this sum would multiply to $600,000. Oscar's brother, also fully convinced, supported his mother's decision. The duo left after assuring Mrs Hartzell that they would return in a few days to hand over the formal legal assignment and other documents for her share.

Oscar, who had also listened to both the visitors, did not feel as much at ease as his mother and brother. But he didn't say anything, largely because he had no money of his own to invest and didn't want to interfere with his mother's or brother's financial decisions.

After a few days, Mrs. Hartzell began to wonder why Sudie hadn't come back yet with the documents as promised. This was when Oscar realized how many people in this little town alone had gladly put all their savings into the scheme. Interestingly, even at this point, none of them, including his mother and brother, were ready to consider the slightest possibility of having been cheated. In fact, many people there were still kicking themselves for passing up the investment opportunity!

Curiosity piqued, he went to the local library in Sioux and read everything he could find about Sir Francis Drake, including his ancestry. After going through all the available information, Oscar concluded that the existence of such a large unclaimed estate was highly unlikely. He was now convinced that Sudie and Milo had pulled off a well-planned con. Though initially annoyed that his mother had been cheated out of her life savings, his sentiments soon changed into admiration for Sudie and Milo's methods.

From his stint on the police force, Oscar had believed that many people had an innate tendency to be cheated easily. But it was the first time he had witnessed so many people succumb to the allure of larger-than-life gains with scant regard for reality. It was even more astonishing that virtually everyone remained confident in their decision. Oscar was marvelling at this psyche when he suddenly realized there was something here that could be used to his advantage if played wisely.

Suspecting that Sudie and Milo were still somewhere in the Iowa area, he decided to use his old police contacts and skills to track them down. When Oscar first met them in Des Moines, they were both embarrassed and apologetic, offering to repay his mother's investment in full.

But Oscar's reaction to their offer proved surprising.

Laughing loudly, he told them they could keep all of it.

'My mother still firmly believes that she'll receive a portion of the Drake Estate. So let it be,' he said.

What he said next was even more astonishing. 'I've studied everything about Sir Drake's estate and am certain that it does not exist. But I think you've both been country jerks to sell such a brilliant thing for a pittance when there's so much to be had. I have much bigger plans for this, and if you trust me, we can start working together right away.'

Tale at work

Having sparked their interest, Oscar proceeded to share his idea.

Instead of targeting small investors like their current scheme, he felt that they ought to aim much higher. As before, they would begin by claiming to have identified a legal heir to Sir Francis Drake, though this time under the name of Ernest Drake. They would also list other people bearing the same surname, though unlike before this would not be confined to only a few such persons. The idea was that instead of knocking on common doors to seek small one-time sums, they would launch a regular scheme which would call for much larger collections. This would be structured like a regular scheme, but be available only to selective people. Oscar's plan was that initially just those with the surname 'Drake' would be invited to join the scheme in their capacity as rightful legal heirs to the estate.

These people would be called on to make a contribution either in lump sums or instalments on the plea that this money was required to defray the legal and other costs of transmitting the estate located in England to them with a proper title. The promise would be that based on the amounts contributed, they would be given shares in the estate once the legal formalities were completed. Then, depending on the success of the scheme, they could think of scaling it up to include other people as well.

Making Sudie and Milo see how much more they could earn with the modified scheme, Oscar soon convinced them to work with him. It was also agreed that Oscar would lead the operations, for which he would be paid an additional sum of $1,000 every month and under his direction, they began to work on the new plan.

From various sources, including telephone directories, they began to identify people with the surname 'Drake' and to their delight, were able to quickly enlist nearly 20,000 candidates from nearby areas itself. Oscar personally wrote to each of them with the story of Sir Francis Drake, the massive estate lying unclaimed since his death in 1596 and how their relationship with the famed buccaneer had now been traced through the roots of one Ernest Drake. Oscar presented the convincing picture of a massive estate covering the entirety of Plymouth, which the British government was now legally obligated to hand back to the legal heirs. He informed them that Ernest Drake (being the first heir identified) had authorized him to set up a common body styled Sir Francis Drake Association to actively pursue the collective interests of all the eligible claimants with the British government. Expressing confidence in completing the legal formalities and getting the estate transferred in a reasonable time frame, he also advised that this could be a complex process entailing significant legal and other expenses. A joint corpus was being set up to defray these costs collectively and each family member entitled to receive a share of the inheritance was called on to make an initial contribution towards this to facilitate the completion of the legal transfer.

Flashing an enormous value of $22.5 billion as the minimum market price estimated of the estate now, he made the request that considering the legal complications anticipated, the minimum value of contribution was fixed at $2,500. This could be paid either as a one-time down payment or through periodic contributions. Additional contributions were welcome, which would of course be given credit when the shares in the estate were finally allocated.

Oscar's assurance was that even by rough estimates, each contributor would receive at least $500 for every dollar paid once the estate's shares were settled. In conclusion, he reiterated that this was not to be seen as a contribution, but instead as an investment itself that would reap tremendous returns.

Oscar's communication was so convincing that almost everyone who received it readily paid the 'small' contribution as requested. In fact, most people contributed larger sums.

The response was so encouraging that Oscar decided to expand the scheme beyond those named 'Drake'.

He now wrote to people at random, informing them that their lineage had also been traced back to Sir Francis Drake and they were entitled to a share in the estate. He even created elaborate family trees to show them how their surnames had changed from 'Drake' over time, mostly through marriages. Inevitably, more people continued to join the Sir Francis Drake Association and willingly contributed to reclaim their estate.

Oscar continued to introduce strategies to ensure the association's membership grew quickly. He appointed field agents who were trained to find and recruit new 'contributors' to the inheritance story in various locations. Regular meetings were convened in different cities, which Oscar personally attended to explain the scheme to the attendees. Each time, he also shared the 'latest status of legal activities' that were supposedly underway to regain the estate. He became so skilled at delivering these speeches that soon he was able to persuade very large audiences to join the Sir Drake Association. In fact, the crowds jostling to hear him grew to a point that finding large enough venues became difficult.

During the scheme's fantastic progress in America, sometime in 1924, Oscar suddenly announced a decision to shift to Britain.

And he had a good reason for making this move.

Oscar had always made it a point to dissuade his 'investors' from talking about the scheme in public. The ostensible reason he shared was that he foresaw plenty of resistance from both the American and British governments in allowing the estate to be reclaimed. He explained that when this much money entered the country, the American leadership would lose all its importance, while the Bank of England would undoubtedly collapse when they had to discharge the huge financial liability to settle the estate.

But Oscar was clearly aware that keeping everyone's mouth shut was not an option, and that as the scheme's popularity grew, there would inevitably be some regulatory scrutiny. Not long ago, some overzealous American embassy officials had written to the British Home Department enquiring about such an elusive estate and were told that, to the best of their knowledge, no such unclaimed properties existed.

Oscar had strongly refuted this information, though he had also needed to use his influence and monetary resources to have the matter dropped without too much ado from the authorities. But from that point on, he began to believe it would be safer to continue his operations from outside of America. Furthermore, he had repeatedly informed the investors that he would have to personally travel to Britain at an appropriate point to resolve matters quickly. Oscar now thought this move would address all these issues, while also adding credibility to his claims.

On arriving in London, he disguised himself as a rich duke and moved into a lavish mansion. But even as he enjoyed his newfound luxuries, he kept the plan going. Shortly after settling in, he made an announcement from London, which was widely publicized among the investors in America.

He shared the heartening news that he had found a true modern-day descendant of the late Sir Francis Drake in Britain. He claimed to have learnt through extensive efforts that though the control of the late admiral's estate had been fraudulently seized by one of his brothers after his sudden death, Sir Francis had a son who was the rightful heir.

Moving down the family tree from this son, Oscar claimed to have discovered that a military officer named Colonel Dexter Drake in London was a direct descendant of Sir Francis and, hence, an immediate legal heir. A little later, Oscar sent another communique stating that the genealogy affirming the colonel's legal heirship had also been sanctioned by the highest authorities in Britain, including the Lord's and the King's Commission and the Crown's Commission. Meaning, it could no longer be contested in official forums.

Oscar continued to send more letters reassuring the American investors that he had formally secured an assignment of the estate and noting that the British government had also formally acknowledged their obligation to account for the estate and return it to the rightful owners. He informed the excited investors that according to official sources, the estate comprising money, properties, timber, rock quarries, fishing rights, heirlooms and other personal assets, together with the income generated on these assets over the past three centuries, was easily enough to buy and ring-fence the entire state of Iowa or Des Moines and still leave plenty behind. Oscar also allayed doubts that Britain may not have the wherewithal to discharge such a large debt, as this was now a Crown commitment. He padded up the fiction with the announcement that he had recently been bestowed a baronetcy by the British government in recognition of his role in settling the long-pending legal matter.

After setting the perfect stage, Oscar made a renewed monetary request.

He wrote to investors that to bring matters to legal fruition and complete the final handover of the estate, he would need to incur some additional expenses for legal and other charges. He estimated this at $2,500 per week, reminding them this was just an incremental investment compared to the much larger gains awaiting. He specifically assured that this would be repaid at the rate of $1,000 for every dollar contributed when the estate was finally settled.

In his next announcement, Oscar wrote that only King George V's final approval was now pending and promised to share a copy of the official *London Gazette* as soon as it was announced. Once again, he requested that they maintain strict confidentiality to avoid generating unnecessary hype in these final stages.

Things were going swimmingly well until Oscar began to receive some worrying news from America.

For some time now, regulations in America were being tightened to address issues like the illegal collection of public deposits and the use of postal services to promote fraudulent schemes. Oscar was disturbed to learn that the activities of the Francis Drake Association were also increasingly coming under official scrutiny. Complaints were mounting from collection agents and the field staff that the regulatory actions and investigations had begun to hamper operations; though, thankfully, collections had not yet taken a hit and continued to grow, both from existing and new investors. Nevertheless, Oscar knew this was a growing fire that needed to be controlled swiftly.

Another troubling development was that in his prolonged absence, his fellow partners, Sudie Whitaker and Milo Lewis, had resorted to various dubious activities of their own. Oscar had long felt that he didn't need either of them but wasn't sure how to best tackle this situation, especially from London. He was still toying with his options when an unexpected piece of news from America offered a way to kill the proverbial two birds with one stone.

Milo Lewis had been found guilty of professional misfeasance and barred from all legal activities. Realizing this would immediately increase the attention on the Sir Francis Drake Association as well, Oscar decided to rush back to America with a plan to manage the situation.

Back home, he seized on the latest news to swiftly turn the tables on both of his partners. Immediately upon arrival, Oscar levelled allegations that both Sudie and Milo had consistently misrepresented facts regarding the estate for some time now. He claimed that they had cheated him and the investors alike over the years through their wily guiles. They had also allegedly introduced him to a cousin of Sudie Whitaker named George Drake, who was purportedly Sir Drake's heir, though all along she had known this was not true.

He agreed to a settlement with the officials after sensing that the investigating authorities in Illinois would also be happy to find someone connected with the Drake Association to initiate action against. Oscar voluntarily admitted to making some inadvertent mistakes while running the association's affairs, but maintained that his actions were in good faith. And Sudie and Milo alone were to blame for attempting to defraud the public. Once again, Oscar used all his contacts and wealth to have both Sudie and Milo taken into custody. As per the arrangement with the officials, Oscar also faced preliminary charges, but he was quickly absolved from all punitive action in exchange for cooperating with the investigation. The press, with whom Oscar had built excellent relations, backed him, providing such extensive coverage that following the indictment of Sudie Whitaker and Milo Lewis, all regulatory doubts about the Drake Association were fully resolved. Even so, before returning to Britain, Oscar went around meeting the investors personally and reassuring them that the matter of the estate was moving satisfactorily towards a planned closure. Aside from the success of his plans, he also felt significantly satisfied by the public support he now enjoyed everywhere. Once he was confident the business in America was in order, Oscar returned to England.

It's only a tale

Oscar had informed the investors he would remain in England until the final affairs of the estate were settled. To keep up the trust and morale of the investors in America, he would send them periodic reports and updates of the 'progress'.

In his letters, he wrote about being present in meetings at the highest levels, including with the British prime minister, where he claimed to have sorted out all issues around the persisting bureaucratic delays. He told them that a team of experts was working on quantifying the huge interest payable by the British government from 1596 onwards on account of the delay in settling the estate. At every stage, Oscar's personal involvement was so great that if he learnt about even one investor becoming mildly disgruntled, he would immediately write to the person directly to assuage their concerns.

Oscar's latest moves had the effect of opening the floodgates even more, as huge sums kept flowing in from investors. Interest in the scheme went up even more when the Great Wall Street Crash of 1929 drove speculators and investors away from securities. When the eminent economist John Keynes wrote a positive article about the Drake Association scheme, new investments poured in through the roof.

The only major challenge Oscar now faced was finding enough staff members to manage both the huge demand for new memberships and the enormous sums flowing in.

But things were due to change soon.

Following the Great Depression, the pace of legislative and regulatory developments in the American financial system accelerated considerably. President Franklin D. Roosevelt, who took office in 1933, oversaw massive economic reforms. Significant new laws, including the 1933 Banking Act, the Securities Act of 1933 and the Securities Exchange Act of 1934, were quickly enacted, with astute officers being pressed into the task of ensuring strict compliance. Many investigations were also launched, especially into institutions collecting public funds.

To Oscar's chagrin, the Sir Francis Drake Association was prominently featured on this list, yet he remained optimistic.

But this time, the American authorities were much more thorough. The officials investigating the Drake Estate scheme pushed hard to collect all possible information, seeking confidential information from their British counterparts about the mysterious estate. Once again, the official response from Britain was that no such estate existed. When it became evident that Oscar was using the postal system to promote his scheme, the US Postal Department also swung into action.

They took legal action against several of Oscar's confidants and staff members in America. Those willing to cooperate by providing information were granted leniency, while serious charges were filed against the others for mail fraud.

Scotland Yard was also keeping a watch on Oscar's activities in Britain, working in tandem with the American authorities. When they learnt how a fictitious estate was being used for a massive fraud, they decided to initiate stern action.

Many of Oscar's British accomplices and assistants were taken into custody for questioning, including even a lady mind reader with whom Oscar had forged financial ties. Though there was little in the form of recorded information, the authorities learnt that Oscar had received large sums ranging from $700,000 to $8,00,000 from America in violation of laws. To bolster the charges, the British authorities also retrieved all possible records from their historical archives to show that whatever Sir Francis Drake had left behind on his death, which was nothing on the scale projected by Oscar, had been duly shared amongst his family members at the time and nothing remained of it now.

Based on these findings, it soon became clear that everything Oscar had promised was a big hoax.

As the official actions began to catch media and public attention, Oscar decided that even if he did not have all the information, enough trouble was brewing to warrant urgent reprisal. Under the circumstances, he decided the best option was to reactivate the enormous public confidence he enjoyed.

In the past, too, when similar situations had arisen, Oscar had inveigled the investor masses to create a huge show of support, forcing the politicians and authorities to back down to avoid risking further escalation of public sentiments. A case in point was the investor-level resistance he had initiated earlier to dissuade a powerful group of elected representatives led by Iowa Secretary of State Ed Smith. This was because this group had been demanding stricter laws to regulate the acceptance of public contributions and donations in schemes like his.

To his credit, Oscar had always warned his investors that they would have to collectively deal with many official moves to scuttle the scheme, and he knew it would be easy to convince them that the current official actions were also merely another manifestation of the expected threat.

Deciding it was safest to remain in England, Oscar issued messages validating the scheme while deploring the government's attempts to bring him down. He even made some outrageous claims, such as the Great Depression being a creation of the government to target his scheme. But he promised that no matter what the governments of America and Britain tried, he would be able to keep his promise as long as he had the people's support. Using his connections with the media and other influencers, he began to issue war cries, pleading for people to support him aggressively in opposing all government actions against the scheme. His efforts resulted in a large amount of public support for him in America.

But this time, the US authorities remained unfazed. As soon as they had enough incriminating evidence, they formally requested the British government to extradite Oscar back to America for legal action. Oscar tried his best to resist the move, but the request was approved, with Sir J. Gilmour, the Home Secretary of the United Kingdom, affirming, '*I decided in February last, on the advice of the Aliens Deportation Advisory Committee, to make a Deportation Order against Oscar Hartzell, on the ground that, as he had no genuine occupation and was holding himself out as carrying on a scheme for the recovery of the so-called Drake estate alleged to be dormant in Chancery, it was not conducive to the public good that he should be allowed to remain in this country. So far as His Majesty's Government is aware, there is no unsettled or unappropriated estate in existence which formerly belonged to Sir Francis Drake or to any member of his family.*'

Oscar was arrested on arrival in America and taken to the Sioux City Prison in Iowa for further interrogation. During questioning, he remained elusive about everything related to the estate, sticking to vague answers with an air of nonchalance.

When Post Office Inspector O. B. Williamson asked him where exactly the Drake estate was located, Oscar merely waved his hands and said, '*I cannot tell you that offhand, it is all over the place.*'

When the Assistant United States District Attorney asked him, '*How is the unclaimed Drake estate coming along?*' he answered, '*There is no such thing as an unclaimed Drake estate. Sir Francis Drake had a wife and child who were not known and that his claim came through them.*'

Upon being asked for the names of the admiral's wife and child, he said, '*I cannot tell you.*'

He also refuted all charges of mail fraud, claiming he had not directly perpetrated the scheme in America, as he had been in England for a long time.

But the officials persisted in their investigation, summoning many of Oscar's collection agents as well as others who worked closely with him in the Sir Drake Association. Backed by their testimonies, the case against him grew stronger.

During the trial, none of Oscar's arguments were accepted and, based on the information presented by the investigators, he was found guilty of committing fraud and sentenced to ten years at the Leavenworth Penitentiary in Kansas. Some of his key accomplices were also awarded sentences, though for a shorter period of one year.

Oscar staunchly maintained even before the Supreme Court that he was being falsely implicated as part of a political smear campaign and that he could bring the Drake Estate to America if allowed to proceed with his plans. These arguments were also summarily rejected.

During his prison term, Oscar tried to keep up his spirits, hoping the continued public support would come to his rescue. But when nothing of the sort happened, he appeared to be steadily losing his mind after a few years. He now insisted that there was a large Drake estate that belonged fully to him and complained to everyone in prison that putting him behind bars was a ploy to steal his estate. Oscar's obsession with the estate grew into an overpowering psychosis, and he was eventually transferred to the prison medical centre for mental care. He died in 1943 after spending the last few years of his life at the institution.

Perhaps the most surprising phenomenon among these developments was that the public faith in Oscar had not dented significantly. Many investors refused to denounce the scheme as fraudulent or divulge details of the amounts they invested during questioning. Several people continued to make contributions, with some even claiming to have been repaid in full with the promised returns. Investor awareness measures like a formal advisory from Attorney General John Fletcher stating that the Drake Association was a fraudulent organization were rejected with disdain. All actions against Oscar were furiously denounced as attempts to deny ordinary people their rights.

According to unconfirmed sources, Oscar defrauded over 70,000 Americans over the years to the extent of approximately $2 million. Due to a general lack of cooperation from the investors, and non-availability of any proper records, the authorities could not assess the exact extent of the fraud or work on any form of recovery and restitution.

Like many con artists before and after his time, a majority of investors who blindly trusted Oscar Hartzell went to their graves insisting that the state had grievously erred in bringing down this person, who, if only allowed a little more time, would have surely brought the multibillion-dollar Drake Estate to America and made them all wealthy.

Perhaps, if anyone with the right glib were to seize upon this idea anew, there would still be willing 'investors' ready to invest their entire life savings for at least a small share in Sir Francis Drake's ever-elusive estate.

9

Natwarlal

The Master Manipulator

'No jail is enough to hold me for too long.'

– NATWARLAL

Forging is simple

Siwan, in the present-day Indian state of Bihar, is said to have been part of Lord Rama's Kosala empire and the birthplace of the great guru from the Mahabharata, Dronacharya. Historically, it passed through the hands of many marauders, including the Lodis, the Moghuls, the Dutch and the English, before playing a prominent role in the 1857 mutiny and later independence struggles. The land, along with being associated with many famous temples, has also been home to great spiritual and thought leaders, including India's first president, Rajendra Prasad.

Natwarlal, India's most notorious conman, was also born here.

Raghunath Prasad Srivastava, the local railway station master in Bangra, Siwan District, led a simple and honest life. Mithilesh Kumar, his older son, was born in 1912, and Ganga Prasad, his younger son, a few years later. Though money was a concern, the family never had major financial problems, and the benevolent station master's house was always known as a place where one could get at least a handful of wheat and pulses. Like many proud Indians, even while serving under the British regime, Raghunath Prasad hoped to see his country free one day.

Mithilesh was enrolled at the local village school, where football became his first love, though he also enjoyed chess. He did not however find much to interest him in academics, clearing matriculation only in his second attempt. Raghunath, who felt it was futile to send the boy for higher studies to the nearest town of Calcutta (now Kolkatta), decided to get him a job locally, ideally at the same railway station. He had often taken the boy to the station, and Mithilesh was well-known among the staff and senior officials there. So, when Raghunath requested that his son be accommodated in some capacity at the station, the management readily agreed. Now that the boy had a 'decent' job, Raghunath proceeded to identify a 'good' girl from the village to be his wife.

But Mithilesh himself remained unhappy. Living in the tiny village like his father was never in his plans, and he yearned to move to Calcutta. But with the financial constraints, he had no other realistic options for now. At the station, while performing odd jobs, Mithilesh would keenly observe the operations, including the systems for handling large loads of cargo.

He also often accompanied his father to the faraway bank, where Raghunath taught him how to undertake regular transactions, like depositing money, encashing cheques and taking out demand drafts. Soon he began to handle these matters for the family on his own and also assisted elderly villagers who found it difficult to walk to the bank each time.

But in rendering this service, he had to frequently deal with one issue: an elderly relative or neighbour forgetting to sign the cheque or the demand draft requisition, making it impossible to complete the transaction. Unfortunately, the elder's need would usually be so urgent that the young man would have to return to the village and go back immediately to the bank after obtaining the signature. During the sweltering summer months, especially, this journey was no mean feat.

Then, on one particularly hot day, Mithilesh tried a simpler approach. He faked the neighbour's signature on the demand draft requisition. After handing over the form, he waited anxiously for the cashier to raise his eyebrows over the mismatch in signature. But the expressionless man in the box handed over the draft to him. From thereon, Mithilesh made it a regular practice to avoid scrambling back to the village just to get the original signatures. His confidence was also growing that forging signatures was a simple task, though the thought of using it for personal ends did not occur to him.

As life went on, Mithilesh's dissatisfaction also grew. With each passing day, his longing for a better life became a desperate urge to somehow make enough money to get out of the village.

This was when he came up with an idea.

For the first time, he decided to forge a signature to get some money of his own. Using the much-rehearsed signature of their next-door neighbour, Sahay, he drew ₹1,000 in cash from the man's bank account using a temporary withdrawal slip. The bank staff, used to the boy transacting on behalf of others, did not bat an eyelid.

But even as he was figuring out his next move, the neighbour visited the bank. On checking his account, the unsuspecting Sahay had the shock of his life when he found his balance significantly depleted. Certain that this was a mistake in the bank's statement, the man was horrified to learn that a bank slip bearing his signature had very recently been used for this withdrawal. It was only a matter of time before he found that it was his trusted neighbour who had forged the instrument and encashed it.

Raghunath Prasad, a pious and honest man, saw this as a terrible offence and gave Mithilesh the worst beating of his life. The boy was also ordered to fall at Sahay's feet in repentance and repay the money the very next morning. Mithilesh, however, did not take kindly to the punishment and, emboldened by the money he still had on hand, decided to flee that same evening.

It was to Calcutta he went.

Calcutta lessons

Mithilesh enrolled in the Bachelor of Commerce course at a small city college, believing that a degree in commerce was the best way forward. Unfortunately, though, he quickly ran out of money and was forced to look for a part-time job.

After several attempts, he was hired by Keshav Ram, a cotton merchant, to do various chores at his shop. Besides the poor pay, just enough for three meals, Mithilesh had a small corner to sleep in. Soon enough, he decided to augment this income. Relying on his knowledge of English and math, he offered his services as a private tutor to the merchant's son and daughter. He even claimed to have taught at a large school earlier and made out letters of commendation from parents of other students to convince Keshav Ram to hire him. The additional fee helped him continue college even if some of the fees remained in arrears.

By the time he was in his final year, the college administration insisted that the arrears be cleared before he could take the completion exams. Mithilesh's only option was to approach Keshav Ram for an advance, promising to pay it back after he graduated and moved to a better position in the merchant's office. However, Keshav Ram ridiculed him in front of the other employees for expecting a promotion in the office after he graduated. Enraged by the response, Mithilesh quietly resolved to make the man pay.

Recognizing the scarcity of high-quality cloth, he informed the merchant that one of his close relatives wanted to sell a large quantity of material. Mithilesh offered to negotiate the deal and confirmed that the seller was ready to accept a price of ₹4.50 lakh, which he knew was low enough to bait the greedy merchant. The understanding was that Mithilesh would accompany Keshav Ram's buying agent to Bombay to close the deal, where he would take delivery of the material. But Mithilesh convinced the agent to stay behind in their hotel room while he settled the transaction. The next thing Keshav Ram knew, the young man had decamped with the entire cash. He tried sending his goons after Mithilesh, but it was futile. The young man even turned the tables on his former employer by reporting that much of Keshav Ram's business was illegal, ensuring the merchant would make no noise about his loss.

Mithilesh was now confident that he had learnt enough to do business on his own. He invested the entire sum stolen from Keshav Ram in a textile business at Calcutta's famous Burra Bazar. But he soon found that replicating successful businesses was harder than it seemed. In just a few months, cunning sharks in the Calcutta cotton market were all over Mithilesh, and the business suffered heavily. Shutting down became inevitable, though, luckily, he managed to settle all the debts amicably using whatever resources he could clobber together.

Left with nothing, Mithilesh pursued a new line of activity. He had noticed the buzz in Calcutta around stock market activities, with people increasingly investing in shares in the hope of huge gains. Since it was well beyond his means to become a regular member of the exchange, he decided to join the exchange as a sub-broker working under a full-time member. In addition to his brokerage duties, he decided to enrol in law school. While working in the stock market, he learnt the nuances of commercial banking and managed to put through some good deals as well. But principal brokers generally granted only paltry sums as commission to sub-brokers like Mithilesh, and he remained on the lookout for better opportunities.

The quest took him to the bustling Howrah Station, where he hoped to use his knowledge of railway operations to find something worthwhile. His first impression was that everything was so much bigger there, including the rail traffic, the crowds and the quantity of cargo being handled. Nobody paid attention as he walked around the different sections, watching how things worked. At the massive cargo area, he also discovered that the systems for clearing goods were a lot like those at his old station. But given the huge volume, no one bothered to double-check when a consignee submitted the original railway receipt and got a release order after paying the freight and other dues. Interestingly, the officials were willing to even accept cheques as full payment for the charges.

In no time Mithilesh was working on a money-making proposition from this operation. He made a few more visits to the cargo section and took detailed notes of all the documents and forms being used there, including the official signatures and seals.

Mithilesh returned only when he was fully ready for his plan, walking around the yard once again, this time looking closely at the goods lying there. His mission was to select something for his pilot operation and, eventually, he chose a harmonium. Light enough to carry away without drawing attention and easily sellable as well. He left after collecting all the information related to this item – the consignee's name, the address and the amount payable for clearance.

Two days later, Mithilesh came back with a release order that looked exactly like the original and bore a realistic signature with the seal of the authorized railway official. He was also carrying a masterful replication of a bank cheque he had elaborately created. Relieved that the harmonium had not been cleared yet, he completed all the formalities and calmly walked out with the musical instrument. The sale fetched only ₹135, but there was great satisfaction in knowing that a lucrative revenue stream had opened up.

He remained careful to not go back to the freight station immediately and, thereafter, only at reasonable intervals. But on each subsequent visit, the value of goods he took out went up. His favourite items were metal goods and other assorted parts, and once he got away with a whole Benz engine.

The earnings were growing, but still not enough for the lifestyle he yearned.

Mastering the trade

Visiting some of the popular brothels in town was a new pleasurable discovery; though, he never imagined this pastime could actually offer him a chance to make money.

Mithilesh knew that some of the prostitutes he frequented were doing quite well for themselves. Learning that they kept all their money and gold in personal custody, he decided to lace the bottle of liquor he usually carried to the brothel with a strong sedative and, after doping the woman with him, decamped with her money and jewels. He repeated the trick over and over, each time choosing a different brothel, until a woman identified him in a public place and called the police. Mithilesh was taken into custody and put on trial. But before the case could be heard by a judge, the woman who had identified him took her life, and he was released for want of evidence. The brush with the law, however, meant he knew this was no longer a safe line of activity to pursue, and so he decided to move on.

Even while continuing the occasional con at the railway station, Mithilesh would often keep an eye on other places in the city with an abundance of heavy items. Soon, he was targeting bulk goods like iron and cloth, which had a reasonable market and couldn't be easily traced to the real owners. He forged invoices, transportation and warehouse receipts establishing ownership of these goods and posing as a businessman, entered into sale arrangements for the goods at huge profits. The money he was now making was better than ever before, and Mithilesh was able to step up his lifestyle.

But this venture ground to an unexpected halt in 1937.

Mithilesh had identified a large lot of iron – nearly nine

tonnes – lying at a corner of Metcalfe Street. He made out the forged documents and approached a scrap dealer with a sale offer, but before the transaction could be completed, the buyer received a tip-off from somebody who had fallen prey to a similar fraud earlier and reported it to the police. When the unsuspecting Mithilesh arrived to close the sale, the police were ready for him. He was arrested and sentenced to rigorous imprisonment for six months.

This was the first time Mithilesh went to jail, though there would be many more memorable instances to follow. But, far from being a reforming experience, his time in prison gave him more confidence to continue his activities – strengthened by the knowledge that jails were not half as secure as he had always presumed.

Upon release, he decided that running petty schemes in Calcutta alone was not enough and began to look for bigger opportunities. This was when he met someone who shared his vision – a Gujarati man named Natwarlal, who was also on the police records as a wanted fraudster. The pair immediately struck up a friendship, especially when they discussed their plans for the future.

Aware of the acute shortage of cotton in the market, the Gujarati man had formulated a plan to defraud large textile manufacturers who were badly in need of material. But he was also aware that he lacked the skills and stature to carry off such a con on his own, particularly as it required posing as a senior government official, besides forging documents. When Mithilesh heard the plan, it seemed like a perfect fit for him to partner in.

The duo decided to launch the scheme in Bombay (now Mumbai), with Mithilesh donning the role of a senior officer in the textile commissioner's office and Natwarlal his junior assistant. Their plan was to call on large textile manufacturers and merchants under this guise and make them an offer.

'The textile commissioner wishes to make a special offer to a leading businessman like you,' Mithilesh would say officiously. 'If you're interested, we can arrange special allocations of cotton for you. All highly confidential, of course.'

Seeing the businessman's eyes light up, he would continue, 'If you are ready to make full payment for the material now, we can immediately give you all the documents ... including railway receipts and the release order to lift the load.'

The duo also took another wily decision to minimize their risk. The merchants were told that to ensure full secrecy, delivery of the cotton stocks would be made only at one specified location – the Azamgarh railway station. Given that this was a good 300 kilometres from the nearest town of Lucknow, they reasoned it would give them ample time to get far away before the merchant arrived and discovered himself duped.

In most cases, the greedy businessmen quickly fell into their trap. Even when someone seemed hesitant, Mithilesh would immediately rise and pretend to walk away, inevitably ensuring that the confused businessman came running after him. But they were also careful to choose victims across different cities.

Life became much better for Mithilesh and Natwarlal after the success of this scheme.

But soon the police received a tip-off that Natwarlal, the Gujarati criminal they had been pursuing for a while, had been seen in a specific area, and they tracked him down. Natwarlal managed to somehow elude capture, and instead Mithilesh was taken into custody. It took a few days for the police to be convinced that the person they had caught was not Natwarlal, but Mithilesh Kumar from Bihar, who had nothing to do with their cases.

He was released from custody, but after this incident, a new name appeared. One that would stick with him until the end, at least for official purposes. From here on, Mithilesh Kumar Srivastava became Natwarlal.

Raising the bar

The success of the cotton goods scheme gave Mithilesh (or Natwarlal) the confidence to plan even bigger scams. He committed several frauds while using more than fifty different aliases, including Surinder Kumar, Mithilesh Agarwal, Ambika Pandey, Shankar Lal, B. N. Mayur and Sitaram Aadi with multiple addresses, including those of leading businessmen and political leaders such as the Uttar Pradesh chief minister. He expanded his operations to include many prominent business cities in north and south India.

Bankers were among his favourite targets, and many gullible executives fell prey to his antics. One of his favourite cons was as a fake merchant dealing in sugar, grains and pulses. He would book a small lot of material for transportation by rail using a false name and address. The original delivery note would then be convincingly altered to make it a much larger load, even hundreds of bags. Posing as a big merchant, he would approach the bank and, presenting the forged delivery note, get the manager to sanction a large loan against the goods. The first time he tried this was at the Patna branch of the Punjab National Bank, where he drew a huge loan of ₹6.50 lakh and vanished. Following that, he used several variations of this scheme, including finalizing large commodity sale contracts against advance payments only to deliver bag loads of sand or bricks to the poor buyers! He even rented out posh offices to persuade counterparties and bank managers to do business with him.

Along with bankers, many jewellers and traders were also drawn in by his dignity and poise.

He once hired a white Ambassador car and directed the driver to take him to the shop of a leading jeweller and watch dealer named Surendra Sharma in New Delhi's upmarket Connaught Place. Dressed in all-whites, as was customary for senior government officials, he walked in with an air of great importance.

'I'm D. N. Tiwari, private secretary to the finance minister,' he said, introducing himself to the shop owner, who was visibly in awe of this high-level visitor.

'As part of our upcoming parliamentary meeting, the prime minister wants to present all senior party leaders with high-quality wristwatches. It will be a very large order, but I'm told you might be able to supply it in a day,' Natwarlal said in all majesty.

Surendra Sharma had no reservations about accepting such a large order, despite being concerned about how to arrange ninety-three expensive watches in a single day. He'd already calculated the huge profit he'd make, even with the generous discount he planned to offer. The earnest hope was that at least the finance minister, if not the prime minister, would hear about his generosity. The order was confirmed, and Natwarlal agreed to come back in person to collect the watches.

'I'll also make your payment tomorrow,' he affirmed in parting, assuaging Sharma's concerns about timely payments in a politically connected arrangement.

Surendra Sharma duly arranged the watches and was ready to receive the VIP customer the next day, as committed.

Natwarlal, alias D. N. Tiwari, arrived in the same vehicle once again, took delivery of the ninety-three watches, and left after handing over a bank draft for ₹32,829 (a large sum at the time). Surendra Sharma was on cloud nine when the important customer also assured him that the generous discount he had thrown in would reach higher ears.

Only two days later, the poor watch dealer learnt that the bank draft was forged and that there was no one named D. N. Tiwari in the entire North Block office of the finance minister.

Later, Natwarlal rolled out the same con, this time impersonating an officer at the Varanasi district judge's office who wanted to purchase eighty watches for their staff. In similar ways he nicked forty-eight watches at Shahjahanpur and another eighty-three in Kanpur. Apart from expensive watches, Natwarlal also siphoned away ornaments, including from the well-known Raja Jewellers, by telling them that a union minister wanted to buy jewellery for his son's wedding. Natwarlal even made the jeweller wait outside the said minister's office blocks while he went inside pretending to collect the draft from his boss.

Another role Natwarlal assumed was that of a social worker seeking funding for large charitable projects. He presented benevolent donors with plans, budgets and other documents to convince them to make large contributions. This way he managed to defraud even some of the country's best-known business houses and industrialists.

Wealthy foreigners were also a favourite target, and though many such scams went unreported, Natwarlal is known to have embezzled large amounts by actually 'selling' some of India's historical monuments and buildings to them. He would select individuals or small groups of rich foreigners who knew little about India and meet them in the guise of a senior government official. Backed with historic records and other documents like site plans, structural drawings, and official approvals, he would convince them that the Government of India had decided to sell an important monument to fund repayment of the country's large foreign currency debts.

'The buyers must, however, agree not to demolish the monument and to allow continued access to visitors,' he would tell them, assuring them that the government was willing to discuss rentals and other terms once the sale was completed. Natwarlal allegedly used this tactic to sell the Taj Mahal three times and the Red Fort twice to such 'investors'. If this is hard to believe, he is also known to have sold the Rashtrapati Bhavan (official seat of the President of India) and the Parliament the same way. To the added joy of the buyer, even 'throwing in' the 545 elected members of parliament who sat in session there!

Natwarlal, flush with cash, now lived in great comfort and style. To some extent, these extravagances also validated his affluent persona, which he frequently assumed when interacting with wealthy and prominent people. To his credit, at least some people saw him as a benefactor of the needy as well. Especially those in and around his village. He would frequently go there with his wife and daughter, much like the old Mithilesh, and interact freely with everyone. During these visits, he would also plan large celebrations with lavish feasts and generous gifts. It was no surprise that the villagers soon referred to him with great respect and pride as Mr Natwarlal.

Natwarlal was also an expert at foreseeing impending problems and changing course to avoid them. He ensured that all his schemes were distinct and original, paying attention to the finest detail: At the same time, there were also the odd instances where he faltered and landed in trouble.

One such incident occurred while he was riding high from cheating many jewellers and watch dealers using government aliases. Given the scale of his earlier operations, news about such a forger had gone around, and when Natwarlal tried to repeat the same stunt at a jewellery shop in Gorakhpur, the proprietor saw through the con, making sure that the police were ready for him when he returned the next day to collect the booty.

Great escapes

During his prolonged fraudster career, Natwarlal was arrested nine times in all. He was charged in over a hundred criminal cases by multiple courts and received several lifetime sentences. But, as per official records, he only served an entire prison term once. Eight times he broke out using various guiles, earning him yet another title: a master escape artist. Even while incarcerated, he is known to have secured many special privileges, such as specially cooked meals and regular bottles of liquor.

And his jailbreak stories are as baffling as those of his scams and deceptions.

In 1957, while he was lodged in Lucknow Jail, he offered eleven members of the prison staff bribes of ₹5 lakh each if they helped him by smuggling in a senior police officer's uniform. He walked out of jail proudly dressed in this uniform, with many police officers saluting him, never to be seen by them again. At the Kakinada Jail in 1975, he offered large bribes to the prison staff and arranged for a vehicle to be waiting outside the prison gate with a briefcase containing the promised money. When the excited policemen dug into the briefcase after Natwarlal's departure, all they found were old newspapers covered by a single layer of currency!

Many of his escapes occurred while being transported for questioning or shifting prisons from railway stations. Given that the usual procedure was to send three policemen to accompany such prisoners, one common tactic he used was to fake a sudden ailment, causing one of the policemen to rush for medicine while another went to get him some water. Natwarlal would then easily outsmart the lone police officer left behind, generally by abruptly snatching the rope out of his hands and disappearing into the station crowd.

He was known for ignoring the law, once telling a judge in Kanpur Court that he never stole anything and that people simply gave their assets to him.

'What do you mean?' the annoyed judge asked.

'I'll tell you, sir ... but only if you give me one rupee,' he said.

The judge, who was slightly amused, handed down a rupee coin and said, 'Okay. Tell me now.'

'I just showed you, sir,' Natwarlal said calmly, returning the coin with deference.

At times, he pulled stunts just to get something done.

During a stint at Lucknow Central Jail, he received many letters from his wife, in which she complained about the lack of funds to plough their farmland. Natwarlal, who knew that the prison staff read all incoming and outgoing communication, ignored all his wife's letters and eventually sent her a solitary reply. Consoling her, he wrote in strict confidence that he had secretly buried valuable goods in their farmland that would last them a lifetime. Just as he'd expected, the animated jailor who read this, immediately ordered his team of policemen to dig up the entire land. Obviously, the search yielded no results, but it ensured that the entire farm was prepared for cultivation by the police for free!

During his numerous brushes with the law, he also made flashy statements aimed at capturing the attention of the media and the public, such as offers to help the Government of India repay all its foreign debt. He also claimed to be a devout man and insisted that everything he did was based on his faith. But he never caused serious physical injury to anyone, not even the policemen he regularly foxed. In fact, some of the officers, like Sardar Hari Singh of the Lucknow Police and Mohammed Sabir Khan, the deputy superintendent of CID, who came into close contact with him, later acknowledged some of his positive traits.

Much like everything about him, Natwarlal's death also remains a puzzle.

When the police finally apprehended him after another long hunt in 1996, it was assumed that the old, pot-bellied man they had apprehended was not the famous Natwarlal. But when his accomplices led the authorities to a printing press that Natwarlal was using for creating forges, the policemen were convinced that they had the right man.

He was tried and sent to Kanpur Jail, where, given his age and failing health, the authorities felt that another escape was infeasible. He couldn't walk and had to rely on a wheelchair to get around because he was in so much pain. Despite receiving medical care, his pain and discomfort worsened, and the prison doctors eventually recommended that he be seen by a specialist at the AIIMS hospital in Delhi. Moving him in his present condition was not easy, and it took three police officers assigned to the task considerable effort to get him on the train to Delhi.

At the Delhi railway station, one of the policemen went to buy their return tickets, leaving the sick Natwarlal with the two others. The train journey had exacerbated his condition, and the elderly man was in terrible pain, repeatedly calling for painkillers. Finally, one of the policemen agreed to go to the nearest medical shop and get some pain relievers until they reached the hospital. But Natwarlal's condition was further deteriorating, and he was now writhing and screaming in agony. The lone policeman left on duty with him was finding it impossible to calm him down.

'Sir, please get me at least a tea from the nearby stall,' Natwarlal now pleaded.

Turning around, the policeman saw that the tea stall was only a few steps away from where they stood. But the crowd on the platform was so dense that pushing the sick man in a wheelchair through it would be difficult. As Natwarlal continued to scream, the hapless policeman decided that a cup of hot tea might calm him down and dashed to the stall to return in a couple of minutes with the tea.

The wheelchair was exactly where he had left it. But, to his horror, it was empty.

Nobody knows how Natwarlal managed to flee, including whether he was truly in pain or had planned for someone to be waiting for him at the Delhi station.

This was the last time he was seen, at least according to official records.

Many years later, his lawyer formally requested that all charges against Natwarlal be dropped as his client had passed away on 25 July 2009.

When this news came out, however, Natwarlal's (or Mithilesh's) brother, Ganga Prasad, responded that this was incorrect and that his elder brother had actually died in 1996 itself, soon after the escape from the Delhi station. He even claimed his body had been cremated in Ranchi.

These arguments remain unresolved to date, ensuring that, much like his life, Mr Natwarlal's end retains the same uncertainty and suspense.

10

Charles Ponzi

The Poor Millionaire

'I landed in this country with $2.50 in cash and $1 million in hopes, and those hopes never left me.'

– CHARLES PONZI

On 18 January 1949, an Italian pauper who had migrated to Brazil for a decent living and failed was buried at the Caju Cemetery in Rio de Janeiro. There were no friends or family in attendance, with the interment fee of $75 being paid by the deceased's part-time employer. There was no headstone and hence no epitaph at the grave either, though a possible one may have read:

'*Here Lies Charles Ponzi, Whom All of America Once Trusted.*'

Early dreams

3 March 1882: It was a joyous day in the tiny Italian home of Oreste Ponzi, the local postman in Lugo, and his wife, Imelda. The newborn boy was named Carlo. Oreste had always led

a simple and religious life, working hard for his daily bread. But Imelda was different. Born into an aristocratic family in Parma, she had grown up in considerable comfort. Even after marriage, despite her husband's monetary limitations, she continued to foster high dreams. Reluctant to forego the title 'Donna' (meant for Italian noble ladies), she lived hoping that one day her family would gain respectability and wealth.

Imelda impressed these ideas on her son from birth, and little Carlo grew up believing he was not meant to live humbly forever. She also pushed Oreste to shift to Parma, and though they could not afford it, enrolled Carlo at a private boarding school there. To her delight, the boy did well, and even when Oreste died suddenly without leaving behind much for his wife and son, Carlo was allowed to continue at the school with management support. Thanks to his good performance, as soon as he finished school, he was offered a seat at Sapienza, one of the most prestigious universities in Rome.

Fees and living expenses in the metropolis presented a challenge, but Imelda viewed it as a worthy investment to mould Carlo into the man she envisioned, setting aside a large portion of the family's resources towards this.

Life in Rome brought many new experiences, though Carlo was quickly sucked into the immense pleasures offered by the city, which took over his scholarly and learning pursuits. To gain acceptance among the wealthy young men and ladies, he spun tales about his family's elite status, hiding his real background. He also began to emulate their style and affluence. Shunning all interest in academic matters, he squandered his time galivanting around town in their company and making merry. Predictably, it was expensive to maintain this lifestyle and he soon spent the entire sum his mother had set aside for his college on pretty girls, fine wines and operas. It was only a matter of time before he was expelled from the university as well.

Carlo returned to Parma with empty hands, except for fluency in some European languages and a little sophistication picked up from privileged friends. He was also filled with shame and guilt, especially for the grief he had caused his trusting mother. But when the compunctions settled, he became determined to find something meaningful to do, which could make him a lot of money.

Just when he was giving up on options in Parma, he heard of America. It was described as a land of opportunities, where men and women from anywhere in the world had a fair chance of becoming as rich as royalty. There were even rumours of money strewn about the streets, simply waiting to be picked up. After convincing his mother of the idea, Carlo coaxed her to put together the money for his passage and prepared to leave.

Travelling in a second-class cabin of the *SS Vancouver* was considered a symbol of class distinction at the time, as those in the first class wallowed in all conceivable luxuries, while the unfortunate third-class travellers slept amidst the stink of urine. Carlo met many people on board who were also sailing in search of greener pastures, one of whom was an expert gambler. They struck up a quick friendship, although when the ship sailed into Boston harbour after two weeks at sea, the wily gamester had reduced the $200 Imelda gave him to start his life in America to $2.50.

Carlo disembarked on American soil carrying petty change and a lot of hope. Thanks to her premonition about his fiscal discipline, Imelda had also pre-booked Carlo's train ticket to a distant relative in Pittsburgh, where the young man was headed.

The initial days in America were enough to see that not only was there no money lying around, but making a living itself posed a huge challenge. Immigrants from various parts of the world had flocked to America with grand dreams and quickly discovered the harsh realities. In the absence of any other support, ethnic groups had formed clusters to collectively forge a living. Some of the early Italian settlers had also set up 'Little Italys' of their own. Although these were typically run by mafia-style regimes, Carlo realized that his only immediate option was to join such a commune.

Adapting his name to an Americanized version, Carlo, now Charles Ponzi, used these newfound ties to hunt for jobs in many cities along the East Coast, finally landing one as a dishwasher at a restaurant. His fluency in English and French, in addition to Italian, came in handy, and he was soon promoted as a waiter. However, the money was measly, forcing him to keep looking for extra income opportunities.

After noting that many diners at the restaurant did not bother to collect the small change after settling their bills, Ponzi began to pocket these amounts for himself. He continued the practice until a watchful floor manager caught him in the act and immediately sacked him. Finding a new job was even more difficult now, so, gathering whatever savings he had, Ponzi decided to try his luck elsewhere.

Based on the tales he had heard about the opportunities in the city, he chose Montreal, the financial capital of Canada. But on arrival, Ponzi found that it was not very different from America, with the Francophones (French-speaking) and the Anglophones (English-speaking) controlling most commercial activities and businesses. Thankfully, the

Italians were also a significant community, though most of them worked at lower levels, including as labourers at the new Canadian Pacific Railway sites under construction. It came as no surprise that a self-styled Italian don had steadily established control over these labour supply arrangements and become one of the most prominent people in the city. Antonio Cardasco, this mafia-esque leader, had also established other business interests, like his own bank which mostly catered to fellow immigrants. Ponzi did not want to work for Cardasco based on what he had heard about him and continued to look for other opportunities.

That's when he spotted another bank, Banco Zarossi. Much smaller than Cardasco's in size and prominence, this was also run by an Italian immigrant named Luigi Zarossi, with a better public reputation. Ponzi used his best charms to impress Zarossi, who took him on as a clerk. In this unexpected position, he worked hard to pick up the nuances of banking while building good relations with the customers, earning Zarossi's praise and quick promotions to managerial levels.

However, the bank's business was not going well, especially in comparison with Cardasco's, who had more clout. It did not help that both banks were essentially targeting the same group of Italians and similar immigrants for their business. Many times, Ponzi and the team would believe that they had a lucrative account or a large deposit heading their way, only to have it rudely snatched away.

Then, one day, Zarossi came up with an unusual idea and decided to make an immediate public announcement – surprising even Ponzi, now one of his most trusted staff members.

'Henceforth, we will pay 6 per cent interest on all deposits,' Zarossi told the press, adding, 'as I'm not a greedy banker ... unlike some others!'

The reference was evidently to Cardasco's, which offered a return of only 2 per cent, although this was generally the prevailing rate across all other banks.

'Zarossi is bluffing ... No one can offer such rates,' Cardasco retaliated.

He also made a public announcement to explain that all banks in Montreal only received 3 per cent income from their investments in government securities, and if another 1 per cent was factored in to cover operating expenses and a minimal profit, no one could pay more than 2 per cent as interest on customer deposits. Cardasco also pointed out that Zarossi Bank, too, had offered only 2 per cent until now.

People on the streets of Montreal were soon echoing Cardasco's sentiment, wondering if Zarossi knew some kind of magic trick to have made such a fantastical promise. Paradoxically, even those working at the bank, including Ponzi, remained sceptical of their boss's plan.

But suspicions dissipated as Zarossi began to honour his commitment. Word spread that Zarossi was paying 6 per cent returns, and Cardasco's large immigrant customer base began to move their accounts to its competitor. Though business grew exponentially, Ponzi continued to wonder how this would work financially, until he realized Zarossi's plan – simple, though not legitimate.

Ponzi learnt that Zarossi had started using the new deposits made in the bank to pay the high interest on maturing deposits. Zarossi was also diverting remittances made by the immigrants to their families in Italy and elsewhere, since it would take time for the depositors to hear from their relatives back home. This way, money continued to flow in and out of the book. Ponzi felt extremely uncomfortable, but Zarossi repeatedly assured him that it was only a temporary push until they got a fillip in growth and fully regularized their business.

Then, one morning, the staff at Zarossi Bank woke up to the news that their boss had fled to Mexico, taking all the bank funds with him and leaving nothing behind in Montreal except his wife and young children. Zarossi Bank was shuttered the same day.

Unable to face the public outrage, many of the staff ran away, while some who had put all their savings in the bank took their lives. Ponzi, however, decided to stay behind and face the heat, mainly because he felt it was his moral duty to help the badly shattered Zarossi family, with whom he had become emotionally close. Fortunately, people started to accept that he, too, had been cheated by Zarossi, and no charges were eventually raised against him. But with the bank closed for good, he was out of money again, especially now that he was shouldering the responsibility of the broken Zarossi family. It was out of desperation that he forged the cheque of a former client.

Canadian Warehousing was a former customer of the Zarossi Bank, and Ponzi kept in touch with its director even after the bank shut down. Ponzi could freely walk into the director's cabin, even when he wasn't in, and wait for him there. From his visits, he knew exactly where the director kept the company's cheque leaves. One day, after making sure that the man was not in the office, Ponzi went in, took out a blank cheque and forged the director's signature, which he knew well from experience. Using this, he drew out $400 from the company's bank account. But an unusual withdrawal on a day when the director was not in office piqued the attention of a clerk, who suspected fraud.

Ponzi was soon arrested and, for the first time in his life, convicted to a three-year prison term. But at the St Vincent-de-Paul Federal Penitentiary, he deployed his linguistic skills and charm to win over the prison staff. He was soon assisting the warden with the prison records and general correspondence. The influence also helped him secure an early release, though he decided to leave Montreal and go back to America. He was also confident that his banking skills would help him secure a job. With the little money he had, Ponzi bought a train ticket to New York, telling himself firmly that his problems had passed. But his troubles would continue.

While he was getting ready for the trip, a former colleague at the Zarossi Bank, Antonio Salviati, approached him with a request. Five of Salviati's Italian friends had arrived in Montreal illegally and were looking for a passage into America. None of them spoke English, so Salviati sought Ponzi's assistance in getting their fellow countrymen across the border safely. Ponzi agreed and boarded the train with the men. But during the journey, some fellow passengers caught wind and sounded the alarm. When the train reached the outskirts of the New York state border, Ponzi was arrested by American Customs and Immigration and once again convicted – this time to serve two years at the Atlanta Federal Prison on charges of smuggling illegal immigrants.

Leveraging his previous experience, Ponzi offered his support to the prison staff again and ensured a generally comfortable stay. This time, he also encountered a few fellow prisoners who interested him considerably. These included gangster Ignazio Lupo, who ran a large underworld operation, and Charles Morse, a shrewd businessman known for major financial frauds. Ponzi formed close friendships with both of them, acquiring many lessons, notably the power of charm over brute force in accomplishing goals. By the end of his prison term, his dream of becoming a successful and wealthy gentleman, as his mother had desired, was reignited.

Next, Ponzi ventured to the mining city of Alabama. Here, he spent a few days with friends who ran an insurance racket by inflating the medical bills of the workers at the nearby large coal mines. But, recognizing the high risk of this operation and possible re-imprisonment, he declined the offer to partner with them.

Relocating to Blocton, another large mining area, Ponzi was struck by the pathetic living conditions of the workers and saw a potential business opportunity there.

Failed plans

Even though the mine workers earned a decent income from their hard labour, Ponzi observed that they lived in shoddy log houses without power or running water. He believed that given an option, these people would willingly pay a reasonable sum for these amenities. He worked out a proposal to set up a small power plant to supply electricity, together with a mechanized facility that would distribute water from the nearby pond to their houses. When presenting his plans, he assured the workers that a small, one-time investment could facilitate a collectively owned venture to provide these amenities. Besides a significant improvement in their lives, he promised that the value of their investment would also appreciate over time. Convinced of their wholehearted support, Ponzi decided to proceed with the project.

But things did not take off as planned due to an unexpected incident. One day, a doctor at the local hospital approached Ponzi with a request. Pearl Grosset, a dedicated nurse at the hospital, had suffered major burns in an accident and urgently needed a skin graft. Unfortunately, the damage was so severe that large chunks of fresh skin were required, and they were desperately looking for donors. Despite not knowing Pearl, Ponzi offered to donate any amount of skin required. She survived, though the doctors had to eventually take a lot more skin off Ponzi's body than planned, leaving him in an extremely fragile state for some time. By the time he was back on his feet, his infrastructure project had been appropriated by somebody else, and a utility, backed by the mineworkers and owners, was already underway.

While Ponzi harboured no regret about helping Pearl, the failure of his envisioned project profoundly disappointed him, prompting him to contemplate his next move – this time to Florida.

But the impacts of World War I were echoing across the world, relegating him to various odd jobs, including as a sign painter. It was only when he landed a desk job as a librarian at a medical college that he felt genuinely happy and stable after a long while. Finally, the pay was good enough for a decent rental accommodation, and the work stimulated him intellectually. His comfort was short-lived as he found himself unwittingly embroiled in a controversy between the government doctors at his college and private practitioners. When Ponzi suspected that one of the senior doctors at the college was behaving unethically, he began to secretly read the doctor's confidential correspondence. Once his doubts were validated, he reported the matter to the college administration. Unfortunately, while punishing the doctor, Ponzi's unauthorized action of reading personal mail was also found inappropriate, and he was asked to leave.

Out of work again, he considered returning to Italy to enlist in the army when he found a position as a clerk in the office of J. R. Poole & Co, a shipping company based in Boston.

In Boston, too, though not in the league of the wealthy Anglo-Saxon Brahmins who controlled the large businesses, the Italians were an influential community. His work at the shipping company was dull, but the weekly pay provided for basic comforts, including an occasional beer and dinner at a decent Irish pub. It was during one such outing that Ponzi ran into Rose.

Rose Gnecco, the daughter of a small-time fruit merchant, was an educated girl who believed in a modest, honest life. While her views on life, especially the importance of money, differed from his own, Ponzi was impressed by many of her thoughts and decided she was the woman he wanted to marry. Thankfully, Rose shared this view and, after a brief courtship, on a cold February day in 1918, Ponzi and Rose were married at an Italian church. Ponzi was sure his mother would be pleased, so he wrote her a detailed letter describing Rose and her family.

What Ponzi would never learn is that apart from a missive congratulating and blessing the new couple, Imelda also wrote a separate letter addressed to her daughter-in-law. She shared everything she had heard about her son from the immigrants who returned from Canada and the United States, including his prison terms. Her maternal instincts may have rationalized some of these as selfless deeds, but when Rose learnt about her husband's acts, and the reason he was so heavily scarred, she found her love and respect for him grow. But there remained a tacit understanding that Rose would never mention any of this to her husband.

In a modestly furnished first-floor rented apartment, the young couple started their lives, sharing many common interests. Serious disagreements stemmed mostly from their contrasting views on money. To Rose, money was essential for sustenance. Any surplus was needless and, by her religious standards, wishing for more was itself a sin. Ponzi, of course, had a disparate perspective. Despite several drawn-out arguments, they generally accepted their differing standings.

Rose's family ran a fruit business that was continuously losing money. One day, her father approached Ponzi with a request to try to revive the establishment. Bored with the mundane work at J. R. Poole & Co, the latter welcomed the challenge. However, even after several efforts, Ponzi could not turn around the heavily debt-ridden business, and he was soon forced to tell his father-in-law that bankruptcy was their only feasible option.

Jobless once again, Ponzi knew that J. R. Poole would be glad to take back their efficient clerk; however, he decided to try his hand at something new – commodity broking. Ponzi launched the operations in a small office strategically stationed to attract attention. He also rented some godown space where customers could stock their goods pending clearance. Business fared reasonably well, but Ponzi realized that he could not make too much money from broking commissions. It was evident the real money lay in transacting directly with the goods. Unfortunately, this approach required a lot of inventory and, consequently, much more investment than he could muster. While looking for ways to augment resources, an idea struck him.

At any point in time, stocks belonging to the customers awaiting clearance were routinely held at his godowns. If he could use them to execute short-term deals that would be settled before clearance was due, he could earn substantial profits. Soon, Ponzi was carrying on many such trades and was pleased with the money he was making. A little later, some of the port officials smelled a rat and, during a sudden inspection, discovered unauthorized transactions undertaken by Ponzi using several cases of cheese belonging to a customer. Prison clouds started rolling in again, though this time luck was on his side. By some oversight, the authorities made an error in reporting his name correctly to the law, and Ponzi managed to escape conviction.

Businesses in Boston were prospering, with international trade experiencing a huge upswing. Seeing this as a promising opportunity, Ponzi decided to enter this line of activity. A first step was to obtain a more prominent office that such customers could relate to, and though he could ill-afford it, rented out a first-floor office on the posh School Street. He also negotiated an arrangement with a furniture dealer named Joseph Daniels to furnish the office, promising to pay $50 upfront and the balance $300 at the rate of $5 per month over the next five years. In the summer of 1919, 'Ponzi Exporters and Importers' started business. Shortly after its launch, though, Ponzi was forced to shut it down, as operations failed to take off at any significant scale.

The experience gave him yet another idea – launching a trade magazine to attract advertisements from local as well as overseas businessmen. Yet again, the project seemed destined to be a non-starter, as low circulation of the new magazine did not appeal to advertisers. Ponzi took an immediate decision to address this issue. He planned to print several copies of the magazine and circulate it free of charge to people both within and outside America. For the record, these copies would be shown as sold subscription copies. The biggest challenge, though, was securing the capital, particularly to fund the printing and shipping costs. Having lost virtually all his earnings on his failed ventures, Ponzi requested the Hanover Trust Bank in Boston for a small loan. He was optimistic as he had maintained a personal account at the bank for some time now. But when he called on them, Ponzi was rudely shown the door, and told that his small checking account with an insignificant balance was not fit for loans from such a prominent bank.

Reply coupons

Back in the office, while despondently running through letters from some of the overseas customers he had approached to promote the magazine, Ponzi noticed an unusual enclosure. Attached to a letter from a Spanish businessman was a small stamp-sized object, though on a closer look, it did not seem to be a regular postal stamp.

This was the first time Ponzi had seen such an instrument. He discovered that it was a specialized postal coupon known as an 'international reply coupon'. His interests sparked, Ponzi learnt that as international correspondence around the world had begun to increase, in 1874 many countries had collaboratively established the Universal Postal Union to facilitate these activities smoothly. It was later in 1906 that the union introduced IRCs so that the letter sender could prepay the cost of receiving a reply.

A sender from a member country could buy these coupons at their own post office and forward them with the letter for the overseas recipient to use in their reply (just as his Spanish customer had done). The recipient could then exchange the coupon for stamps at their own post office to send the reply. He also learnt that the rate at which a coupon could be exchanged for stamps in each country had been prefixed by the union and implemented across post offices in all the member countries. From his shipping company days and attempts to set up an overseas trading venture, Ponzi was well aware of the significant impact that foreign currency exchange variations had on international transactions. It was from this understanding that he suddenly spotted an anomaly in the reply coupon system.

Ponzi noticed that the postal union had originally fixed the rate for conversion of coupons into stamps based on the forex rates prevailing in each member country at the time of the scheme's inception. These rates had not been revised thereafter, probably due to the insignificant impact of normal currency fluctuations. But after World War I, the US dollar had strengthened significantly against the currencies of many European countries, especially the traditional superpowers like Italy and Austria, which were badly affected by the war. Amidst a multitude of post-war matters, Ponzi surmised, revising coupon rates may not have seemed a priority for the postal union.

Scenting a monetary proposition, he conceived a scheme. While testing his theory, he was delighted to realize a margin of around 25 per cent on converting the Spanish coupon into American stamps at the Boston post office. It was evident that this was entirely on account of the exchange difference of around 25 per cent prevailing between the US dollar and the Spanish peseta then.

The most exciting prospect was that if this seemed like a

large difference, the approximate conversion rate of his home currency (the Italian lira) to the US dollar was as low as 0.004878, which meant that the fall in value was more than a whopping 200 per cent.

Doing the actual math, he realized that:

- 1 US dollar could buy twenty American stamps, each worth 5 cents, at any American post office (investment for computation purposes = $1).
- At the prevailing exchange rates, the Italian lira equivalent of 1 USD could purchase sixty-six international reply coupons at any Italian post office.
- Sixty-six international coupons purchased in Italy could be exchanged at any US post office into sixty-six American stamps, each worth 5 cents (increased value now = $3.30).
- Hence, 1 USD converted into lira and used to buy coupons in Italy could be turned into American stamps worth $3.30, resulting in an extraordinary return of 230 per cent.

If this worked successfully with the lira, Ponzi knew it would work with many other European currencies, including the Austrian schilling, which had been similarly battered against the US dollar.

Never had Ponzi heard of any investment offering such high returns. He excitedly began work on a proposal for this huge arbitrage opportunity. The scheme he formulated was to invite deposits, which would carry a guaranteed return of 50 per cent after a minimum term of ninety days. These funds would be used to buy IRCs in countries like Italy or Austria. The coupons could then be converted and sold as postal stamps in America to earn margins over 200 per cent, as seen. Ponzi had no doubts the scheme would be a huge success. Possibly in excitement, he decided to shelve all practical challenges for now, including how to physically handle and ship such a large number of coupons.

He was confident that the affluent Boston Brahmins would be eager to invest heavily, so he decided to approach them first with the scheme. The worry, though, was whether the information would somehow leak out and tempt competitors to launch similar schemes before things got moving. To pre-empt this, he decided to withhold the specifics of the scheme when discussing with potential investors.

But none of the wealthy individuals showed any interest in the scheme. Even his claim to pay 50 per cent interest in a shorter period of forty-five days, effectively doubling the rate of return, failed to catch their eye.

The situation looked rather bleak until he had an unexpected visitor one day. It was Joseph Daniels, the furniture dealer. Ponzi had settled a portion of the liability as agreed, but recent challenges had caused him to default on some payments, and he still owed the man $100.

Daniels barged in, demanding his pending dues and threatening to take back all the furniture unless he was paid immediately. Ponzi knew that settling the amount right away was out of the question. But if Daniels wasn't placated somehow, there would be no furniture left in the office. Aware that Daniels had a penchant for quick money, Ponzi offered a new proposition.

He conveyed to Daniels that he was on the verge of launching a new scheme that would undoubtedly see large investments coming in very soon. Then he extended a special offer for the settlement of his dues. Ponzi would issue a six-month promissory note for a sum of $200, which Daniels could immediately discount with his bank. He could retain the $100 due to him but pay back Ponzi the remaining $100 over five months in $20 instalments, without accruing any interest. At the end of six months, Ponzi would honour the promissory note together with the bank's charges to settle the transaction fully.

Just as Ponzi had hoped, Daniels was enticed by the offer and agreed to the deal, without even needing a formal agreement.

Though he had failed to convince the wealthy Boston Brahmins to invest with him, Daniels' investment had restored Ponzi's faith in his plan. He decided to formally register a company to roll out the scheme, which he called the Securities Exchange Company (SEC). Ponzi then commissioned a printer to produce a large wad of blank investment certificates in the name of the company, pledging to repay the investment with an interest of 50 per cent after ninety days.

In the new year of 1920, Ponzi publicly announced his new company and formally launched the deposit scheme.

SEC

However, despite significant publicity that the SEC scheme offered a return of 100 per cent – vastly superior to the 5 per cent offered by banks – the response from investors remained poor. Instead of wasting more time courting big investors, Ponzi decided he would try to rope in at least some small investments to kickstart the operation.

He chose an Italian immigrant, Giberti, who ran a popular grocery store, and invited him to join the scheme with a small investment of $10. Ponzi's offer was that the entire amount would be paid back to him as commission if Giberti could canvass more people to join in. This strategy clicked, and modest amounts – never more than $10 from each investor – started to trickle in from the locals. Though dissatisfied, Ponzi kept hoping that a quantum jump would occur when the initial investments came up for redemption, at which point he'd honour the promise of paying high returns.

But he could no longer ignore a looming concern – he had not yet found a way to invest the deposits collected in international reply coupons as planned. He had always felt that the operational aspects of the scheme could be sorted out once things got rolling. But it was closer to reality that some of these matters reared up as much bigger challenges. The main issue at hand was how to manage regular purchases of so many coupons in faraway countries and arrange for them to be shipped to America. Furthermore, there was great risk in converting all these coupons into stamps in America with a clear profiteering objective – something the US postal authorities would not see kindly.

For the time being, though, Ponzi set aside the original investment plan and tried to figure out how to manage the incoming funds. One thing was crystal clear – under no circumstances could there be any default in honouring the liability. As the due dates for repayment of the first tranche of deposits drew closer, Ponzi's panic escalated.

A straightforward option was to coax the depositors into reinvesting for another term, but, even with the bait of higher returns, Ponzi knew he could not bank on this strategy.

Over sleepless nights, he contemplated many options, including running away from Boston like his former boss Zarossi. But he couldn't bring himself to it. Just as he was reaching his wits' end, an idea struck him – a flashback from his banking days.

Just like Zarossi, Ponzi decided that the only option now was to repay the maturing deposits using the influx of deposits. He reassured himself this was a temporary measure until he worked out a way to buy the coupons.

As Ponzi had anticipated, repaying the due deposits with the promised interest worked wonders to boost the depositor' confidence in the scheme.

News spread of the trustworthy gentleman who could double investments in record time, and new deposits began to pour in. In fact, when the next round of deposits fell due, most of the investors chose to renew their matured deposits rather than exit the scheme. What was also changing was that while the ten-dollar investments still came in large numbers, people were also investing larger sums. Even many of the Boston Brahmins, who had earlier spurned the scheme, seemed to be slowly joining in.

Receipts for February 1920, only the second month of regular operations, touched $5,000, and even Ponzi was pleasantly surprised to see the amount rise sharply to cross $25,000 by March.

As the momentum continued, he had to make rapid changes to stay in step. The company headquarters was shifted to a larger, better-furnished office in the upscale Niles Building on School Street. New branches sprouted regularly, initially within Massachusetts area but soon expanding to other towns and suburbs. Large teams of salesmen were hired to extend the business even further, and liberal commissions were paid to all those who brought in new deposits. Security guards were deployed at all the SEC branches to manage the increasing crowds as new depositors heavily outweighed those wanting redemptions. Ponzi even had to call in the Pinkerton guards to maintain order when the crowds swelled excessively. Deposits in the tens of thousands of dollars no longer excited Ponzi and the SEC team.

Over the ensuing months, as collections galloped at a furious pace, Ponzi could not handle the staggering volume of business on his own anymore. Consequently, he appointed some efficient and trustworthy people, including a bright young chief accountant named Lucy, to manage key financial functions within the SEC.

Amidst this surge in operations, Ponzi made sure to stay in personal touch with all the existing and prospective customers. It soon became a standard practice at SEC to offer all the guests special doughnuts and coffee, which Ponzi himself often shared with them.

Ponzi still kept a close watch on the daily fund position. Even while relying on the numbers shared by Lucy, he personally kept tabs on all incoming deposits as well as those due for repayment each day. Ensuring that adequate cash was always available across all offices and branches to meet redemptions without fail was always his top-most priority. And instructions to the team were loud and clear – no depositor should leave with a complaint.

The sudden influx of so much money also brought significant changes in Ponzi's lifestyle, like an array of designer suits, an exquisitely furnished villa and a chauffeured luxury locomobile. Predictably, he also began to receive regular invitations to dinners and events involving the town's elites and soon became one of Boston's most illustrious business figures.

With the windfall, Ponzi opened SEC accounts at all major banks in Boston, such as Fidelity, Hanover, Tremont,

Old South and Cosmopolitan, to park the funds. He was receiving requests from large banks in the adjoining areas as well, eager to get a share of the huge business. Ponzi took particular pleasure in the occasional visit to these banks, where he would be greeted with the utmost respect and ushered directly into the chairman's office for coffee while his business requests were promptly assisted by deferential managers and senior staff. Among these, it was visiting Hanover Trust Bank that brought Ponzi the greatest satisfaction, reminding him that it had not been long since he was denied a paltry loan request of $2,000 there – a fact no one at the bank seemed to remember or chose to forget.

The only disappointment, though, was his wife's sceptical view of the progress. In fact, many times Rose questioned if they needed such opulence to be happy and repeatedly cautioned him to be careful. Ponzi brushed these concerns aside with the gentle assurance that they were the same people, only extremely successful now. But increasingly, he, too, gave up on trying to appease her.

When the collections for April 1920 outdid the preceding month by a long way, it was a further validation of the huge acceptance of his scheme. Even so, he could not fully shake off the occasional inner voice reminding him that SEC was still servicing old deposits from new ones. And he had still not found ways to invest in the coupons as planned. Recently, he had read the disturbing news that many post offices in Europe, including those in Italy, were discontinuing further issuance of IRCs. It raised a concern in his mind about whether there would be enough reply coupons available around the world to invest all the money SEC was now collecting.

But the way collections were swelling, Ponzi knew there were few other alternatives to immediately consider. For now, the new investments had to continue paying the older ones. He also kept up the facade with regular affirmations that the SEC staff were constantly sailing between America and Europe to bring loads of reply coupons and that several large warehouses had been hired out to store them – even publicly sharing the idea of actually chartering some ships to run this exclusive service.

But these apprehensions prompted him to initiate certain changes in SEC's ownership structure, entirely to alleviate any risk of personal threats. On records, Ponzi shifted legal ownership of the entity to Rose's uncle, who was only an employee, and a family friend in Italy, who, by Ponzi's estimates, was old enough to have died long ago, while redesignating himself merely as a manager. No one else heard about these amendments.

Confidence Building

As public hype around the SEC burgeoned, regulators and law enforcers also started taking notice. Ponzi was increasingly faced with the task of dealing with police inspectors, postal officials and other officers. He used his affability and charisma so well that not only were the officials convinced, but many of them even enrolled as investors. Newspapers also came sniffing, at times threatening to get too close for comfort with sharp queries, prompting Ponzi to hire specialists to handle media and public relations matters.

Thanks to all these, it was soon not only in Boston but also other places that people were singing praises about the new financial king. And in complete ratification of the acclaimed status, collections kept growing at a prodigious pace, with

June 1920 collections spiralling towards $2,500,000 against $420,000 in May 1920.

With so much money at hand, the discomfort of not having any avenues to park the funds profitably was also mounting. Ponzi began to look around for some good companies to invest in. Since he knew the move would also enhance their public credibility, he acquired controlling interests in a traditional Italian pasta-making company called the Napoli Macaroni Manufacturing and a construction company called C&R Construction. He also bought out his former boss's stake in J. R. Poole & Co. But even these new investments could not dip SEC's ever-expanding bank balance, and it was with some consternation that Ponzi read Lucy's latest report that the accumulated balance was more than $6 million.

Another concern during this period was the emergence of numerous fly-by-night operators who modelled their schemes after the SEC and started to collect public money. Ponzi knew these were all slimy characters who could vanish anytime with the collections, putting a lot of pressure on SEC's much larger operations.

He was still trying to solve these issues when his relationships with some of the main bankers took an unexpected turn.

Ponzi was always clear that no depositor who came for redemption was to be turned away, The instructions were that even if they came without prior notice, as was customary, the requests were to be honoured on the same day. This meant that Lucy and the team would have to make large withdrawals from the SEC bank accounts on at least some days, and the bankers had recently expressed concerns about arranging so much funding on such short notice.

While apologetic, they explained that the bank's policy was to invest their funds for longer tenures to generate higher returns for customers, and it was not possible to have such liquid funds readily on hand day after day. But, as the SEC was also unable to find solutions to this regular issue, the banks began to impose restrictions on daily withdrawals.

Ponzi was not keen to disturb relations with the bankers at this critical juncture, but after a while, their adamance began to infuriate him, and cordiality started to sour.

It also opened Ponzi's eyes to the reality that he could no longer remain an outsider in the banking system and depend on their kindness to get things done. With this in mind, he began to invest in some of the major banks in the city – not controlling interests, though large enough to ensure he received the special treatment reserved for prominent stakeholders. Relations improved to some extent, but they also showed him that even this was not enough to ensure a completely sure footing. He realized that for this to happen, it had to be nothing short of complete management control over at least one major bank very soon.

Acquiring control over banks like Fidelity Trust or Tremont Trust was difficult, as they had strong management teams. So, Ponzi fixed his attention on Hanover Trust Bank. Of course, there was an added thrill since this was his old bank that had kicked him out over a minor loan request.

Ponzi was gathering all possible information about Hanover when he discovered that the bank was in the early stages of issuing new voting shares to expand its business. Ponzi immediately began to transfer the SEC's large deposits with other banks into Hanover. He only stopped when he was certain that closing his accounts would cause the Hanover Trust Bank to fail. With this power, he approached the major stockholders in private, promising to play an active role in the bank's future. Once he had their support, Ponzi moved to enlist the help of the bank's two senior executives, Henry Chmielinski, the president, and William McNary, the treasurer. Using a deft mix of carrots and sticks, he persuaded the bank's board to give him a sizeable portion of the new voting shares. Large enough to make him the Hanover Trust Bank's largest investor and chairman.

During every stage of the seventeen years since he boarded the *SS Vancouver* from Naples, Ponzi had missed his mother. Many times, he had contemplated going back home to visit her with Rose but had been unable to do so for various reasons. Now, he wished his mother could see the new Charles Ponzi that her little Carlo had become. Imelda sailed to Boston in first class and spent many months with Rose and him, and by the time she returned, Ponzi was pleased that he had proven worthy of all her aspirations for him.

As activities at the SEC kept growing, Ponzi once again felt the pressure to find new options to manage the massive funds accumulated with them. He tried many things, including coaxing investors to put their money in the Hanover Trust Bank, which he now controlled, instead of into the SEC. He organized a deposit mobilization campaign and offered large commissions to those canvassing new deposits for Hanover. Henry Chmielinski, a trusted insider who had been asked by Ponzi to continue as the president of the bank, was deputed on a secret mission when the latter heard there were some reply coupons available for sale in Poland. Ponzi even planned to buy a three-thousand-ship fleet from the US Shipping Board after the war by issuing ten-year bonds that could be repaid by operating the ships commercially. However, none of these schemes provided significant relief to the SEC's ever-increasing bank balances, and the firefighting continued.

Around this time, Daniels, the old-time furniture dealer, turned up one day at the SEC office with an audacious claim. According to him, the $100 he had given to Ponzi as five instalments of $20 each at the commencement of the SEC was actually his 'investment' in the scheme as per their original understanding. He refused to accept the shell-shocked Ponzi's contention that the arrangement back then was only for a loan, which had also been repaid in full. The astute Daniels now insisted that he, too, was entitled to a share in all the money that SEC was making as a founding investor and demanded payment. Unfortunately for Ponzi, the 'friendly' deal back then was not documented, and Daniels proceeded to file a $1 million suit claiming his share of the profits of SEC. To Ponzi's horror, Daniels used this to also secure a freeze on some of the SEC bank accounts.

Most of the Boston media chose to ignore this news as drivel. But one newspaper decided to investigate further – the *Boston Post*.

Enemy

When Edwin Grozier, the respected newspaper baron who ran the *Boston Post*, was unexpectedly taken ill, his son Richard found himself thrust to the fore. Feeling the weight of his father's boots, Richard Grozier was determined to quickly find his own feet in the media world. Beginning to hunt for something sensational, his eyes fell on the new financial whiz man in Boston. Finding it difficult to digest the stories he heard about the Italian immigrant's miraculous rise, Richard urged his team to start posing serious questions about the SEC. Soon, the *Boston Post* started publishing several articles questioning the bona fide of Ponzi's operations.

The articles triggered an immediate panic among the investors. But Ponzi responded quickly by instructing all the branches of SEC to stay open until the last depositor who desired encashment was paid in full, while personally moving around to meet those who rushed there to assuage their fears. Though the crisis management required some additional withdrawals to be made urgently from the banks, by the end of the day itself, Ponzi was able to quickly regain investor faith, and once again, confidence on the street was back with him.

But Richard Grozier was determined to keep the fire going. Unsatisfied with the responses to the *Boston Post*'s articles, he commissioned external experts like Clarence W. Barron of the *Wall Street Journal* to write about the flaws in Ponzi's venture. Ponzi also stood firm against the renewed offensives, knowing that even if public opinion shifted slightly, their overall trust was not shaken. The most compelling evidence was that despite the negative publicity, investments continued to flow into SEC at a rate of more than $1 million per day, with aggregate deposits approaching $15 million. However, after a little while, when Richard showed no intentions of letting go, Ponzi decided to devise a permanent solution.

He sought an immediate meeting with the two senior-most legal authorities in Boston: Daniel J. Gallagher, the State Attorney for the District of Massachusetts, and Joseph Pelletier, the Suffolk District Attorney, and made a strange request to them:

> Gentlemen, given the recent negative publicity around me, may I request your offices to order a full-fledged audit of my accounts and financial position?

People volunteering to go through such an audit was unusual, but much to his listener's surprise, Ponzi stuck to this seemingly transparent request.

He readily agreed to everything they demanded, including that the independent auditor would be appointed by them without any interference on his part and that the audit fees be fully defrayed by him. Obviously, the men had no inkling of any hidden motives behind this odd move.

Ponzi reasoned that if he could secure a satisfactory report from an official audit, it would put an end to all criticism of SEC's operations. Undoubtedly, the *Boston Post*'s crusades would also have to come to an end. Besides, Ponzi believed that the law officials could be coaxed to order similar audits of his competitors, most of whom would not survive such scrutiny.

A few days later, a senior auditor named Edwin Pride was appointed by the law officials to the task of verifying financial matters at the SEC and certifying the company's solvency.

Ponzi was confident that the audit would find nothing amiss in Lucy's and her team's meticulous accounting systems, especially their elaborate mechanisms of issuing receipts for deposits, retaining the stubs and colour-coding them to track redemptions. Despite this, he instructed that the audit team had to be accommodated in every possible way. So, when Pride expressed his concern that it would be practically difficult to verify the deposits when so many large transactions continued to take place every day, Ponzi surprised even his own team by immediately offering to stop accepting all new deposits until the audit was completed.

Given the massive volume of transactions, Ponzi knew that the senior auditor would only be able to verify selected samples. He knew that suspending acceptance of new deposits would make prospective investors restless, and it would only be a matter of days before the people thronging the SEC offices turned into a law-and-order situation. Something that neither the legal officials nor other authorities in Boston would find desirable. In such a situation, the authorities themselves could be compelled to push for a speedier conclusion to the audit.

But Ponzi also knew that the truly critical aspect of this entire exercise was to assure Pride of SEC's solvency, which would affirm to the world that there were enough funds available with the company to discharge all its liabilities.

His problem was that, unfortunately, this was not the actual position of the company.

As per Lucy's latest numbers, the aggregate liability due to deposit holders, comprising principal and interest payable after forty-five days, was approximately $15 million. But, as per bank statements, the aggregate balance available across all accounts was only $8 million, resulting in a gap of $7 million, which Ponzi had to somehow bridge before Pride got around to verifying it.

In fact, even while scheming for the audit to address the external issues, Ponzi had another agenda – something that could bring down the current liability due to depositors. As per the official scheme, SEC was liable to pay interest only if the depositor remained invested for at least forty-five days, and no interest was payable for early redemption before this period. Ponzi assessed that when news of the mandatory audit was announced, the media, led by the *Boston Post*, would launch another rampage against SEC, triggering large withdrawal requests as usual. But unlike earlier times, Ponzi's gambit was that no efforts would be made to stop the mass withdrawals. At least not from depositors with terms below forty-five days. He even sent a confidential message to his people stating that such deposit holders were to be specifically targeted and, to the best possible extent, intimidated into redeeming their deposits immediately for fear of losing even their principal. Ponzi estimated that by doing so, SEC could save around $4 million towards interest otherwise payable after forty-five days.

If this happened, the shortfall between deposits due and available funds would fall to a more manageable level of $3 million. So, even as Pride continued verifying the deposits, Ponzi turned his attention towards bridging this shortfall.

His biggest source of solace now was having acquired Hanover Trust Bank and it was there that Ponzi headed now. The demand he now made to Chmielinski and McNary was patently outrageous, but they were forced to comply with the bank chairman's request. And even if most hesitantly, the two senior bankers agreed to grant the chairman a short-term accommodation of $3 million from the bank's reserve funds on the day he needed it. Ponzi's assurance was that because the money was marked in bank bundles, Pride could easily count $3 million in a few hours and the money would be returned before the end of banking hours the same day, necessitating no record of this transaction anywhere.

War

At the *Boston Post*, though, Richard Grozier remained disturbed that they were unable to make any significant impact in the Ponzi matter and directed the chief editor, Edward Dunn, to exclusively up the diatribe. Apart from Clarence Barron, they now asked other influential figures like Simon Swig, the chairman of the Tremont Trust Bank, to write critically about Ponzi and SEC's schemes.

The news of a mandatory audit ordered by judicial authorities came as a shot in the arm, and Richard was happy to learn that this time the newspaper had triggered a fairly large run on SEC following this announcement. Little did he know that this was exactly what Ponzi wanted.

Ponzi had now ensured that deposits of less than forty-five days could be repaid without any interest liability, knocking down the gap in available funds quite close to the desired level. With Pride's audit also progressing satisfactorily, he felt much more confident about sealing the matter in favour of SEC.

Renewed by this confidence, Ponzi also decided to take the battle into Richard Grozier's camp for the first time. Through his connections in the media, he ridiculed the *Boston Post*'s reportage. A dedicated public relations operation led by a former journalist, William McMaster, was undertaken, in which Ponzi's team tore into what they called 'bits and pieces' articles that deliberately hid the truth. They also raised serious aspersions about the genuine understanding of the 'so-called experts' like Barron and Swig in international postal matters and even subtly questioned their intentions behind spreading such fake news.

Ponzi now made a fervent plea to Daniel Gallagher, the state attorney, that with the tense scenes playing out at the SEC offices every day from turning away new investors, Pride should be directed to complete the audit at the earliest. When Gallagher seemed confused about issuing such a direction, Ponzi played yet another card. Knowing that Pride could only provide positive assurances about his audit findings at this stage, Ponzi modified the plea. He asked Gallagher to keep public sentiments at least temporarily under check, Pride be directed to issue an interim announcement regarding his observations.

The state attorney had also received reports about the crowds collecting in front of SEC offices, sometimes even requiring the police's intervention to disperse them. Fearing a more serious mob backlash, Gallagher decided that the second request from Ponzi was reasonable and directed Edwin Pride to issue an interim report immediately.

Exactly as Ponzi predicted, Pride confirmed that the audit had thus far shown no significant deviations in the operations of SEC. Needless to say, Ponzi and his team made sure that the entire Boston media, barring, of course, one paper, celebrated this victory vociferously.

All the latest developments, and Ponzi's clever moves, incensed Richard Grozier further, making him even more determined to go after Ponzi. Deploying every weapon in their arsenal, Richard's team managed to bribe William McMaster, Ponzi's publicity agent, to make sensitive disclosures against his boss.

Ponzi reacted immediately by filing large libel suits against the *Boston Post* and McMaster. He also raised charges against the other major critics, like Clarence Barron.

Forced to backtrack again, Richard Grozier knew that it would be foolhardy to continue publishing anything that was not backed by proper evidence and once again ordered his best investigative journalists to learn everything they could about the man they were after.

Then, one day, Richard received information that some

years ago, a certain Charles Ponzi had served a jail term in Montreal for cheque fraud. When he checked on it, he insisted that all the details, including the identity of the person, be confirmed before they broke the sensational news. But once again, Ponzi turned this to his advantage.

A teary-eyed Ponzi went on to share the circumstances that forced him to do something like this, readily admitting that the cheque fraud incident and his arrest were true. He told the packed press conference that he had stayed back in Montreal only to help his former boss Zarossi's family, forced to resort to fraudulent means to provide for them. By the end he reiterated that he had served the punishment for the illegal act in the right spirit, and he was still unsure about the true morality of his actions.

The next morning, all the newspaper reports – once again, barring one – waxed lyrical about how the philanthropic Ponzi had braved imprisonment to help the beleaguered family of a former boss who had cheated so many people, even Ponzi himself.

To Richard Grozier's fury, Charles Ponzi was practically a martyr now.

Throughout these triumphs, though, Ponzi remained focused on the ongoing audit, which was moving as planned.

The major discomfort, however, was the frequent complaints from Lucy and her team about the tightness in their daily fund positions, particularly because new deposits were paused. If only the freeze imposed on the SEC accounts due to the ongoing dispute with Joseph Daniels could be lifted, they complained, their challenges would be alleviated.

Despite his aversion to the idea of a compromise with Daniels, under the circumstances, Ponzi decided to concede. He called on the unsuspecting furniture dealer, sharing his plans for an imminent, larger venture shortly. Daniels was assured he would be made a promoter in this project without having to make any initial financial commitment. Having won him over, Ponzi arm-twisted Daniels into settling his present claims. The understanding released $700,000 blocked from the court attachment, and Ponzi was delighted the winds were blowing in their direction again. The business and banking world were keenly following the financial developments in Boston, especially the Ponzi versus *Boston Post* battle. Among the officials tracking things closely was the banking commissioner of Massachusetts, Joseph Allen. Allen had been of the view that since the SEC was not a bank, his office did not have a direct regulatory role in this case. But, when the *Boston Post* articles started to link the affairs of the SEC with the Hanover Trust Bank, the commissioner took a closer look.

His initial directive was to make general inquiries about the transactions between Hanover Trust Bank and SEC. But when he learnt that certain transactions, particularly some large withdrawals, seemed questionable, the commissioner realized the case warranted a thorough investigation. To Allen's discomfort, the examination revealed several irregularities, notably the frequent fund transfers to the chairman, Charles Ponzi, and his company, SEC. Allen issued an immediate order limiting such withdrawals and directed his officers to monitor all transactions at the Hanover Trust Bank regularly.

This latest bolt from the blue came as a shock to Ponzi. Aware that SEC could not continue operations without the large fund withdrawals from Hanover, Ponzi rushed back to Chmielinski and McNary to seek their support. With no way to refuse the insistent chairman, the two agreed to continue financing SEC as before. To cover this, they began to create fictitious transactions and false accounting adjustments to cover this in the bank's records.

When Joseph Allen found that operations at SEC had not been significantly affected despite the restraining order, he smelled a rat. The commissioner was shocked to learn that Hanover was now using illegal practices to fund Ponzi's operation. His concerns skyrocketed when he was informed that the amounts granted to SEC over the last few days alone were as high as $2.5 million. Sensing serious trouble, the commissioner was also afraid of the news leaking out. With the media, particularly the *Boston Post* waiting to pounce on any discrepancy, Allen had little doubt of this news triggering a massive run on the Hanover Bank. In its current precarious state, this would inevitably lead to the bank's collapse. So, too, was the possibility of the effects of the fallout spilling over to the entire banking industry and turning into a financial catastrophe.

Without further thought, Allen issued a directive to stop payment for all cheques issued by Charles Ponzi and SEC. He additionally ordered all senior officials, including Chmielinski and McNary, to vacate their posts at Hanover Bank with immediate effect, and took over the bank's day-to-day operations.

The End

Panic-stricken, Ponzi decided the best course of action was to create a smoke screen through the press, at least until he figured out how to handle his predicaments.

Learning that Ponzi was planning to convene a press conference shortly, Allen decided to intervene before the duplicitous financier could further mislead the public. Summoning an immediate press meet, Joseph Allen presented all his investigative findings as well as the actions taken against SEC by his office. He also publicized how his office had been necessitated to take urgent control of Hanover Trust Bank's management due to the fraud involving SEC.

The *Boston Post* spearheaded the public outcry, with other press outlets also baying for Ponzi's blood now. The postal service and local police, which had supported Ponzi thus far, also demanded their pound of flesh now. Edwin Pride, too, rushed to finish the audit and issue his final report.

The final liability due to depositors as per Pride's assessment was found to be around $7 million, just as Ponzi had planned. But the funds available across all of SEC's bank accounts were at $4 million, falling short by approximately $3 million. Price's report also revealed that the value of IRCs Ponzi had acquired during the entire tenure of the SEC was worth just $30. All the maturing deposits were being repaid only with incoming deposits.

Ponzi spent one more day trying to mobilize all the resources he could. But he was all alone now. Desperate phone calls went unanswered, and nobody agreed to meet him. The next morning, dressed smartly as usual, he directed his chauffeur to take him to the state attorney's office, where he turned himself in. From there, Ponzi's life took several unexpected turns.

'Even if they never got anything for it, it was cheap at that price. Without malice aforethought I had given them the best show that was ever staged in their territory since the landing of the Pilgrims! It was easily worth fifteen million bucks to watch me put the thing over,' Ponzi later argued during the trial.

All of his pleas claiming that everything was done in good faith were ignored, and he was sentenced to five years in Plymouth Jail for mail fraud.

Because of his good behaviour, he was found eligible for early release after only four years. But new charges of larceny were filed against him almost immediately, resulting in yet another sentence, this time for nine years at the Massachusetts State Prison. By this point Ponzi had lost a lot of his vitality and, with almost no resources left, was even forced to argue his case in court.

During this time, he learnt that the Hanover Trust Bank had succumbed to massive depositor runs, affecting five other large Boston banks. Even the banking commissioner or other regulators could not salvage the situation. According to reports, investors lost more than $20 million.

Everywhere, one person, Charles Ponzi, was being held singularly responsible for all this.

'*I went looking for trouble, and found it*,' he once admitted.

Ponzi attempted to flee by violating the bail set for him when he realized he couldn't. He fled to Florida, hoping that the state's lax laws would grant him immunity. There he attempted to resurrect his fortunes by launching another investment scheme – this time backed by the promise of huge real estate gains. However, some people linked this to the SEC scam, and Ponzi was arrested again.

Sentenced to prison in Florida, he once again violated the bail granted to him on compassionate grounds to visit his family and tried to escape to Italy under a false alias by faking his death. Unfortunately, true to his nature, he couldn't resist bragging about his skills to some people he met while attempting to board the vessel. He was recognized and arrested once more.

During the seven years he served at Massachusetts State Prison, Ponzi also learnt about the death of his beloved mother in Italy.

After his release, all the authorities in America were firm that they were done with Charles Ponzi. All his pleas to be allowed to continue living in America were denied and he was put on board the *SS Vulcania* to be deported back to Italy.

Ponzi sailed alone, as Rose had decided to stay back with her own family in Boston for good. A few years later, they officially divorced.

After being unable to find a meaningful job in Italy, Ponzi accepted a friend's offer to work as an agent for an Italian airline company in Brazil. He spent a few quiet years in Rio de Janeiro, living in solitude off his frugal remuneration. When the Second World War broke out, the airline was suspected of aiding Mussolini's activities through smuggling and other illegal means and was immediately shut down. As an employee, Ponzi also faced some allegations and, despite not being charged, found himself back on the job market in a foreign land.

A pale imitation of the man he once was, it was only through the kindness of well-meaning individuals in the city that he was able to make a living. He earned a meagre income from odd jobs, such as running a small boarding house and tutoring children. His health also deteriorated rapidly, and without other options, some kind-hearted city-dwellers admitted him to the public ward of the Rio government hospital.

On 18 January 1949, Charles Ponzi, once a millionaire and celebrated financial innovator, died as a penniless beggar.

His remains were interred in an unmarked grave at a public cemetery in Rio de Janeiro.

Many believe that if Ponzi had been properly understood and given a fair chance, global financial history might have unfolded differently. Unfortunately, this remains anybody's guess. It is also uncertain whether even Charles Ponzi could have anticipated how influential his work would become, as his legacy carries on through the numerous disciples who emerged and continue to surface worldwide, ensuring that the notoriety of 'Ponzi' schemes endures through time.

Acknowledgements

Thanks to Achan and Amma, Gayathri and the boys, everyone in the family and those close to me – who knew that even if I was wasting time before the laptop, at least it was keeping things quiet.

Sujith Uncle – so much more than our family doctor, who first hinted that I should try writing short stories.

The researchers, editors, journalists and authors whose brilliant work over time has provided invaluable inputs for each case in this book. I trust I've given all of them due credit in the bibliography section. Padmajachechi – in her role as senior librarian at Nanyang Technological University, Singapore – and the big worldwide web for making available all the original historical and library records, newspaper reports and articles I needed in digitized form. It was amazing to learn how much research can be reliably done online.

Smita Khanna of the Jacaranda Literary Agency – for her belief which I began to share only when one day she said, 'We have an offer!' Her unwavering support throughout this process is so much more than I could wish for.

Isha Banerji, editor at Pan Macmillan India – prayer couldn't have brought down a better professional guide, supporter and friend in such an arduous journey. Each word in this book is more hers than mine.

The wonderfully skilled team at Pan Macmillan India, who created this book – Amartaya Gupta, who formatted the long bibliography; R. Ajith Kumar, who typeset the book; Haitenlo Semy, who designed the brilliant cover; and the sales and publicity team who will manage the next part of the book's journey – Vijay Sharma, the sales director; Saburi Sumran, the marketing manager; and Pooja Sharma, the social media manager. A big thank you to all of you.

S. Hussain Zaidi – the country's best-known crime writer – who has generously taken the time to read the final manuscript and offer his encouraging words. His support and blessings mean so much.

Finally, to each one of you who has read the book, whether you liked it or not – I remain beholden to you. And I promise that the second book in the series will be better or worse, or perhaps both.

Bibliography

Chapter 1: William Chaloner: The Coin Connoisseur

Historical Records

Brown, Id, Chris Comber and Walter Wilkinson. *The Hammered Silver Coins produced at the Tower Mint during the Reign of Elizabeth I*. Galata Print Ltd. Available: https://www.galata.co.uk/the-hammered-silver-coins-produced-at-the-tower-mint-during-the-reign-of-elizabeth-i.

Chaloner, William. *The Defects in the present Constitution of the Mint Humbly Offered to the Consideration of the Honourable House of Commons*. London: 1697. Accessed through Newton Project, Faculty of History, University of Oxford. Available: https://www.newtonproject.ox.ac.uk/view/texts/normalized/MINT01536.

———. *To the Honourable, the knights, citizens, and burgesses, in Parliament assembled proposals humbly offered, for passing an act to prevent clipping and counterfeiting of money*. MINT 01535. Accessed through Newton Project, Faculty of History, University of Oxford, 11 February 1694. Available: https://www.newtonproject.ox.ac.uk/view/texts/diplomatic/MINT01535.

———. *William Chaloner's Letters to the Warden of the Mint, to Justice Railton, to Isaac Newton, and to Justice Railton*. MINT 15/17/133. National Archives, Kew, Richmond, Surrey, UK. Accessed through Newton Project, Faculty of History, University of Oxford, 20–24 January 1698. Available: https://www.newtonproject.ox.ac.uk/view/texts/normalized/MINT00917.

———. *William Chaloner's Letter to Isaac Newton.* MINT 15/17/205. National Archives, Kew, Richmond, Surrey, UK. Accessed through Newton Project, Faculty of History, University of Oxford, early March 1698. Available: https://www.newtonproject.ox.ac.uk/view/texts/normalized/MINT00918.

———. *Chaloner's Letter to Mr. Secretary Vernon.* MINT 15/17/126. National Archives, Kew, Richmond, Surrey, UK. Accessed through Newton Project, Faculty of History, University of Oxford, February 1699. Available: https://www.newtonproject.ox.ac.uk/view/texts/diplomatic/MINT01379.

———. *William Chaloner's Letter to Isaac Newton.* MINT 15/17/174. National Archives, Kew, Richmond, Surrey, UK. Accessed through Newton Project, Faculty of History, University of Oxford, January 1699. Available: https://www.newtonproject.ox.ac.uk/view/texts/normalized/MINT00918.

———. *Chaloner's petition to Parliament.* MINT 19/1/497. National Archives, Kew, Richmond, Surrey, UK. Accessed through Newton Project, Faculty of History, University of Oxford, late 1697 and early 1698. Available: https://newtonandthemint.history.ox.ac.uk/transcriptions/normalised/MINT00845.

Lee, Charles. *Elizabeth Holloway: The Information of Elizabeth the wife of Thomas Holloway late of the parish of St Martins in the Fields in the county of Middlesex Cane Chair Maker.* 10 January 1698/9.' MINT 15/17/81. National Archives, Kew, Richmond, Surrey, UK. Accessed through Newton Project, Faculty of History, University of Oxford, 10 January 1698.

Newton, Isaac. *Sir Isaac Newton's Mint Reports (1701–1725).* Pierre Marteau's Publishing House, Cologne. Available: *http://www.*pierre-marteau.com/editions/1701-25-mint-reports.html.

———. *Holograph summary of the submissions put to a committee examining Chaloner's case.* MINT 19/1/503. National Archives, Kew, Richmond, Surrey, UK. Accessed through Newton Project, Faculty of History, University of Oxford, 1698.

———. *Papers of Isaac Newton. Cambridge University Digital Library.* https://www.lib.cam.ac.uk/collections/departments/manuscripts-university-archives/significant-archival-collections/papers-sir.

———. *Order of the Commons Committee on the Miscarriages of the Mint (forwarded to Newton by the Committee's chairman, Arnold) for [William] Chaloner [Challoner] to demonstrate before them his method of making guineas.* MINT 19/1/506. National Archives, Kew, Richmond, Surrey, UK. Accessed through Newton Project, Faculty of History, University of Oxford, 15 February 1696. Available: https://www.newtonproject.ox.ac.uk/view/texts/diplomatic/MINT00843.

———. *'Chaloner's Case'. A history of Chaloner's crimes since 1690, largely summarising the confessions of other coiners.* MINT 19/1/501–2. National Archives, Kew, Richmond, Surrey, UK. Accessed through Newton Project, Faculty of History, University of Oxford, before 22 March 1699. Available: https://www.newtonproject.ox.ac.uk/view/texts/diplomatic/MINT00849.

———. *Draft list of editorial amendments to be made to a report on Chaloner.* MINT 19/2/265. National Archives, Kew, Richmond, Surrey, UK. Accessed through Newton Project, Faculty of History, University of Oxford, Before 22 March 1699. Available: https://www.newtonproject.ox.ac.uk/view/texts/normalized/MINT01914.

———. 'Newton's response to Chaloner petition to Parliament. MINT 19/1/497v-498. National Archives, Kew, Richmond, Surrey, UK'. Accessed through Newton Project, Faculty of History, University of Oxford, Late 1697 and early 1698. Available: https://www.newtonproject.ox.ac.uk/view/texts/normalized/MINT01868.

Turnbull, H. W., J. F. Scott, A. R. Hall and Laura Tilling. 'The Correspondence of Isaac Newton'. *Cambridge University Press*, 1959–1977.

Unknown. *Guzman Redivivus. A short view of the life of Will. Chaloner, the notorious coyner, who was executed at Tyburn on Wednesday the 22d. of March 1698/9.* Published for J. Hayns, 1699. Original from: British Library, 1699. Available: https://www.newtonproject.ox.ac.uk/view/texts/normalized/MINT01534.

Books

Ackroyd, Peter. *Newton: Ackroyd's Brief Lives.* New York: Nan A. Talese, 2008.

Challis, C. E. *A New History of The Royal Mint.* New York: Cambridge University Press, 1992.

Craig, John Herbert McCutcheon, Sir. *Newton at the Mint.* New York: Cambridge University Press, 1946.

Fauvel, John, Flood, Raymond, Shortland, Michael & Wilson, Robin. *Let Newton Be!*. Oxford: Oxford University Press, 1989.

Gjertsen, Derek. *The Newton Handbook*. London: Routledge, 1986.

Levenson, Thomas. *Newton and the Counterfeiter*. New York: Faber & Faber, 2010.

Li, Ming-Hsun. *The Great Recoinage of 1696 to 1699*. London: Weidenfeld and Nicolson, 1963.

Stukeley, William. *Memoirs of Sir Isaac Newton's Life*. London: Taylor & Francis, 1936.

Westfall, Richard S. *Never at Rest: A Biography of Isaac Newton*. Cambridge: Cambridge University Press, 1981.

Newspaper, Magazine and Journal Articles

Chodos, Alan. 'March 16, 1699: William Chaloner, Counterfeiter, Hanged'. *American Physical Society*. Available: https://www.aps.org/publications/apsnews/201103/physicshistory.cfm.

Conliffe, Ciaran. 'William Chaloner, Master Counterfeiter'. *Headstuff*, 11 April 2017. Available: https://headstuff.org/culture/history/william-chaloner-master-counterfeiter/.

Craig, John Herbert Mccutcheon. 'Isaac Newton-Crime Investigator'. *Nature*, vol. 182, no. 4629, 1 July 1958. Available: https://doi.org/10.1038/182149a0.

———. 'Isaac Newton and the counterfeiters'. *Notes and Records of the Royal Society of London*, vol. 18, 1963. Available: https://royalsocietypublishing.org/doi/10.1098/rsnr.1963.0017.

———. and G. Findlay Shirras. 'Sir Isaac Newton and the Currency'. *Economic Journal*, vol. 55, no. 218/219, June–September 1945. Available: https://www.jstor.org/stable/2226082.

Hiebendaal, Sam. 'The Counterfeit Presentment of Two Britons: Isaac Newton and Currency Crime in Modem England.' *Auckland Law Review*, 2009. Available: http://www.nzlii.org/nz/journals/AukULRev/2009/5.pdf.

Hopkins, Paul and Handley, Stuart. 'Chaloner, William (d. 1699)'. *Oxford Dictionary of National Biography*, 23 September 2004. Available: https://www.oxforddnb.com/display/10.1093/ref:odnb/9780198614128.001.0001/odnb-9780198614128-e-66841.

Lee D'mato. 'Issac Newton's Historic Feud with a Conman'. *Archive*, 28

September 2022. Available: https://explorethearchive.com/william-chaloner.

Robinson, Justin. 'Sir Isaac Newton – Master of the Mint'. *Coins & History Foundation*, 30 April 2021. Available: https://coinsandhistoryfoundation.org/tag/william-chaloner/.

Westfall, Richard S. 'Newton Defends His First Publication: The Newton-Lucas Correspondence.' *ISIS*, vol. 57, no. 3, University of Chicago Press, Autumn 1966. Available: https://www.journals.uchicago.edu/doi/abs/10.1086/350140.

William Chaloner. Wikipedia. https://en.wikipedia.org/wiki/William_Chaloner.

Chapter 2: Haridas Mundhra: The Great Investor

Legal and Authoritative Documents

Champarun Sugar Co. Ltd. and Another vs Haridas Mundhra and Others. Calcutta High Court, AIR 1966 Cal 134. 5 May 1965. Available: https://indiankanoon.org/doc/320528/?type=print.

Haridas Mundra vs National and Grindlays Bank Ltd. Calcutta High Court, AIR 1963 Cal 132. 31 July 1962. Available: https://indiankanoon.org/doc/673186/.

Hungerford Investment Trust Limited vs Haridas Mundhra & Ors. Supreme Court of India, AIR 1826 1972 SCR (3). 9 March 1972. Available: https://www.advocatekhoj.com/library/judgments/index.php?go=1972/march/7.php.

Legal Remembrance of Govt. of W.B. vs Haridas Mundra. Supreme Court of India. Appeals Nos. 115, 256 & 257 of 197. 9 December 1975. Available: https://indiankanoon.org/doc/413624/.

The State vs Haridas Mundra and Anr. Calcutta High Court, AIR 1970 Cal, 16 June 1970. Available: https://indiankanoon.org/doc/1825909/.

The State vs Haridas Mundhra and Others. Calcutta High Court. 17 July 1974. Available: https://www.casemine.com/judgement/in/56095f34e4b01497112c9b43.

Books

Balachandran, G. *The Bank and Mundhra Affair.* Appendix D, Reserve Bank of India, II, 1951–1967.

Bhushan, Shashi. *Feroze Gandhi: A Political Biography, Progressive People's Sector Publications*. New Delhi: Progressive People's Sector Publications, 1977.

Falk, Bertil. *Feroze Gandhi: The Forgotten Gandhi*. New Delhi: Roli Books, 2016.

Swain, Smarak. *The Great Indian Fraud: Serious Frauds Which Shook the Economy*. New Delhi: Bloomsbury India, 2020.

Newspaper, Magazine and Journal Articles

Chandrachud, Abhinav. 'Nehru's Apology to Justice Bose: How A 'Fledgling Democracy Passed A Major Test' Had it not been for a swift & graceful apology by Nehru, a constitutional crisis could have ensued', *BQ Prime*, 5 July 2021. Available: https://www.bqprime.com/opinion/nehrus-apology-to-justice-bose-how-indias-fledgling-democracy-passed-a-major-test-by-abhinav-chandrachud.

Desai, Ashok. 'Afterthoughts on the Mundhra Affair'. *Economic & Political Weekly*, vol. 11, no. 28–29–30, 11 July 1959. Available: https://www.yumpu.com/en/document/view/22030299/afterthoughts-on-the-mundhra-affair-economic-and-political-weekly.

Falk, Bertil. 'The Gandhi in The Opposition'. *Outlook*, 30 September 2016. Available: https://www.outlookindia.com/magazine/story/the-gandhi-in-the-opposition/297914.

Haridas Mundra. Wikipedia. Available: https://en.wikipedia.org/wiki/Haridas_Mundhra.

Misra, Siddharth. 'British India Corporation and Mundhra Affair'. *The Bizdom*, 12 December 2020. Available: https://www.thebizdom.in/british-india-corporation-and-mundhra-affair/.

Pandey, Sheo Nandan. 'India's Tryst with Corruption Menace'. Berline: *The Institute for Strategic, Political, Security and Economic Consulting (ISPSW)*, September 2016. Available: https://www.files.ethz.ch/isn/98806/India_Corruption_Menace.pdf.

'The Mundhra Scandal'. Scamleaks. Available: https://scamsleaks.blogspot.com/2014/04/the-mundhra-scandal.html.

Subramanian, Samanth. 'Long View: India's Very First Corruption Scandal'. *New York Times*, 9 May 2012. Available: https://archive.nytimes.com/india.blogs.nytimes.com/2012/05/09/long-view-indias-very-first-corruption-scandal/.

'Independent India's First Big Financial Scam: Mundhra Scandal'. *Logical Indian*, 19 March 2016. Available: https://thelogicalindian.com/news/independent-indias-first-big-financial-scam-mundhra-scandal.

'The People's Premiums'. *Time*, 3 March 1958. Available: https://archive.org/details/the-peoples-premiums.

Tyabji, Nasir. 'Private Industry and the Second Five-Year Plan: The Mundhra Episode as Exemplar of Capitalist Myopia.' *Munich Personal RePEc Archive*, 7 August 2010. Available: https://papers.ssrn.com/sol3/papers.cfm?abstract_id=2367925.

Wasu, Riddhi Ravindra. 'Facets Of White-Collar Crime In The Indian Legal System'. *International Journal of Legal Science and Innovation*, vol. 3, no. 3. Available: https://www.ijlsi.com/wp-content/uploads/Facets-of-White-Collar-Crime-in-the-Indian-Legal-System.pdf.

Chapter 3: Hugh Cameron: The Artful Manager

Legal and Authoritative Documents

A Word to the Shareholders and Depositors in the Royal British Bank containing a Scheme for the Arrangement of its Affairs without Litigation by David Elwin Colombine, Solicitor. 1856. Available: https://www.google.co.in/books/edition/A_Word_to_the_Shareholders_and_Depositor/PspVAAAAcAAJ?q=A+Word+to+the+Shareholders+and+Depositors+in+the+Royal+British+Bank+containing+a+Scheme+for+the+Arrangement+of+its+Affairs+without+Litigation+by+David+Elwin+Colombine,+Solicitor&gbpv=1#f=false.

Deed of Constitution of the Royal British Bank, London. J. King, Printer, 1849. Available: https://www.google.co.in/books/edition/Deed_of_Constitution_of_the_British_Bank/8MFVAAAAcAAJ?hl=en.

Royal British Bank vs Turquand. 6 E&B 327, All ER 435 5, 1 May 1856. Available: http://www.commonlii.org/uk/cases/EngR/1856/470.pdf.

The Annual Register. Rivingtons, 1863. Available: https://archive.org/details/annualregister118unkngoog/page/2/mode/2up.

Trial of the Directors of the Royal British Bank Viz. Humphry Brown, Edward Esdaile... [et Al.] at the Court of Queen's Bench, Guildhall, Before Lord Campbell and a Special Jury Humphry Brown. 1857. Available: https://babel.hathitrust.org/cgi/pt?id=mdp.39015001078792&seq=17.

The Curious and Remarkable History of the Royal British Bank, Showing 'How We Got It Up' and 'How It Went Down': The Suppressed Pamphlet. Effingham Wilson, Royal Exchange, 1856. Available: https://archive.org/details/curiousremarkabl00londuoft.

Books

Evans, James Cook. *Report of The Trial of The Information Filed by Her Majesty's Attorney-General, (Sir R. Bethell,) against Humphrey Brown and Others, The Directors and General Manager of The Royal British Bank, before Lord Campbell and a Special Jury, at Guildhall, on the 13th of February, 1858, and twelve following days.* The Making of the Modern Law: Trials, 1600–1926. Michigan: Gale Ecco, Making of Modern Law, 1 February 2012.

Garber, Peter M. *Famous First Bubbles: The Fundamentals of Early Manias.* Cambridge: The MIT Press, October 2001.

Gaskill, Malcolm. *Crime and Mentalities in Early Modern England.* Cambridge: Cambridge University Press, 2012.

Orbell, Ron. *British Banking: A Guide to Historical Records, Studies in British Business Archives.* London: Ashgate Publishing Limited, August 2001.

Taylor, James. *Boardroom Scandal: The Criminalization of Company Fraud in Nineteenth Century Britain.* Oxford: Oxford University Press, 25 April 2013.

Turner, John D. *Banking in Crisis: The Rise and Fall of British Banking Stability 1800 to the Present.* Cambridge Studies in Economic History, Cambridge University Press, July 2014.

Newspaper, Magazine and Journal Articles

Alborn, Timothy L. 'The Moral of the Failed Bank: Professional Plots in the Victorian Money Market'. *Victorian Studies*, vol. 38, no. 2, 1995, 199–226. Indiana University Press. Available: https://www.jstor.org/stable/3829168.

Foreman-Peck, James and Leslie Hannah. 'Some Consequences of the Early Twentieth Century British Divorce of Ownership from Control'. *Business History*, vol. 55, no. 4, 2013, 543–564. Available: https://econpapers.repec.org/article/tafbushst/v_3a55_3ay_3a2013_3ai_3a4_3ap_3a543-564.htm.

'The Frauds on the Great Northern Railway'. *Illustrated London News*, British Newspaper Archives, 22 November 1856. Available: https://www.britishnewspaperarchive.co.uk/.

'The Royal British Bank'. *Illustrated London News*, British Newspaper Archives, 10 January 1857. Available: https://www.britishnewspaperarchive.co.uk/.

'The British Bank Conspirators'. *Illustrated London News*, British Newspaper Archives, 23 May 1857. Available: https://www.britishnewspaperarchive.co.uk/.

'Fraudulent Breaches of Trust'. *Illustrated London News*, British Newspaper Archives, 23 May 1857. Available: https://www.britishnewspaperarchive.co.uk/.

'Joint Stocks Out of Joint'.19 September 1857. Available: https://www.britishnewspaperarchive.co.uk/.

'Savings Banks'. *Illustrated London News*, British Newspaper Archives, 20 June 1857. Available: https://www.britishnewspaperarchive.co.uk/.

'Trial of the British Bank Directors'. *Illustrated London News*, British Newspaper Archives, 20 February 1858. Available: https://www.britishnewspaperarchive.co.uk/.

'The Royal British Bank Trial'. *Illustrated London News*, British Newspaper Archives, 6 March 1858. Available: https://www.britishnewspaperarchive.co.uk/.

The British Museum. *Royal British Bank*. Available: https://www.britishmuseum.org/collection/term/BIOG114599.

Royal British Bank. Wikipedia. Available at https://en.wikipedia.org/wiki/Royal_British_Bank.

Taylor, James. 'Company Fraud in Victorian Britain: The Royal British Bank Scandal of 1856'. *English Historical Review*, vol. 122, no. 497, Oxford Academic, June 2007. Available: https://academic.oup.com/ehr/article-abstract/CXXII/497/700/391074?redirectedFrom=fulltext.

'The Royal British Bank: Examination of The Governor- Extraordinary Disclosures'. *Argus* (Melbourne, Victoria), 27 May 1857, 6. Available: https://trove.nla.gov.au/newspaper/article/12995794.

The Perth Gazette. 'History of the Royal British Bank'. *Perth Gazette and Independent Journal of Politics and News*, 29 May 1857, 5. Available: https://trove.nla.gov.au/newspaper/article/2930004.

'Royal British Bank'. *Spectator Archive*, 13 September 1856. Available:

http://archive.spectator.co.uk/article/13th-september-1856/11/the-royal-british-bank.

Turner, John and Graeme Acheson. 'The death blow to unlimited liability in Victorian Britain: The City of Glasgow failure'. *Explorations in Economic History*, vol. 45, no. 3, 2008. Available: https://www.sciencedirect.com/science/article/abs/pii/S0014498307000411?via%3Dihub.

Williams, Geoffrey Fain. 'Trust But Verify: Fraud in Victorian Banking and Its Diminishment'. *Transylvania University*. Available: https://papers.ssrn.com/sol3/papers.cfm?abstract_id=1983633.

Chapter 4: Chia Teck Leng: The King of Gamblers

Legal and Authoritative Documents

Director of Public Prosecutions (Cth) vs Teck Leng Chia. Supreme Court of Victoria, Gaming Law Review, vol. 9, no. 5, Mary Ann Liebert Inc., 20 June 2005. Available: https://www.liebertpub.com/doi/10.1089/glr.2005.9.470.

Ministry of Trade And Industry, Singapore. Statement By The Minister For Home Affairs Wong Kan Seng On The Development Of Integrated Resorts. 18 April 2005. Available: https://www.mti.gov.sg/-/media/MTI/Legislation/Public-Consultations/2012/Additional-Information-on-the-Integrated-Resorts/ministerial-statement---wks-18apr05.pdf?la=en&hash=B9DF2B6E1E016C3600929B7F6BE07782.

Public Prosecutor vs Chia Teck Leng. CC 12/2004, 2004 SGHC 68. 2 April 2004. Available: https://www.elitigation.sg/gdviewer/s/2004_SGHC_68.

Public Prosecutor vs Chia Teck Leng, High Court of Singapore. SGHC 68, CC 12/2004. 2 April 2004. Available: http://www.singaporelaw.sg/sglaw/laws-of-singapore/case-law.

Skandinaviska Enskilda Banken AB (Publ), Singapore Branch vs Asia Pacific Breweries (Singapore) Pte Ltd and another. Civil Appeals Nos 121 and 122 of 2009, 4 SLR(R) 788. 19 May 2011. Available: https://www.elitigation.sg/gdviewer/s/2011_SGCA_22.

Newspaper, Magazine and Journal Articles

Ahmad, Nureza. 'Longest jail term for the worst case of commercial fraud'. *Singapore Infopedia*, May 2016. Available: https://eresources.nlb.gov.sg/infopedia/articles/SIP_422_2005-01-25.html.

Anparasan, K. 'White-collar crime in Singapore: Then and Now'. *Singapore Academy of Law Journal*, vol. 21, 2009. Available: https://journalsonline.academypublishing.org.sg/Journals/Singapore-Academy-of-Law-Journal/e-Archive/ctl/eFirstSALPDFJournalView/mid/495/ArticleId/622/Citation/JournalsOnlinePDF.

Apple Podcast. 'The Casino Dragon: Chia Teck Leng'. *Heinous – An Asian True Crime Podcast*, 2004.

Chan, James. Steering Clear of Corporate Frauds. *Crowe*. Available: https://www.crowe.com/my/-/media/Crowe/Firms/Asia-Pacific/my/CroweMY/Insights/Steering-Clear-of-Corporate-Frauds_Audit.pdf?la=en-GB&hash=18984A8A06BC2DF3007D7A8384CFE75D676AAF71.

Chia Teck Leng, Wikipedia. Available: https://en.wikipedia.org/wiki/Chia_Teck_Leng.

'Singapore: HVB allowed to seize $38m from Chia Teck Leng's assets'. *Corruption.Net*. 16 March 2012. Available: https://corruption.net/singapore-hvb-allowed-to-seize-38m-from-chia-teck-lengs-assets/.

Hafiz, Abdul. 'Guilty As Charged 25 Crimes That Have Shaken Singapore Since 1965'. *Straits Times Press Pvt Ltd.*, 24 July 2017.

Leng, Chia Teck. 'Taming the Casino Dragon'. April 2005. Available: https://www.scribd.com/document/84799581/Gambling-Inside-Story#.

Liang. Tan Sin. 'An Overview of the Anti-Money Laundering and Anti-Terrorist Financing Laws in Singapore'. *Singapore Law Gazette*. Available: https://v1.lawgazette.com.sg/2005-2/Feb05-feature5.htm.

'Behind The Poker Face: Chia Teck Leng'. *Money FM 89.3*, 4 January 2021. Available: https://www.facebook.com/moneyfm893/videos/734566203828074/.

'Singapore: Chia Teck'. *News 5 Tonight*. Available: https://www.nas.gov.sg/archivesonline/audiovisual_records/record-details/57dd8a54-1164-11e3-83d5-0050568939ad.

'S'pore judge dismisses SEB, HVB suit vs Asia Pacific Breweries'. *Reuters Staff*, 19 May 2011. Available: https://www.reuters.com/article/apb-idUKL4E7GJ1WY20110519.

'Asia Pacific Breweries: We were a victim of fraud'. *Singapore Business Review*, 2012. Available: https://sbr.com.sg/manufacturing/in-focus/asia-pacific-breweries-we-were-victim-fraud.

Tan, Gerard. 'Don't Forget the Internal Threats'. *Singapore Institute of Directors*. https://www.sid.org.sg/images/PDFS/Publications/BoardroomMatters/Vii/33.%20Boardroom%20Matters%20Vol%20II-Don't%20Forget%20The%20Internal%20Threats.pdf.

Tan, Valarie. 'Home Affairs Ministry releases Chia Teck Leng's paper'. *Channel NewsAsia*, 19 April 2005. Available: https://sgforums.com/forums/10/topics/127721/.

'Swindler's assets: 10-year saga ends with settlement'. *Straight Times*, 8 August 2012. Available: https://eresources.nlb.gov.sg/newspapers/browse/straitstimes.

'Passport lands exec's woman friend in court'. *Straight Times*, 13 December 2003. Available: https://eresources.nlb.gov.sg/newspapers/browse/straitstimes.

'APB exec charged with forging papers'. *Straight Times*, 5 September 2003. Available: https://eresources.nlb.gov.sg/newspapers/browse/straitstimes.

'Brewery man held over huge alleged fraud'. *Straight Times*, 6 September 2003. Available: https://eresources.nlb.gov.sg/newspapers/browse/straitstimes.

'$230m in brewery man's casino account'. *Straight Times*, 18 October 2003. Available: https://eresources.nlb.gov.sg/newspapers/browse/straitstimes.

'She was brewery man's good luck charm'. *Straight Times*, 12 March 2004. Available: https://eresources.nlb.gov.sg/newspapers/browse/straitstimes.

'Brewery man gets 42 years'. *Straight Times*, 3 April 2004. Available: https://eresources.nlb.gov.sg/newspapers/browse/straitstimes.

Vanessa Ng. 'Meet Singapore's Biggest White Collar Criminal'. *Kopi*. Available: https://thekopi.co/2020/01/15/white-collar-criminal/.

White & Case. 'A higher standard of financial prudence and responsibility for banks – Singapore Court of Appeal dismisses claims of defrauded banks'. *Lexology*. Available: https://www.lexology.com/library/detail.aspx?g=3c5eb051-646a-4a21-b029-25461152215b.

Chapter 5: Hegestratos: The First Fraudster

Historical Records

Demosthenes. *Orations*. Translated by J.H. Vince, C.A. Vince, A.T. Murray, N.W. DeWitt, and N.J. DeWitt. Massachusetts: Harvard University Pres, 1939.

Dobson, John Frederic. *The Greek Orators*. London: Methuen & Company Limited, 1919. Available: https://archive.org/details/greekorators00dobs/page/98/mode/2up.

Evans, D. Morier. *Banking Almanac and Directory*. Islington: Richard Groombridge and Sons, 1861.

Herodotus. Translated by Robin Waterfield. *The Histories*. Oxford: Oxford University Press, 10 February 2010.

Paley, F. A. and J. E. Sandys. *Select Private Orations of Demosthenes with Notes 1886*. Published online by Cambridge University Press, 27 October 2009.

Smith, William. *Dictionary of Greek and Roman Geography*. Massachusetts: Harvard University, 1856.

Tourloukis, Vangelis, and Katerina Harvati. 'The Palaeolithic record of Greece: A synthesis of the evidence and a research agenda for the future'. *Quaternary International*, 1 May 2017.

Books

Joint Association of Classical Teachers. *Reading Greek*. Cambridge: Cambridge University Press, 2007.

Karambelas, Athina; Helmis, Andreas & Karambelas, Dimitris. *Law and Rhetoric in Commercial Shipwreck Cases: Isolating the Facts*. Studies in Ancient Greek and Roman Law, 2020.

Pomeroy, Sarah B; Burstein, Stanley M. & Donlan, Walter. *A Brief History of Ancient Greece: Politics, Society, and Culture*. Oxford: Oxford University Press, 2019.

Newspaper, Magazine and Journal Articles

Dill, Christopher. 'History of Fraud: Greek Grain Merchant Thwarted – 300 B.C'. *ICW Group Insurance Companies*, 30 June 2022. Available: https://blog.icwgroup.com/fraud/history-of-fraud-greek-grain-merchant-thwarted-300-b-c/.

'Crime in Ancient Greece'. *Police Journal: Theory, Practice and Principles, vol. 2, no. 3, July 1929*. Available: https://journals.sagepub.com/doi/abs/10.1177/0032258X2900200309.

Union, Radiant. 'The First Recorded Scam'. *Radiant Blog*, 18 August 2021. Available: https://factsandhistory.com/the-first-recorded-scam/.

Vinogradoff, Paul. 'The Legal background of Demosthenes' speech in Zenothemis vs Demon'. *Legal History Review*, vol. 3, 1 January 1922. Available: https://brill.com/view/journals/lega/3/2/article-p163_2.xml.

Zane, John M. 'A Modern Instance of Zenothemis vs Demon'. *Michigan Law Review*, vol. 23, February, 1925. Available: https://www.jstor.org/stable/pdf/1278553.pdf.

Chapter 6: Jeanne de Valois: The Friendly Imposter

Historical Records

Beugnot, Comte Jacques Claude. *Life and Adventures of Count Beugnot: Minister of State Under Napoleon I*. Translated by C.M. Yonge, Hurst and Blackett, 1871. Available: https://archive.org/details/cu31924077096471/page/n7/mode/2up.

Hausset, Du, Mme. *Memoirs of the Courts of Louis XV and XVI. Being Secret Memoirs of Madame Du Hausset, Lady's Maid to Madame de Pompadour, and of the Princess Lamballe*. L. C. Page, 1899.

Lamballe, Marie Thérèse Louise De Savoie-Carignan. Edited by Catherine Hyde. *Secret Memoirs of Princess Lamballe: Being Her Journals, Letters and Conversations During Her Confidential Relations With Marie Antoinette*. M. Walter Dunne, 1901.

Macmahon, Parkyns (Translator). *Memorial, Or Brief, for the Comte de Cagliostro, Defendant: Against the King's Attorney-General, Plaintiff: in the Cause of the Cardinal de Rohan, Comtesse de la Motte, and Others*. J. Debrett, Macklew & DeBoff, 1786.

Multiple Authors. *Authentic Adventures of the Celebrated Countess de la Motte: from Her Birth to Her Escape from Prison: Including the Whole Transaction with Cardinal de Rohan*. Geo Kersley, 1787. (Jeanne de Valois).

Rocheterie, Maxime De La. Translated by Cora Hamilton Bell. *The Life of Marie Antoinette*. New York: Dodd, Mead & Co, 1893.

Saint-Rémy, Jeanne De (De Valois La Motte). *The Life of Jane de St. Remy de Valois, heretofore Countess de la Motte*. J. Bew, 1791.

Target, Avocat (Translator). *Memorial of Louis-René - Édouard de Rohan, Cardinal of the Holy Roman Church etc Against the Attorney-General in the Presence of Madame de La Motte*. London: J. Jarvis, 1787.

Books

Beckman, Jonathan. *How to Ruin a Queen: Marie Antoinette and the Diamond Necklace Affair*. Da Capo Press. September 2014

Carlyle, Thomas. *The Diamond Necklace*. New York: Houghton Mifflin Company, (1913 Reprint: Cambridge University Press), 2012.

Jeanne De Saint-Remy. *Memoirs of the Countess de Valois de la Motte; Containing a Compleat Justification of Her Conduct and an Explanation of the Intrigues Relative to the Diamond Necklace*. London: Gale Ecco, 2010.

Trowbridge, W R H. *Cagliostro and The Diamond Necklace Affair*. Montana: Kessinger Publishing, 2010.

Vizetelly, Henry. *The Story of the Diamond Necklace*. London: Vizetelly & Co, 1881.

Newspaper, Magazine and Journal Articles

Henley, John. *How to Ruin a Queen by Jonathan Beckman – review*. The Guardian, August 2014. https://www.theguardian.com/books/2014/aug/21/how-to-ruin-queen-jonathan-beckman-review

Jeanne de Valois-Saint-Rémy. Wikipedia. Available: https://en.wikipedia.org/wiki/Jeanne_de_Valois-Saint-R%C3%A9my.

Mark, Harrison W. *Affair of the Diamond Necklace*. World History Encyclopaedia. March 2022 https://www.worldhistory.org/article/1970/affair-of-the-diamond-necklace/92988.

Sorensen, David R. 'Thomas Carlyle's MS Notes for 'The Diamond Necklace'. *Carlyle Studies Annual*, no. 23, Saint Joseph's University Press, 2007. Available: https://www.jstor.org/stable/26592988.

Watts, Sydney. *How to Ruin a Queen: Marie Antoinette and the Diamond Necklace Affair*. By Jonathan Beckman. The Historian. March 2017. https://doi.org/10.1111/hisn.12468

Chapter 7: Kenneth Lay: The Energy Chief

Legal and Authoritative Documents

Andrew S. Fastow, Former Enron Chief Financial Officer, Pleads Guilty, Settles Civil Fraud Charges and Agrees to Cooperate with Ongoing Investigation. Press Release (2004–6). Securities and Exchange Commission, United States of America, 14 January 2004. Available: https://archives.fbi.gov/archives/news/pressrel/press-releases/former-enron-chief-financial-officer-andrew-fastow-pleads-guilty-to-conspiracy-to-commit-securities-and-wire-fraud.

Crime in the Suites A Look Back at the Enron Case. Federal Bureau of Investigation (FBI), United States Government, 13 December 2006. Available: https://archives.fbi.gov/archives/news/stories/2006/december/enron_121306.

Enron Code of Ethics. Federal Bureau of Investigation (FBI), United States Government, 2000. Available: https://www.fbi.gov/history/artifacts/enron-code-of-ethics#:~:text=%E2%80%9CEnron%20was%20a%20company%20where,top%20levels%20of%20the%20company.

Enron Corp., et al. Memorandum Opinion and Order Authorizing External and Intrasystem Financing and Related Transactions; Authorizing Service Agreements; and Reserving Jurisdiction. Release No. 35-27809; 70-10200. Securities and Exchange Commission, United States. 9 March 2004. Available: https://www.sec.gov/rules/other/35-27809.pdf.

Enron Related Press Releases. The United States Department of Justice. 2002–2006. Available: https://www.justice.gov/archive/index-enron.html.

Enron Task Force: Production of List of Witnesses. The United States Department of Justice. 6 January 2006. Available: https://www.justice.gov/archive/enron/pdf/enron.witlist.revised.0106.pdf.

Enron Task Force Charges Three Former British Bankers with Wire Fraud#378. The United States Department of Justice. 27 June 2002. Available: https://www.justice.gov/archive/opa/pr/2002/June/02_crm_377.htm.

Enron Trial Exhibits and Releases. The United States Department of Justice Archives. 1 February – 3 May 2006. Available: https://www.justice.gov/archive/index-enron.html.

Federal Jury Convicts Former Enron Chief Executives Ken Lay, Jeff Skilling on Fraud, Conspiracy and Related Charges#06-328, The United States

Department of Justice. 25 May 2006. Available: https://www.justice.gov/archive/opa/pr/2006/May/06_crm_328.html.

Financial Oversight of Enron: Report Prepared by The Staff Of The Committee On Governmental Affairs United States Senate, The SEC And Private-Sector Watchdogs. October 7, 2002. Securities and Exchange Commission, United States. 7 October 2002. Available: https://www.govinfo.gov/content/pkg/CPRT-107SPRT82147/html/CPRT-107SPRT82147.htm.

Former Enron Chairman and Chief Executive Officer Kenneth L. Lay Charged with Conspiracy, Fraud, False Statement. The United States Department of Justice. 8 July 2004. Available at https://www.justice.gov/archive/opa/pr/2004/July/04_crm_470.htm.

Former Enron Chief Executive Officer Jeffrey K. Skilling Charged with Conspiracy, Securities Fraud, Insider Trading. The United States Department of Justice. 19 February 2004. Available: https://www.justice.gov/archive/opa/pr/2004/February/04_crm_099.htm.

Former Enron Assistant Treasurer Timothy Despain Pleads Guilty to Fraud and Agrees to Cooperate#682. The United States Department of Justice. 5 October 2004. Available: https://www.justice.gov/archive/opa/pr/2004/October/04_crm_682.htm.

Former Enron Broadband Chief Executive Officer Kenneth Rice Sentenced on Securities Fraud Charge#07-433. The United States Department of Justice. 18 June 2007. Available: https://www.justice.gov/archive/opa/pr/2007/June/07_crm_433.html#:~:text=Officer%20Kenneth%20Rice-,Sentenced%20on%20Securities%20Fraud%20Charge,Assistant%20Attorney%20General%20Alice%20S.

Former Enron Broadband Co-Chief Executive Officer Pleads Guilty to Wire Fraud#08-92. The United States Department of Justice. 14 October 2008. Available: https://www.justice.gov/archive/opa/pr/2008/October/08-crm-921.html.

Former Enron Chief Accounting Officer Richard Causey Pleads Guilty to Securities Fraud#05-695. The United States Department of Justice. 28 December 2005. Available: https://www.justice.gov/archive/opa/pr/2005/December/05_crm_695.html.

Former Enron Chief Executive Officer Jeffrey Skilling Sentenced to More Than 24 Years in Prison on Fraud, Conspiracy Charges#06-723. The United States Department of Justice. 23 October 2006. Available: https://www.justice.gov/archive/opa/pr/2006/October/06_crm_723.html.

Former Enron Chief Financial Officer Andrew Fastow Sentenced to Six Years in Prison for Conspiracy to Commit Securities and Wire Fraud#06-647. The United States Department of Justice. 26 September 2006. Available: https://www.justice.gov/archive/opa/pr/2006/September/06_crm_647.html.

Grand Jury in Houston Returns Superseding Indictment Against Former Executives at Enron And Merrill Lynch#430. The United States Department of Justice. 23 June 2004. Available: https://www.justice.gov/archive/opa/pr/2004/June/04_crm_430.htm.

An Overview of The Enron Collapse: Hearing Before the Committee On Commerce, Science, And Transportation. United States Senate One Hundred Seventh Congress. 18 December 2001. Available: https://www.govinfo.gov/content/pkg/CHRG-107shrg82282/pdf/CHRG-107shrg82282.pdf.

Accountability Issues: Lessons Learnt from Enron's Collapse: Hearing Before The Committee On Energy And Commerce, House Of Representatives, One Hundred Seventh Congress, Second Session. Securities and Exchange Commission. United States. 6 February 2002. Available: https://www.govinfo.gov/content/pkg/CHRG-107shrg84416/pdf/CHRG-107shrg84416.pdf.

Memorandum Opinion and Order Approving Plan of Reorganization of Enron Corp Under Section 11(f) and Issuing Report Under Section 11(g) United States Bankruptcy Code. Release No 35-27810; 70-10199. Securities and Exchange Commission, United States. 9 March 2004. Available: https://www.sec.gov/rules/other/35-27810.pdf.

Public Utility Holding Company Act of 1935; Administrative Proceeding; Applications of Enron Corp. for Exemptions Under the Public Utility Holding Company Act of 1935. Nos. 70-9661 and 70-10056). Notice by the Securities and Exchange Commission, Securities and Exchange Commission. United States. 10 November 2002. Available: https://www.federalregister.gov/documents/2002/10/11/02-26025/public-utility-holding-company-act-of-1935-administrative-proceeding-applications-of-enron-corp-for.

Report Of Investigation by The Special Investigative Committee of The Board of Directors of Enron Corp: William C. Powers, Jr., Chair, Raymond S. Troubh, Herbert S. Winokur, J. Securities and Exchange Commission, United States. 1 February 2002. Available: https://www.sec.gov/Archives/edgar/data/1024401/000090951802000089/big.txt.

SEC Charges Jeffrey K. Skilling, Enron's Former President, Chief Executive Officer and Chief Operating Officer, With Fraud. Press Release (2004-18), Securities and Exchange Commission, United States. 19 February 2004. Available: https://www.sec.gov/news/press/2004-18.htm.

Securities and Exchange Commission (Plaintiff) vs Jeffrey K. Skilling, Richard A Causey (Defendants). Civil Action No. H-04-0284 (Harmon), United States District Court, Southern District of Texas, Houston Division, Securities and Exchange Commission, United States. 1 February 2004. Available: https://www.sec.gov/litigation/complaints/comp18582.htm.

Securities and Exchange Commission vs Andrew S. Fastow. Civil Action No H-02-3666 (Hoyt) (S.D. Tx.) SEC settles civil fraud charges filed against Andrew S. Fastow, former Enron Chief Financial Officer, Litigation Release No. 18543 / January 14, 2004, Accounting and Auditing Release No. 1942 / January 14, 2004, Securities and Exchange Commission, United States. 14 January 2004. Available: https://www.sec.gov/litigation/litreleases/lr18543.htm.

Securities and Exchange Commission vs Richard A. Causey, Jeffrey K. Skilling and Kenneth L. Lay. Civil Action No. H-04-0284 (Harmon) (S.D. Tx.). July 8, 2004. Litigation Release No. 18776 / July 8, 2004, Accounting and Auditing Enforcement Release No. 2051 / July 8, 2004, Securities and Exchange Commission, United States. 8 July 2004. Available: https://www.sec.gov/litigation/litreleases/lr18776.htm.

Skilling vs United states 561 U.S. Supreme Court, The United States Department of Justice. 2009–10. Available: https://www.justice.gov/osg/brief/skilling-v-united-states-opposition-0.

Ten-Year Anniversary of the Convictions of Chief Executives in FBI's Largest White-Collar Crime Investigation. Federal Bureau of Investigation, FBI, United States Government. 25 May 2016. Available: https://www.fbi.gov/contact-us/field-offices/houston/news/press-releases/ten-year-anniversary-of-the-convictions-of-chief-executives-in-fbi2019s-largest-white-collar-crime-investigation.

*Three Top Former Merrill Lynch Executives Charged with Conspiracy, Obstruction of Justice, Perjury in Enron Investigation#510.*The United States Department of Justice. 17 September 2003. Available: https://www.justice.gov/archive/opa/pr/2003/September/03_crm_510.htm.

Transcript of Deputy Attorney General Larry Thompson News Conference Regarding the Enron Investigation#. The United States Department of

Justice. 17 October 2002. Available: https://www.justice.gov/archive/dag/speeches/2002/101702dagnewsconferenceenron.htm.

Transcript of Media Availability with Attorney General Alberto R. Gonzales. The United States Department of Justice. 13 March 2007. Available: https://www.justice.gov/archive/ag/speeches/2007/ag_speech_070313.html.

Transcript of Statement by Deputy Attorney General Paul J. McNulty on the Convictions of Former Enron Chief Executive Officers Ken Lay and Jeff Skilling, The United States Department of Justice. 25 May 2006. Available: https://www.justice.gov/archive/enron/pdf/layskillingverdictstatementvydagmcnulty.pdf.

USA vs Jeffrey Skilling, Kenneth Lay (4:04-CR-25) United States District & Bankruptcy Court, Southern District of Texas. The United States Department of Justice. 2006. Available: https://www.justice.gov/osg/brief/skilling-v-united-states-brief-merits.

Books

Arbogast, Stephen V. *Resisting Corporate Corruption: Lessons in Practical Ethics from the Enron Wreckage (Conflicts and Trends in Business Ethics).* MA: M&M Scrivener Press, 2008.

Bauer, Andreas. *The Enron scandal and the Sarbanes-Oxley-Act.* California: Grin Publishing, 2009.

Bhaskar, Krish & Flower, John. *Financial Failures and Scandals: From Enron to Carillion (Disruptions in Financial Reporting and Auditing).* New York: Routledge, 2019.

Coleman, Phil. *Enron: Crooks In Suits: The Story of Enron and the Biggest Corporate Scandal in History.* Independently Published, 2017.

Eichenwald, Kurt. *Conspiracy of Fools: A True Story.* New York: Broadway Books, 2005.

Ellison, Cara. *Blogging Enron: The Enron Broadband Story.* Florida: Rumble Press, 2014.

Fox, Loren. *Enron: The Rise and Fall.* New Jersey: Wiley, 2004.

Kammerer, Matthias. *Creative Accounting, the Enron Case and its impact on Corporate Governance.* Munch: Grin Publishing, 2009.

Markham, Jerry W. *A Financial History of Modern U.S. Corporate Scandals: From Enron to Reform.* New York: Routledge, 2006.

Mclean, Bethany & Elkind, Peter. *The Smartest Guys in the Room: The*

Amazing Rise and Scandalous Fall of Enron Hardcover. London: Penguin, 2013.

Smith, Rebecca & Emshwiller, John R. *24 Days: How Two Wall Street Journal Reporters Uncovered the Lies that Destroyed Faith in Corporate America*. New York: Harper Business, 2004.

Newspaper, Magazine and Journal Articles

Anderson, Michael E. *Recalling the July 8, 2004*. Arrest and Indictment of Enron's Chairman Kenneth Lay on the 15th Anniversary. 8 July 2019. Available: https://www.linkedin.com/pulse/recalling-july-8-2004-arrest-indictment-enrons-lay-michael-e-.

Beasley, Mark S, Carcello, Joseph V, Hermanson, Dana R. and Neal, Terry L. 'Fraudulent financial reporting: 1998–2007: An analysis of U.S. public companies'. *American Institute of Certified Public Accountants (AICPA)*, Association Sections, Divisions, Boards, Teams 453. 1 May 2010. Available: https://egrove.olemiss.edu/aicpa_assoc/453.

Behr, Peter. 'Broadband Strategy Got Enron in Trouble'. *Washington Post Archives*, 1 January 2002. Available: https://www.washingtonpost.com/archive/business/2002/01/01/broadband-strategy-got-enron-in-trouble/86ce87f6-33e6-4efe-90c5-067c795e9e8c/.

Beneish, Messod. 'The Detection of Earnings Manipulation'. *Financial Analysts Journal*, vol. 5, no. 5, Indiana University Bloomington. 1 September 1999, pp. 24–36. Available: https://www.researchgate.net/publication/252059255_The_Detection_of_Earnings_Manipulation.

Brown, Ken and Weil, Jonathan (Staff Reporters). 'How Andersen's Embrace of Consulting Changed the Culture of the Company'. *Wall Street Journal*, 12 March 2002. Available: https://www.wsj.com/articles/SB1015888232231686560.

Catanach Jr, Anthony H. and Rhoades-Catanach, Shelley C. 'Enron: A Financial Reporting Failure?' *Villanova Law Review*, vol. 48, Charles Widger School of Law, 2003. Available: https://digitalcommons.law.villanova.edu/vlr/vol48/iss4/3/.

Davis, Michael. 'Enron: Making of the Market-maker'. *Houston Chronicle*, 2001. Available: https://www.chron.com/business/article/enron-making-of-the-market-maker-2013245.php.

Emshwiller, John R. and Rebecca Smith (Staff Reporters). 'Behind Enron's Fall, a Culture of Secrecy Which Cost the Firm Its Investors' Trust'.

Wall Street Journal, 5 December 2001. Available: https://www.wsj.com/articles/SB1007502843500372680.

Enron. Wikipedia. Available: https://en.wikipedia.org/wiki/Enron.

Gerstein, Josh. 'Enron's Close Ties to Bush'. *ABC News*. 7 January 2006. Available: https://abcnews.go.com/Politics/story?id=121269&page=1.

Goodwyn, Wade and Lynn Neary. 'Fraud Conviction Changed Lay Personality'. *National Public Radio*, 5 July 2006. Available: https://www.npr.org/2006/07/05/5534881/fraud-conviction-changed-lay-personality.

Johnson, Carrie. 'Prosecutors Link Enron Fall to 1987 Scandal'. *Washington Post*, 5 November 2005. Available: https://www.washingtonpost.com/archive/politics/2005/11/05/prosecutors-link-enron-fall-to-1987-scandal/1cc9a9d0-0a88-43f9-8d11-16972f2e9a87/.

Ken Lay. Wikipedia. Available: https://en.wikipedia.org/wiki/Kenneth_Lay.

'Portraits in Oversight: Congress and the Enron Scandal'. *Levin Center at Wayne Law*, 10 December 2021. Available: https://levin-center.org/what-is-oversight/portraits/congress-and-the-enron-scandal/.

Mclean, Bethany. 'Why Enron Went Bust Start with arrogance. Add greed, deceit, and financial chicanery. What do you get? A company that wasn't what it was cracked up to be'. *Fortune Magazine*, 24 December 2001. Available: https://money.cnn.com/magazines/fortune/fortune_archive/2001/12/24/315319/index.htm.

Moshinsky, Ben, Doan, Lynn and Jim Brunsden. 'Enron no lesson to traders as EU probes oil-price manipulation'. *Bloomberg News*, 21 May 2013. Available: https://www.mresearch.com/pdfs/519.pdf.

'Timeline: Ken Lay and the Arc of Enron'. *National Public Radio*, 5 July 2006. Available: https://www.npr.org/2006/07/05/5535821/timeline-ken-lay-and-the-arc-of-enron.

'The History of Regulation'. *Naturalgas.org*, 20 September 2013. Available: http://naturalgas.org/regulation/history/.

Norris, Floyd and Kurt Eichenwald. 'Enron's Many Strands: The Accounting: Fuzzy Rules of Accounting And Enron'. *New York Times*, 30 January 2002. Available: https://www.nytimes.com/2002/01/30/business/enron-s-many-strands-the-accounting-fuzzy-rules-of-accounting-and-enron.html.

Oppel, Richard A. Jr and Don Van Natta. 'Enron's Collapse: The Relationships: Bush and Democrats Disputing Ties to Enron'.

New York Times, 12 January 2002. Available: https://www.nytimes.com/2002/01/12/business/enron-s-collapse-the-relationships-bush-and-democrats-disputing-ties-to-enron.html.

Perri, Frank S. and EDYTA M Mieczkowska. 'I didn't intend to deceive anyone'. *Fraud Magazine*, Association of Certified Fraud Examiners, March/April 2015. Available: https://www.fraud-magazine.com/article.aspx?id=4294987208.

Reporters, Glenn. 'Citigroup, J.P. Morgan Chase Enron Deals Attract Scrutiny'. *Wall Street Journal*, 9 December 2002. Available: https://www.wsj.com/articles/SB103939126763770673.

Smith, Rachel. 'The Enron Scandal'. *Stanford University*, 10 December 2018. Available: http://large.stanford.edu/courses/2018/ph240/smith1/.

Stinson, Todd. 'Arthur Andersen and Enron: Positive Influence on the Accounting Industry'. *Scholars*, no. 4, McKendree University, Spring 2004. Available: https://www.mckendree.edu/academics/scholars/issue4/stinson.htm.

'Looking At Ken Lay And The Lack Of Financial Crisis Cases'. *New York Times*, 5 July 2011. Available: https://archive.nytimes.com/www.nytimes.com.

'Judge Throws Out Kenneth Lay's Conviction'. *New York Times*, 18 October 2006. Available: https://archive.nytimes.com/www.nytimes.com.

'Fastow sentenced to 6 years'. *New York Times*, 27 September 2006. Available: https://archive.nytimes.com/www.nytimes.com.

'Respect And Anger Voiced At Lay Service'. *New York Times*, 13 July 2006. Available: https://archive.nytimes.com/www.nytimes.com.

'A Sense Of Something Rotten In Aspen'. *New York Times*, 10 July 2006. Available: https://archive.nytimes.com/www.nytimes.com.

'Enron Founder, Awaiting Prison, Dies In Colorado'. *New York Times*, 6 July 2006. Available: https://archive.nytimes.com/www.nytimes.com.

'Lay's Death Complicates Efforts To Seize Assets'. *New York Times*, 6 July 2006. Available: https://archive.nytimes.com/www.nytimes.com.

'Ken Lay's Final Act'. *New York Times*, 6 July 2006. Available: https://archive.nytimes.com/www.nytimes.com.

'Even At The End, Ken Lay Didn't Get It'. *New York Times*, 6 July 2006. Available: https://archive.nytimes.com/www.nytimes.com.

'The Enron Case That Almost Wasn't'. *New York Times*, 4 June 2006. Available: https://archive.nytimes.com/www.nytimes.com.

'The Other Legacy of Enron'. *New York Times*, 28 May 2006. Available: https://archive.nytimes.com/www.nytimes.com.

'Tough Justice For Executives In Enron Era'. *New York Times*, 27 May 2006. Available: https://archive.nytimes.com/www.nytimes.com.

'Executives' Downfall: The 'Managing' Of Numbers Turned Into Manipulating Them'. *New York Times*, 27 May 2006. Available: https://archive.nytimes.com/www.nytimes.com.

'Two Enron Chiefs Are Convicted In Fraud And Conspiracy Trial'. *New York Times*, 26 May 2006. Available: https://archive.nytimes.com/www.nytimes.com.

'What fraud? All was fine at Enron'. *New York Times* 19 May 2006. Available: https://archive.nytimes.com/www.nytimes.com.

'Did Ken Lay demonstrate credibility?' *New York Times*, 3 May 2006. Available: https://archive.nytimes.com/www.nytimes.com.

'Lay Blames Financial Officer And Newspaper Articles For Enron's Fall'. *New York Times*, 26 April 2006. Available: https://archive.nytimes.com/www.nytimes.com.

'Ex-Enron Chief Defends Shift Of Contracts'. *New York Times*, 13 April 2006. Available: https://archive.nytimes.com/www.nytimes.com.

'For Ken Lay, Enron's riches turning to ruin'. *New York Times*, 26 February 2006. Available: https://archive.nytimes.com/www.nytimes.com.

'Enron's Chief offers his case'. *New York Times*, 14 December 2005. Available: https://archive.nytimes.com/www.nytimes.com.

'Remember when Ken Lay was a genius?' *New York Times*, 16 January 2005. Available: https://archive.nytimes.com/www.nytimes.com.

'Enron inquiry turns to sales by Lay's wife'. *New York Times*, 17 November 2004. Available: https://archive.nytimes.com/www.nytimes.com.

'Enron's Spiritual Leader'. *New York Times*, 9 July 2004. Available: https://archive.nytimes.com/www.nytimes.com.

'Corporate Conduct: The Overview; Ex-Chief Of Enron Pleads Not Guilty To 11 Felony Counts'. *New York Times*, 9 July 2004. Available: https://archive.nytimes.com/www.nytimes.com.

'Enron ex-chief indicted by U.S. In fraud case'. *New York Times*, 8 July 2004. Available: https://archive.nytimes.com/www.nytimes.com.

'Crimes of others wrecked Enron, ex-chief says'. *New York Times*, 27 June 2004. Available: https://archive.nytimes.com/www.nytimes.com.

'Life without a jet, and other laments'. *New York Times*, 15 December 2002. Available: https://archive.nytimes.com/www.nytimes.com.

'Ex-executives say sham deal helped Enron'. *New York Times*, 8 August 2002. Available: https://archive.nytimes.com/www.nytimes.com.

'Corporate conduct: close links; Merrill banker had many direct ties to Enron.' *New York Times*, 31 July, 2002. Available: https://archive.nytimes.com/www.nytimes.com.

'Officials got a windfall before Enron's collapse'. *New York Times*, 18 June 2002. Available: https://archive.nytimes.com/www.nytimes.com.

'Enron's many strands: correspondence; letters show bush and lay shared much'. *New York Times*, 16 February 2002. Available: https://archive.nytimes.com/www.nytimes.com.

'Enron's many strands: ex-chairman's finances; lay sold shares for $100 million'. *New York Times*, 16 February 2002. Available: https://archive.nytimes.com/www.nytimes.com.

'Enron's many strands: the overview; Enron official says many knew about shaky company finances'. *New York Times*, 15 February 2002. Available: https://archive.nytimes.com/www.nytimes.com.

'Enron's many strands; 'lone voice': excerpts from testimony of executive who challenged Enron'. *New York Times*, 15 February 2002. Available: https://archive.nytimes.com/www.nytimes.com.

'Enron official says she warned lay about financial irregularities'. *New York Times*, 14 February 2002. Available: https://archive.nytimes.com/www.nytimes.com.

'Enron's many strands: the hearings; Enron official expected to say many knew of irregularities'. *New York Times*, 14 February 2002. Available: https://archive.nytimes.com/www.nytimes.com.

'Excerpts from the senate committee hearing'. *New York Times*, 13 February 2002. Available: https://archive.nytimes.com/www.nytimes.com.

'Enron's many strands; excerpts from the senate committee hearing on the collapse of Enron'. *New York Times*, 13 February 2002. Available: https://archive.nytimes.com/www.nytimes.com.

'Enron's ex-chief harshly criticized by senate panel'. *New York Times*, 13 February 2002. Available: https://archive.nytimes.com/www.nytimes.com.

'Enron's many strands: the overview; G.O.P. Studies new rules on companies'. *New York Times*, 12 February 2002. Available: https://archive.nytimes.com/www.nytimes.com.

'Enron's many strands: the investigation; Enron's lay is to appear before panel'. *New York Times*, 9 February 2002. Available: https://archive.nytimes.com/www.nytimes.com.

'Enron's many strands: early warnings; lawyer at Enron warned officials of dubious deals'. *New York Times*, 7 February 2002. Available: https://archive.nytimes.com/www.nytimes.com.

'Enron's many strands: the transactions; the financial wizard tied to Enron's fall'. *New York Times*, 6 February 2002. Available: https://archive.nytimes.com/www.nytimes.com.

'Enron's many strands: the overview; senate panel says it will subpoena ex-chief of Enron'. *New York Times*, 5 February 2002. Available: https://archive.nytimes.com/www.nytimes.com.

'Decoding Enron'. *New York Times*, 5 February 2002. Available: https://archive.nytimes.com/www.nytimes.com.

'Enron's many strands: the auditors; former fed Chief picked to oversee auditor of Enron'. *New York Times*, 3 February 2002. Available: https://archive.nytimes.com/www.nytimes.com.

'Enron's many strands: the politics; at 11th hour, lay refuses to testify as congressional criticism grows more pointed'. *New York Times*, 4 February 2002. Available: https://archive.nytimes.com/www.nytimes.com.

'Enron panel finds inflated profits and few controls'. *New York Times*, 3 February 2002. Available: https://archive.nytimes.com/www.nytimes.com.

'Enron's many strands: the former chairman; his influence lost, lay prepares to answer questions in Washington'. *New York Times*, 3 February 2002. Available: https://archive.nytimes.com/www.nytimes.com.

'Enron's many strands: ex-chief's family; son and sister of Enron chief secured deals'. *New York Times*, 2 February 2002. Available: https://archive.nytimes.com/www.nytimes.com.

'Enron's many strands: the investigation; senator says Enron refuses to cooperate'. *New York Times*, 1 February 2002. Available: https://archive.nytimes.com/www.nytimes.com.

'Police say former Enron executive committed suicide'. *New York Times*, 25 January 2002. Available: https://archive.nytimes.com/www.nytimes.com.

'Enron's collapse: the Chairman; Enron Chief quits under pressure and calls inquiries a distraction'. *New York Times*, 24 January 2002. Available: https://archive.nytimes.com/www.nytimes.com.

'Enron's collapse: the Chairman; Chief's words paint hands-off image, but actions offer different view'. *New York Times*, 23 January 2002, 2002. Available: https://archive.nytimes.com/www.nytimes.com..

'Enron's collapse; kind words for Andersen'. *New York Times*, 23 January 2002. Available: https://archive.nytimes.com/www.nytimes.com.

'Enron's collapse: marketplace; for Chief, $200 million wasn't quite enough cash'. *New York Times*, 22 January 2002. Available: https://archive.nytimes.com/www.nytimes.com.

'Enron's collapse: transactions at issue; Enron Chief says his sale of stock was to pay loans'. *New York Times*, 21 January 2002. Available: https://archive.nytimes.com/www.nytimes.com.

'Enron's collapse: the anger; Enron fired workers for complaining online'. *New York Times*, 21 January 2002. Available: https://archive.nytimes.com/www.nytimes.com.

'Enron's collapse: the overview; despite warning, Enron Chief urged buying of shares'. *New York Times*, 19 January 2002. Available: https://archive.nytimes.com/www.nytimes.com.

'The United States of Enron'. *New York Times*, 19 January 2002. Available: https://archive.nytimes.com/www.nytimes.com.

'Enron's collapse: the auditor; Enron's Chief sold shares after receiving warning letter'. *New York* Times, 18 January 2002. Available: https://archive.nytimes.com/www.nytimes.com.

'Congress rebuffed on energy documents'. *New York Times*, 18 January 2002. Available: https://archive.nytimes.com/www.nytimes.com.

'Enron's collapse: the review; White House says economics adviser saw little risk on Enron'. *New York Times*, 17 January 2002. Available: https://archive.nytimes.com/www.nytimes.com.

'Enron's collapse: the letter; Enron letter suggests $1.3 billion more down the drain'. *New York Times*, 17 January 2002. Available: https://archive.nytimes.com/www.nytimes.com.

'Enron's collapse: the employee; author of letter to Enron Chief is called tough'. *New York Times*, 16 January 2002. Available: https://archive.nytimes.com/www.nytimes.com.

'Text of letter to Enron's chairman after departure of Chief Executive'. *New York Times*, 16 January 2002. Available: https://archive.nytimes.com/www.nytimes.com.

'Enron's collapse: the overview; Arthur Andersen fires an executive for

Enron orders'. *New York Times*, 16 January 2002 Available: https://archive.nytimes.com/www.nytimes.com.

'Enron's collapse: the law firm; legal counsel in many ways mirrors client'. *New York Times*, 16 January 2002. Available: https://archive.nytimes.com/www.nytimes.com.

'Enron's collapse: the donations; Enron's ties to a leader of house republicans went beyond contributions to his campaign'. *New York Times*, 16 January 2002. Available: https://archive.nytimes.com/www.nytimes.com.

'Enron's collapse: the transaction; Chief used stock to repay Enron loan, lawyer says'. *New York Times*, 15 January 2002. Available: https://archive.nytimes.com/www.nytimes.com.

'Enron's collapse: the overview; Enron's chairman received warning about accounting'. *New York Times*, 15 January 2002. Available: https://archive.nytimes.com/www.nytimes.com.

'Enron's collapse; before debacle, Enron insiders cashed in $1.1 billion in shares'. *New York Times*, 13 January 2002. Available: https://archive.nytimes.com/www.nytimes.com.

'Enron's collapse: the relationships; bush and democrats disputing ties to Enron'. *New York Times*, January 12, 2002. Available: https://archive.nytimes.com/www.nytimes.com.

'Enron's president said to have asked treasury official for help'. *New York Times*, 11 January 2002. Available: https://archive.nytimes.com/www.nytimes.com.

'Enron contacted 2 cabinet officers before collapsing'. *New York Times*, 11 January 2002. Available: https://archive.nytimes.com/www.nytimes.com.

'Enron's collapse: the overview; Enron contacted 2 cabinet officers before collapsing'. *New York Times*, 11 January 2002. Available: https://archive.nytimes.com/www.nytimes.com.

'Senate democrats to examine Enron's ties to white house'. *New York Times*, 2 January 2002. Available: https://archive.nytimes.com/www.nytimes.com.

'Fate's ups and downs, 2 December 2001. Available: https://archive.nytimes.com/www.nytimes.com.

'With Enron's fall, many dominoes tremble'. *New York Times*, 2 December 2001. Available: https://archive.nytimes.com/www.nytimes.com.

'Enron's collapse: the directors; eyebrows raised in hindsight about outside ties of some on the board'. *New York Times*, 30 November 2001. Available: https://archive.nytimes.com/www.nytimes.com.

'Enron's collapse: the Chief Executive; foundation gives way on Chief's big dream'. *New York Times*, 29 November 2001. Available: https://archive.nytimes.com/www.nytimes.com.

'Circling the wagons around Enron; risks too great to let trader just die'. *New York Times*, 22 November 2001. Available: https://archive.nytimes.com/www.nytimes.com.

'Employees' retirement plan is a victim as Enron tumbles'. *New York Times*, 22 November 2001. Available: https://archive.nytimes.com/www.nytimes.com.

'The markets: marketplace; Enron Chief will give up severance'. *New York Times*, 14 November 2001. Available: https://archive.nytimes.com/www.nytimes.com.

'Dynegy to acquire fast-sinking rival Enron'. *New York Times*, 9 November 2001. Available: https://archive.nytimes.com/www.nytimes.com.

'Enron tries to dismiss finance doubts'. *New York Times*, 24 October 2001. Available: https://archive.nytimes.com/www.nytimes.com.

'Two are promoted as Enron seeks executive stability'. *New York Times*, 29 August 2001. Available: https://archive.nytimes.com/www.nytimes.com.

'Enron's Chief Executive quits after only 6 months in job'. *New York Times*, 15 Augus 2001. Available: https://archive.nytimes.com/www.nytimes.com.

'Power trader tied to bush finds Washington all ears'. *New York Times*, 25 May 2001. Available: https://archive.nytimes.com/www.nytimes.com.

'Reckonings; power and profits'. *New York Times*, 24 January 2001. Available: https://archive.nytimes.com/www.nytimes.com.

'Enron rewards President with promotion to Chief Executive'. *New York Times*, 14 December 2000. Available: https://archive.nytimes.com/www.nytimes.com.

'President of Enron says he will resign'. *New York Times*, 27 November 1996. Available: https://archive.nytimes.com/www.nytimes.com.

'Bottom-fishing in the gas patch'. *New York Times*, 9 May 1991. Available: https://archive.nytimes.com/www.nytimes.com.

'Transco denies Houston gas link'. *New York Times*, 9 June 1984. Available: https://archive.nytimes.com/www.nytimes.com.

'A Chronology of Enron's Woes'. *Wall Street Journal,* 20 March 2003. Available: https://www.wsj.com/articles/SB101171396110000000.

Thomas, C William. 'The Rise and Fall of Enron – When a company looks too good to be true, it usually is'. *Journal of Accountancy,* 1 April 2002. Available: https://www.journalofaccountancy.com/issues/2002/apr/theriseandfallofenron.html.

Weil, Jonathan (Staff Reporter). 'Enron's Accounting Violated Accepted Financial Practices'. *Wall Street Journal,* 09 November 2001. Available: https://www.wsj.com/articles/SB1005513831533786OO.

Chapter 8: Oscar Hartzell: The Dream Merchant

Legal and Authoritative Documents

Deportation Order (Mr Oscar Hartzell) debated on Thursday. UK Parliament. Hansard, vol. 277, 4 May 1933. Available: https://hansard.parliament.uk/Commons/1933-05-04/debates/221ba29b-4b8c-4578-9d61-e801fb59e26e/DeportationOrder(MrOscarHartzell).

Drake Estate, debated on Thursday 26 April 1934, UK Parliament. Hansard, vol. 288, 26 April 1934. Available: https://hansard.parliament.uk/Commons.

Hartzell vs United States. 72 F.2d 569 (8th Cir. 1934) U.S. Court of Appeals for the Eighth Circuit. August 16, 1934. Available: https://law.justia.com/cases/federal/appellate-courts/F2/72/569/1549626/

"The Sir Francis Drake Estate" fraud: Oscar Hartzell obtained vast sums of money from America. Appointed temporary clerk 1902 Mar 3 and as Assistant Commissioner 1932 Jan 1915; retired 1947, died 1954. Catalogue No: MEPO 3/2765, Held by: The National Archives, Kew. 1919–1936.

Books

Bergreen, Laurence. *In Search of a Kingdom: Francis Drake, Elizabeth I, and the Perilous Birth of the British Empire.* New York: Custom House, 2021.

Brannon, William T. *The Drake Fable: Scoundrels & Scalawags.* The Reader's Digest Association Inc. 1968.

Pressman, Steven (Matulich, Serge & Currie, David M). *Oscar Hartzell and the Estate of Sir Francis Drake, Chapter 3, Handbook of Frauds, Scams, and Swindles: Failures of Ethics in Leadership.* Boca Raton: Routledge, 2008.

Rayner, Richard. *Drake's Fortune: The Fabulous True Story of the World's Greatest Confidence Artist.* New York: Knopf Publishing Group, 2003.

Winkle, Marshall Van. *Believing the unbelievable: The Sir Francis Drake estate swindle, Sixty famous cases: 29 English cases-31 American cases, from 1778 to the present: trials selected and accounts narrated.* New Jersey: Warren S. Ayres, 1956.

Newspaper, Magazine and Journal Articles

Buchan, Don. 'The Great Drake Estate Hoax 'The Money Kept Coming in Until a Judge Pronounced 'go Back to Your Hamlets: The Court Has Judicially Found That There is No Pot of Gold'. *Frontier Times*, 1966. Available: https://www.abebooks.com/magazines-periodicals/Article-Great-Drake-Estate-Hoax-Money/30932525323/bd.

Rayner, Richard. 'The Admiral and the Con Man'. *New Yorker*, April 14, 2002. Available: https://www.newyorker.com/magazine/2002/04/22/the-admiral-and-the-con-man.

'Drake Estate Fraud'. *Macleay Chronicle*, 10 January 1934. Available: https://trove.nla.gov.au/newspaper/article/173631335. Available: https://archive.nytimes.com/www.nytimes.com.

'The Drake Estate--Meeting of the Supposed Heirs'. *New York Times*, 25 August 1870.

'The Drake Estate Myth'. *New York Times*, 16 September 1924. Available: https://archive.nytimes.com/www.nytimes.com.

'DRAKE 'HEIR' IS HELD UNDER $10,000 BOND; Hartzell, Seized on Arrival From England'. *New York Times*. Available: https://archive.nytimes.com/www.nytimes.com.

'Denies Mail Fraud Charge'. *New York Times*, 17 February 1933. Available: https://archive.nytimes.com/www.nytimes.com.

'HARTZELL SAILS FOR HOME; American Deported From Britain for "Drake Estate" Activities'. *New York Times*, 10 February 1933. Available: https://archive.nytimes.com/www.nytimes.com.

'43 INDICTED IN SWINDLE.; Accused of Defrauding 270,000 Persons on Drake Estate Scheme'. *New York Times*, 1 May 1935. Available: https://archive.nytimes.com/www.nytimes.com.

'Guilty of swindling 'Francis Drake heirs'; Hartzell, accused of $700,000 fraud, gets ten years after Iowa trial'. *New York Times*, 16 November

1933. Available: https://archive.nytimes.com/www.nytimes.com.

Walton, David. 'A Depression-Era Swindle'. *News & Record*, 17 Aug 2002. Available: https://greensboro.com/a-depression-era-swindle/article_ec60e6fb-8f3d-50fd-baa1-1698bde254ab.html.

Chapter 9: Natwarlal: The Master Manipulator

Books

Kapoor, Abeer. *The Most Notorious Jailbreakers: Untold Stories of Escaped Convicts*. New Delhi: Rupa Publications, 2020.

Newspaper, Magazine and Journal Articles

Ahmad, Faizan. 'Nuts about Natwarlal'. *Times of India*, 23 April 2011. Available: https://web.archive.org/web/20161116072947/http://www.timescrest.com/opinion/nuts-about-natwarlal-5243.

Bobb, Dilip, Jal, Hoshi, Ahmed, Farzand and Subramanian, Lalitha. 'Natwarlal: A con man par excellence, a master forger, a escape artist to rival Houdini'. *India Today*, 27 January 2014. Available: https://www.indiatoday.in/magazine/crime-stories/story/19800815-natwarlal-a-con-man-par-excellence-a-master-forger-a-escape-artist-to-rival-houdini-821356-2014-01-27.

Chengappa, Raj. 'The life and crimes of a master criminal Natwarlal'. *India Today*, 30 November 1987. Available: https://www.indiatoday.in/magazine/special-report/story/19871130-the-life-and-crimes-of-a-master-criminal-natwarlal-799579-1987-11-29.

Kapoor, Abeer. 'How Natwarlal, the con artist, conned jail officials'. *National Herald*, 13 September 2020. Available: https://www.nationalheraldindia.com/book-extract/how-natwarlal-the-con-artist-conned-jail-officials.

Madhavan, Deepu. '10 Things You Need To Know About The Man Who Sold The Taj Mahal Thrice!!!'. *Indiatimes*, March 23 2017. Available: https://www.indiatimes.com/news/india/10-things-you-need-to-know-about-the-man-who-sold-the-taj-mahal-thrice-247513.html.

Natwarlal. Wikipedia. Available: https://en.wikipedia.org/wiki/Natwarlal.

Naqvi, Haider. 'Natwarlal leaves 'em guessing even in death'. *Hindustan Times*, 29 July 2009. Available: https://www.hindustantimes.com/india/natwarlal-leaves-em-guessing-even-in-death/story-mYkqbv8grOOw0oFEsIryrJ.html.

Pareek, Shabdita. 'The Story of Natwarlal, India's Greatest Conman Who Sold the Taj Mahal Not Once But Thrice!'. *Scoopwhoop*, 10 March 2016. Available: https://www.scoopwhoop.com/news/natwarlal-indias-greatest-conman-who-sold-taj-mahal/.

Parvez, Shayan. 'Natwar Lal: The Man Who Sold The Taj Mahal, Red Fort & Parliament House'. *Scrolldroll*, 29 February 2020. Available: https://www.scrolldroll.com/natwar-lal/.

'Natwarlal'. CrimeWiki. Available: http://crimewiki.in/post/Natwarlal.

'Natwarlal: 10 things about conman who sold Taj Mahal, Parliament several times. Zee News'. *Zee News*, 12 December 2015. Available: https://zeenews.india.com/news/india/natwarlal-10-things-about-conman-who-sold-taj-mahal-parliament-several-times_1833677.html.

Chapter 10: Charles Ponzi: The Poor Millionaire

Legal and Authoritative Documents

Commissioner of Banks vs Hanover Trust Co. 247 Mass. 347 (1924), Massachusetts Supreme Judicial Court. 4 January 1924. Available: https://casetext.com/case/comr-of-banks-v-hanover-trust-co.

Commonwealth vs Ponzi. 256 Mass. 159 (1926), Massachusetts Supreme Judicial Court. 28 May 1926. Available: https://casetext.com/case/commonwealth-v-ponzi.

Commonwealth vs Commissioner of Banks in re Prudential Trust Company; Same vs Same in re Hanover Trust Company; Same vs Same in re Cosmopolitan Trust Company. 240 Mass. 244 (1922). Massachusetts Supreme Judicial Court. 14 January 1922. Available: https://casetext.com/case/commonwealth-v-commissioner-of-banks.

Cunningham Trustee of Ponzi vs Brown. 265 U.S. 44 S. Ct. 424 (1924). Supreme Court of the United States. 28 April 1924. Available: https://casetext.com/case/cunningham-v-brown.

In re Ponzi. 15 F.2d 113 (1926). United States District Court for the District of Massachusetts. 7 September 1926. Available: https://casetext.com/case/in-re-ponzi-2.

In re Ponzi. 268 F. 997 (1920). United States District Court for the District of Massachusetts. 12 November 1920. Available: https://case-law.vlex.com/vid/in-re-ponzi-28063-887782233.

In re Ponzi. 6 F.2d 324 (1925). United States District Court for the District of Massachusetts. 14 May 1925. Available: https://casetext.com/case/in-re-ponzi.

Levenbaum vs Hanover Trust Co. 253 Mass. 19 (1925). Massachusetts Supreme Judicial Court. 25 May 1925. Available: https://casetext.com/case/levenbaum-v-hanover-trust-co.

Ponzi vs Fessenden. 258 U.S. 254 (1922). U.S. Supreme Court. March 27, 1922. Available: https://supreme.justia.com/cases/federal/us/258/254/.

Ponzi vs Ward. 7 F. Supp. 736 (1934). United States District Court for the District of Massachusetts. 30 July 1934. Available: https://casetext.com/case/ponzi-v-ward.

Books

Banker, International. *Charles Ponzi (1920).* History of Financial Crises, 2021.

Dunn, Donald H. *Ponzi! The Boston Swindler also as Ponzi: The Incredible True Story of the King of Financial Cons.* New York: McGraw-Hill, 1975.

Editors, Charles Rivers. *Charles Ponzi and the Ponzi Scheme: The History and Legacy of 20th Century America's Most Famous Con Artist.* Independently Published, 2019.

O'Connor, Thomas H. *Bibles Brahmins and Bosses: A Short History of Boston.* Boston: Boston Public Library, 1991.

Ponzi, Charles. *The Rise of Mr. Ponzi.* Texas: Despair Inc, 2009.

Pressman, Steven (Matulich, Srge & Currie, David M). *Charles Ponzi, Chapter 3, Handbook of Frauds, Scams, and Swindles: Failures of Ethics in Leadership.* New York: Routledge, 2008.

Walsh, James. *You Can't Cheat an Honest Man: How Ponzi Schemes and Pyramid Frauds Work and Why They're More Common Than Ever.* Washington: Silver Lake Publishing, 1998.

Zuckoff, Mitchell. *Ponzi's Scheme: The True Story of a Financial Legend.* London: Random House, 2006.

Newspaper, Magazine and Journal Articles

Bullock, Cora. 'The Man Who Time (Almost) Forgot William H. McMasters Finally Gets His Due for Exposing Ponzi'. *Fraud Magazine,* July/August 2011. Association of Certified Fraud Examiners. https://www.fraud-magazine.com/article.aspx?id=4294970026

Dar, Mary. 'In Ponzi We Trust'. *Smithsonian Magazine*, 1 December 1998. Available: https://www.smithsonianmag.com/history/in-ponzi-we-trust-64016168/.

Knutson, Mark C. 'The Remarkable Criminal Financial Career of Charles Ponzi'. *Investopedia*, 1993. Available: https://vdocuments.mx/the-remarkable-criminal-financial-career-of-charles-n-the-summer-of-1920-charles.html?page=1.

Labaton, Stephen. 'Charles Ponzi: A Pyramid of Postage'. *New York Times*, 7 December 1986. Available: https://www.nytimes.com/1986/12/07/business/archives-of-business-a-rogues-gallery-charles-ponzi-a-pyramid-of-postage.html.

Maloney, Russell. 'Where Are they Now? The Rise of Mr. Ponzi'. *New Yorker*, 8 May 1937. Available: https://www.newyorker.com/magazine/1937/05/08/the-rise-of-mr-ponzi.

'Ponzi Wearing His Smile Even in East Cambridge Jail'. *Boston Globe*, 12 August 1920. Available: https://bostonglobe.newspapers.com.

'Bank Commissioner Takes Charge of Hanover Trust'. *Boston Globe*, 1 August 1920. Available: https://bostonglobe.newspapers.com.

'Ponzi Freed on $35000 Bail on Federal and State Charges'. *Boston Globe*, 1 August 1920. Available: https://bostonglobe.newspapers.com.

'Charles Ponzi and His Wife Arrested Today'. *Boston Globe*, 1 February 1926. Available: https://bostonglobe.newspapers.com.

'Ponzi Stops Payment – Not to Take Up Any Notes Upon Loans'. *Boston Post*, 10 August 1920. Available: https://www.newspapers.com/paper/boston-post.

'Canadian 'Ponsi'. Served Jail Term'. *Boston Post*, 11 August 1920. Available: https://www.newspapers.com/paper/boston-post.

'Arrest in Ponzi's Case May Be Made Today'. *Boston Post*, 12 August 1920. Available: https://www.newspapers.com/paper/boston-post.

'Ponzi Idolised By Jail Mates'. *Boston Post*, 12 December 1920. Available: https://www.newspapers.com/paper/boston-post.

'Ponzi Lodged in Cambridge Jail'. *Boston Post*, 14 August 1920. Available: https://www.newspapers.com/paper/boston-post.

'Ponzi's Records in Girl's Home'. *Boston Post*, 15 August 1920. Available: https://www.newspapers.com/paper/boston-post.

'Ponzi May Be Bailed Today'. *Boston Post*, 16 August 1920. Available: https://www.newspapers.com/paper/boston-post.

'Mrs Ponzi Offers'. *Boston Post*, 17 August 1920. Available: https://www.newspapers.com/paper/boston-post.

'New Hampshire Taking A Hand in Ponzi Probe'. *Boston Post*, 1 August 1920. Available: https://www.newspapers.com/paper/boston-post.

'State Still After Ponzi'. *Boston Post*, 1 December 1920. Available: https://www.newspapers.com/paper/boston-post.

'How the Post Exposed Ponzi'. *Boston Post*, 20 August 1920. Available: https://www.newspapers.com/paper/boston-post.

'More Arrests Coming Today in Ponzi Case'. *Boston Post*, 20 August 1920. Available: https://www.newspapers.com/paper/boston-post.

'Ponzi Must Tell His Assets Today'. *Boston Post*, 21 August 1920. Available: https://www.newspapers.com/paper/boston-post.

'Ponzi Defiant Baulks Efforts of Receivers'. *Boston Post*, 22 August 1920. Available: https://www.newspapers.com/paper/boston-post.

'Doubles the Money Within Three Months'. *Boston Post*, 24 July 1920. Available: https://www.newspapers.com/paper/boston-post.

'Charles Ponzi: Head of Securities Exchange Company who is said to have made $8,500,000 in year'. *Boston Post*, 25 July 1920. Available: https://www.newspapers.com/paper/boston-post.

'$10000 Turned Back by Ponzi's Former Agent'. *Boston Post*, 26 August 1920. Available: https://www.newspapers.com/paper/boston-post.

'Amounts invested with Charles Ponzi'. *Boston Post*, 26 August 1920. Available: https://www.newspapers.com/paper/boston-post.

'Questions The Motive Behind Ponzi Scheme'. *Boston Post*, 26 July 1920. Available: https://www.newspapers.com/paper/boston-post.

'Less than $15000 in Ponzi Vault Boxes'. *Boston Post*, 27 August 1920. Available: https://www.newspapers.com/paper/boston-post.

'Ponzi Closes; Not Likely to Resume'. *Boston Post*, 27 July 1920. Available: https://www.newspapers.com/paper/boston-post.

'State to Try Ponzi'. *Boston Post*, 28 April 1921. Available: https://www.newspapers.com/paper/boston-post.

'Million is Paid Back by Ponzi'. *Boston Post*, 28 July 1920. Available: https://www.newspapers.com/paper/boston-post.

'Discover Many Police Officials Profited Through Ponzi'. *Boston Post*, 29 August 1920. Available: https://www.newspapers.com/paper/boston-post.

'Mrs Ponzi Must Surrender Auto'. *Boston Post*, 29 August 1920. Available: https://www.newspapers.com/paper/boston-post.

'Uncle Sam to get facts of Ponzi's Case'. *Boston Post*, 29 July 1920. Available: https://www.newspapers.com/paper/boston-post.

'Declares Ponzi is Now Hopelessly Insolvent'. *Boston Post*, 02 August 1920. Available: https://www.newspapers.com/paper/boston-post.

'Probe of Ponzi Turns to New Hampshire'. *Boston Post*, 30 August 1920. Available: https://www.newspapers.com/paper/boston-post.

'Officials Baulked by Ponzi Puzzle'. *Boston Post*, 30 July 1920. Available: https://www.newspapers.com/paper/boston-post.

'Pulitzer Prize is Awarded to Post'. *Boston Post*, 30 May 1921. Available: https://www.newspapers.com/paper/boston-post.

'Secretary of Ponzi Arrested'. *Boston Post*, 31 December 1920. Available: https://www.newspapers.com/paper/boston-post.

'Great Run on Ponzi Continues Until Office is Closed For Day'. *Boston Post*, 03 August 1920. Available: https://www.newspapers.com/paper/boston-post.

'Department of Justice Joins in Probe of Ponzi's Business'. *Boston Post*, 04 August 1920. Available: https://www.newspapers.com/paper/boston-post.

'Ponzi Pays as Probers Work'. *Boston Post*, 05 August 1920. Available: https://www.newspapers.com/paper/boston-post.

'Call Lansing in Ponzi Case'. *Boston Post*, 07 August 1920. Available: https://www.newspapers.com/paper/boston-post.

'A Million Paid Back: Ponzi Offers to Aid in Recovering Huge Sum'. *Boston Post*, 08 December 1920. Available: https://www.newspapers.com/paper/boston-post.

'Ponzi Debts Known Today'. *Boston Post*, 09 August 1920. Available: https://www.newspapers.com/paper/boston-post.

'Exchange 'wizard' to fight bankers'. *New York Times*, 29 July 1920. Available: https://archive.nytimes.com/www.nytimes.com.

'Federal officials begin Ponzi inquiry'. *New York Times*, 31 July 1920. Available: https://archive.nytimes.com/www.nytimes.com.

'Ponzi investigation goes on day and night'. *New York Times*, 02 August 1920. Available: https://archive.nytimes.com/www.nytimes.com.

'Big run on Ponzi but all get cash'. *New York Times*, 03 August 1920. Available: https://archive.nytimes.com/www.nytimes.com.

'Another day's run sees Ponzi smiling'. *New York Times*, 04 August 1920. Available: https://archive.nytimes.com/www.nytimes.com.

'Ponzi refuses inquiry to show his assets; run on his Boston office practically ended'. *New York Times*, 05 August 1920. Available: https://archive.nytimes.com/www.nytimes.com.

'Consults Lansing on Ponzi's business'. *New York Times*, 07 August 1920. Available: https://archive.nytimes.com/www.nytimes.com.

'Ponzi tells managers to reopen tomorrow'. *New York Times*, 08 August 1920. Available: https://archive.nytimes.com/www.nytimes.com.

'Stop Ponzi checks; say he's bankrupt; Is solvent, 'wizard' says'. *New York Times*, 10 August 1920. Available: https://archive.nytimes.com/www.nytimes.com.

'Ponzi's talk leaves club still puzzled'. *New York Times*, 11 August 1920. Available: https://archive.nytimes.com/www.nytimes.com.

'Ponzi confesses record in prisons; pleads for chance; took Italians over border'. *New York Times*, 12 August 1920. Available: https://archive.nytimes.com/www.nytimes.com.

'Ponzi arrested; liabilities put at $7,000,000; claims $4,000,000 assets'. *New York Times*, 13 August 1920. Available: https://archive.nytimes.com/www.nytimes.com.

'Ponzi goes to jail; rival operators are also taken; new note holders appear; crowd storms offices'. *New York Times*, 14 August 1920. Available: https://archive.nytimes.com/www.nytimes.com.

'Ponzi says he lost heavily by forgery; Allen asks for receiver'. *New York Times*, 18 August 1920. Available: https://archive.nytimes.com/www.nytimes.com.

'Ponzi arraigned assails banker; crowds are more hostile'. *New York Times*, 20 August 1920. Available: https://archive.nytimes.com/www.nytimes.com.

'Ponzi bankrupt receivers named'. *New York Times*, 21 August 1920. Available: https://archive.nytimes.com/www.nytimes.com.

'Ponzi surrenders $1,000,000 assets'. *New York Times*, 22 August 1920. Available: https://archive.nytimes.com/www.nytimes.com.

'Ponzi jury hearing asked by counsel'. *New York Times*, 24 August 1920. Available: https://archive.nytimes.com/www.nytimes.com.

'Expect Ponzi to pay but half his debts'. *New York Times*, 25 August 1920. Available: https://archive.nytimes.com/www.nytimes.com.

'Six police officials named as Ponzi agents'. *New York Times*, 29 August 1920. Available: https://archive.nytimes.com/www.nytimes.com.

'Ponzi is indicted by a federal jury; 86 counts for using the mails to defraud'. *New York Times*, 02 October 1920. Available: https://archive.nytimes.com/www.nytimes.com.

'Receivers seize home of Ponzi'. *New York Times*, 02 October 1920. Available: https://archive.nytimes.com/www.nytimes.com.

'Ponzi sentenced to 5 years in jail'. *New York Times*, 1 December 1920. Available: https://archive.nytimes.com/www.nytimes.com.

'Ponzi goes to trial'. *New York Times*, 27 May 1921. Available: https://archive.nytimes.com/www.nytimes.com.

'Ponzi accuses Allen'. *New York Times*, 31 July 1921. Available: https://archive.nytimes.com/www.nytimes.com.

'Didn't keep a cent declares Ponzi'. *New York Times*, 28 November 1922. Available: https://archive.nytimes.com/www.nytimes.com.

'Ponzi Creditors Get $400,000; Final disbursement to creditors'. *New York Times*, 30 May 1925. Available: https://archive.nytimes.com/www.nytimes.com.

'Ponzi soon eligible for parole'. *New York Times*, 29 May 1926. Available: https://archive.nytimes.com/www.nytimes.com.

'Reports Ponzi in flight at sea; was awaiting sentence'. *New York Times*, 27 June 1926. Available: https://archive.nytimes.com/www.nytimes.com.

'Coolidge to ignore Ponzi appeal. Pres coolidge to ignore his appeal for pardon'. *New York Times*, 05 July 1926. Available: https://archive.nytimes.com/www.nytimes.com.

'Texas to hold hearing on Ponzi. Hearing on extradition proceedings will be held in Texas'. *New York Times*, 07 July 1926. Available: https://archive.nytimes.com/www.nytimes.com.

'Upholds Ponzi's sentence; conviction upheld'. *New York Times*, 25 September 1926. Available: https://archive.nytimes.com/www.nytimes.com.

'Ponzi will be deported'. *New York Times*, 21 December 1930. Available: https://archive.nytimes.com/www.nytimes.com.

'To rearrest Ponzi today; Boston 'wizard' faces deportation as prison term ends'. *New York Times*, 14 February 1934. Available: https://archive.nytimes.com/www.nytimes.com.

'Deportation of Ponzi affirmed by board: deportation ordered'. *New York Times*, 22 June 1934. Available: https://archive.nytimes.com/www.nytimes.com.

'Ponzi must leave tonight. Must leave country'. *New York Times*, 10 July 1934. Available: https://archive.nytimes.com/www.nytimes.com.

'Ponzi dies in Rio in charity ward'. *New York Times*, 19 January 1949. Available: https://archive.nytimes.com/www.nytimes.com.

'Ponzi to be freed but faces rearrest'. *New York Times*, 16 August 1920. Available: https://archive.nytimes.com/www.nytimes.com.

'Trace Ponzi funds; he stays in jail'. *New York Times*, 17 August 1920. Available: https://archive.nytimes.com/www.nytimes.com.

'Ponzi assets $1,593,834; liabilities fixed at $6,396,000– notes worth $4,264,000'. *New York Times*, 7 'December 1920. Available: https://archive.nytimes.com/www.nytimes.com.

'Made millions by trick in exchange'. *New York Times*, 27 July 1920. Available: https://archive.nytimes.com/www.nytimes.com.

'Ponzi faces operation'. *New York Times*, 12 November 1921. Available: https://archive.nytimes.com/www.nytimes.com.

'Declares Ponzi insolvent'. *New York Times*, 16 October 1920. Available: https://archive.nytimes.com/www.nytimes.com.

'Ponzi Adjudged Bankrupt'. *New York Times*, 26 October 1920. Available: https://archive.nytimes.com/www.nytimes.com.

'Ponzi Denies He's Bankrupt'. *Washington Post*, 24 August 1920. Available: https://newspaperarchive.com/search/location/us/dc/washington/washington-post/.

'Postage Stamp King Defies Federal Government to Learn How He Profits'. *Washington Post*, 30 July 1920. Available: https://newspaperarchive.com/search/location/us/dc/washington/washington-post/.

'Ponzi Pleads Not Guilty'. *Washington Post*, 9 October 1920. Available: https://newspaperarchive.com/search/location/us/dc/washington/washington-post/.

Weisman, Steve. 'The History of Ponzi Schemes Goes Deeper Than the Man Who Gave Them His Name'. *Time*, 12 August 2020. Available: https://time.com/5877434/first-ponzi-scheme/.

Wells, Joseph T. 'How Ponzi Prospered Famous Scheme Produced Millions Before Pyramid Collapsed'. *Fraud Magazine*, Association of Certified Fraud Examiners, March/April 2001. Available: https://www.fraud-magazine.com/article.aspx?id=4294968365.

Common Reference Materials

Books

Angelis, Gina De. *White Collar Crime (Crime Justice and Punishment)*. New York: Chelsea House, 1999.

Bolt, Roelf. *The Encyclopaedia of Liars and* Deceivers. London: Reaktion Books, 2014.

Edwards, John Richard & Walker, Stephen P. *The Routledge Companion to Accounting History*. Oxfordshire: Routledge, 2008.

Farquhar, Michael. *A Treasury of Deception: Liars, Misleaders, Hoodwinkers, and the Extraordinary True Stories of History's Greatest Hoaxes, Fakes and Fraud*. New York: Penguin Books, 2005.

Fine, Ralph Adam. *The How-To-Win Trial Manual*. New York: Juris Publishing, Inc., 2011.

Geis, Gilbert. *White-Collar Crime: Offenses in Business, Politics, and the Professions*. Mumbai: Free Press, 1994.

Gibson, Walter B. *The Fine Art of Swindling*. New York: Grosset and Dunlap, 1966.

Giroux, Gary. *Business Scandals, Corruption, and Reform: An* Encyclopaedia. California: Greenwood, 2013.

Hayward, Arthur L. *Lives of the Most Remarkable Criminals Who Have Been Condemned and Executed for Murder, the Highway, Housebreaking, Street Robberies, Coining or Other Offences*. New York: Dodd, Mead & Company, 1927.

Jones, Michael J. *Creative Accounting, Fraud and International Accounting Scandals*. West Sussex: Wiley, 2010.

Konnikova, Maria. *The Confidence Game: The Psychology of the Con and Why We Fall for It Every Time*. Edinburgh: Canongate Books, 2017.

Matulich, Serge; David M. Currie & Ors. *Handbook of Frauds, Scams and Swindles: Failures of Ethics in Leadership*. Boca Raton: Routledge, 2008.

Maurer, David. *The Big Con: The Story of the Confidence Man*. North Carolina: Anchor, 1999.

Nash, Jay Robert. *Hustlers and Con Men*. New York: M. Evans & Co, 1982.

Reinhart, Carmen & Kenneth, Rogoff. *This Time is Different: Eight Centuries of Financial Folly*. Princeton: Princeton University Press, 2011.

Rorie, Melissa L. *The Handbook of White-Collar Crime John*. New Jersey: Wiley & Sons Inc, 2020.

Thomas, David. *Beggars, Cheats and Forgers: A History of Frauds Through the Ages*. South Yorkshire: Pen & Sword Books Ltd, 2014.

Sarna, David E. Y. *History of Greed: Financial Fraud from Tulip Mania to Bernie Madoff*. West Sussex: Wiley, 2010.

Shadel, D. *Outsmarting the Scam Artists How to Protect Yourself From the Most Clever Cons*. West Sussex: Wiley, 2012.

Slyke, Shanna Van: Benson, Michael & Cullen, Francis T. *The Oxford Handbook of White-Collar Crime*. Oxford: Oxford University Press, 2016.

Stratmann, Linda. *Fraudsters and Charlatans: A Peek at some of History's Greatest Rogues*. Cheltenham: The History Press Ltd, 2010.

Subramanian, Revathi. *Bank Fraud: Using Technology to Combat Losses*. New Jersey: Wiley, 2014.

Sutherland, Edwin H. *White Collar Crime*. Westport: Praeger Publishers Inc, 1983.

Swain, Smarak. *Applied Psychology*. Gurugram: OakBridge Publishing. 2019

Train, John. *Famous Financial Fiascos*. London: Fraser Pub Co, 1995.

Wells, Joseph T. *Corporate Fraud Handbook: Prevention and Detection*. New Jersey: Wiley, 2017.

Wilson, R. Paul. *The Art of the Con*. Connecticut: Lyons Press, 2020.

Newspaper, Magazine and Journal Articles

Association of Certified Fraud Examiners. *2020 Report to the Nations Report to the Nation on Occupational Fraud and Abuse (11th edition)*. Available: https://legacy.acfe.com/report-to-the-nations/2020/.

Braithwaite, J. 'Poverty, Power, White-Collar Crime, and the Paradoxes of Criminological Theory'. *Journal of Criminology*, vol. 24, Sage Journals, March 1991. Available: https://journals.sagepub.com/doi/abs/10.1177/000486589102400104.

Cotton, David L., Johnigan, Sandra and Givarz, Leslye. *Fraud Risk Management Guide*. Committee of Sponsoring Organizations of the Treadway Commission (COSO) and Association of Certified Fraud Examiners, 1 September 2016. Available: https://www.acfe.com/home/fraud-resources/fraud-risk-tools---coso/~/-/media/38f9248262f14c0da0ce27bc4c89cc88.ashx.

Crumbley, Donald Larry. 'Forensic accounting: Older than you think'. *Journal of Forensic Accounting*, no. 2, January 2001, 181–202. Available:

https://www.researchgate.net/publication/238659496_Forensic_Accounting_Older_Than_You_Think.

Matthews, Derek. 'Oral history, accounting history and an interview with Sir John Grenside'. *Accounting History Review*, 1 March 2000, vol. 10, no. 1, 57–83. Available: https://www.researchgate.net/publication/24067115_Oral_history_accounting_history_and_an_interview_with_Sir_John_Grenside.

Pressman, Steven. 'On Financial Frauds and Their Causes: Investor Overconfidence'. *The American Journal of Economics and Sociology*, vol. 57, no. 4, October 1998. Available: https://www.jstor.org/stable/3487115.

Steven, Toms. 'Fraud and Financial Scandals: A Historical Analysis of Opportunity and Impediment'. *SSRN Electronic Journal*, January 2015. 10.2139/ssrn.2694962, 2015. Available: https://papers.ssrn.com/sol3/papers.cfm?abstract_id=2694962.

Websites

ABC News (https://abcnews.go.com/)

Advocate Khoj (https://www.advocatekhoj.com)

American Bankers Association (www.aba.com/)

American Finance Association (afajof.org/)

American Heritage (https://www.americanheritage.com/)

American Institute of Certified Public Accountants (www.aicpa.org/)

American National Biography (https://www.anb.org/)

Anti-Fraud Alliance (www.antifraudalliance.org/)

Asian Journal of Economics and Banking (www.emeraldgrouppublishing.com/journal/ajeb)

Association of Accounting Technicians (www.aat.org.uk/)

Association of Certified Fraud Examiners (www.acfe.com)

Association of Chartered Certified Accountants (www.accaglobal.com)

Association of Corporate Treasurers (www.treasurers.org/)

Association of International Accountants (www.aiaworldwide.com/)

Auckland Law Review (http://www.nzlii.org/)

Australian Banking Association (www.ausbanking.org.au/)

Bankers' Magazine (https://www.thebanker.com/)

Bartelby (https://www.bartleby.com/)

BBC News (https://www.bbc.com/news/)

Bibliomania (http://www.bibliomania.com/)
Bizdom (https://www.thebizdom.in/)
Bloomberg (https://www.bloomberg.com/)
Book Depository (https://www.bookdepository.com/)
Boston Globe (www.bostonglobe.com/)
Boston Post (thebostonpost.com/)
Brill (https://brill.com/view/journals/)
British Library (https://www.bl.uk/)
British News Paper Archive (https://www.britishnewspaperarchive.co.uk)
Business Standard (www.tbsnews.net)
California Digital Library (https://cdlib.org/)
Canadian Institute of Chartered Accountants (www.cpacanada.ca/)
Casemine (https://www.casemine.com/judgement/in)
CaseText (https://casetext.com)
Certified General Accountants Association of Canada (www.cpacanada)
CFA Institute (www.cfainstitute.org/)
Channel NewsAsia (https://sgforums.com/)
Chartered Accountants Australia and New Zealand (www.charteredaccountantsanz.com/)
Chartered Accountants Ireland (www.charteredaccountants.ie/)
Chartered Banker Institute (www.charteredbanker.com/)
Chartered Banker Institute (www.charteredbanker.com/)
Chartered Institute of Internal Auditors (www.iia.org.uk/)
Chartered Institute of Management Accountants (www.cimaglobal.com/)
Chartered Institute of Public Finance and Accountancy (www.cipfa.org/)
Chartered Management Institute (www.managers.org.uk/)
CNN Money (https://money.cnn.com/magazines/fortune/fortune_archive/)
Coin Archives (https://www.coinarchives.com/)
Colonial Society of Massachusetts (https://www.colonialsociety.org/)
Committee of Sponsoring Organizations of the Treadway Commission (www.coso.org/)
Confederation of Asian and Pacific Accountants (http://www.capa.com.my/)
CPA Australia (www.cpaaustralia.com.au/)
DataCite (datacite.org/)
Department of Accounting, Finance and Management University of Essex (https://repository.essex.ac.uk)

Directory of Open Access Journals (doaj.org/)
Econ Papers (https://econpapers.repec.org)
Economic & Political Weekly (https://www.epw.in/)
Economist (www.economist.com/)
ELitigation (https://www.elitigation.sg/)
Encyclopaedia Britannica (www.britannica.com)
Encyclopedia.com (www.encyclopedia.com)
English Historical Review, Oxford Academic (https://academic.oup.com/ehr/)
Facebook (https://www.facebook.com/)
FBI, United States Government (https://archives.fbi.gov/)
Financial Action Task Force (www.fatf-gafi.org/)
Forbes (https://www.forbes.com)
Gale (https://www.gale.com/)
Genealogist (https://www.thegenealogist.com/)
Global Association of Risk Professionals (www.garp.org/)
Global Financial Data (https://globalfinancialdata.com/)
Google Books (books.google.co.in/)
Google Scholar (scholar.google.com/)
Guardian (https://www.theguardian.com)
Hansard, UK Parliament (https://hansard.parliament.uk/)
Harvard Business Law Review (www.hblr.org/)
Harvard Business School (https://www.hbs.edu/)
Hindustan Times(https://www.hindustantimes.com/india/)
Historic Newspapers (https://www.historic-newspapers.co.uk)
Historical Horizons, Calvin University Historical Studies Department (https://historicalhorizons.org/)
Hong Kong Institute of Certified Public Accountants (www.hkicpa.org.hk/)
Houston Chronicle (https://www.chron.com/business/article/)
Ibiblio (https://www.ibiblio.org/)
ICW Group Insurance Companies (https://blog.icwgroup.com/)
India Kanoon (https://indiankanoon.org/)
India Today (https://www.indiatoday.in/)
Indian Institute of Banking and Finance (www.iibf.org.in/)
Indian Journal of Finance (http://www.indianjournaloffinance.co.in/)
Indiana University Bloomington Library (https://libraries.indiana.edu)
Indiatimes (https://www.indiatimes.com/)

Infoplease (www.infoplease.com)
Information Systems Audit and Control Association (www.isaca.org)
Institute of Chartered Accountants Australia (www.charteredaccountantsanz.com/)
Institute of Chartered Accountants in England and Wales (www.icaew.com)
Institute of Chartered Accountants of India (www.icai.org)
Institute of Chartered Accountants of Scotland (www.icas.com)
Institute of Internal Auditors (na.theiia.org/)
Institute of Management Accountants (www.imanet.org/)
Institute of Public Accountants (www.publicaccountants.org.au/)
Institute of Singapore Chartered Accountants (isca.org.sg/)
International Federation of Accountants (www.ifac.org/)
Internet Archive (https://archive.org/)
Internet Public Library (www.ipl.org)
ISPSW, Berlin (https://www.files.ethz.ch/isn/)
Jamaica Observer (https://www.jamaicaobserver.com/)
Journal of Accountancy (https://www.journalofaccountancy.com/)
Journal of Banking and Finance (www.journals.elsevier.com/journal-of-banking-and-finance)
Journal of Criminology, Sage Journals (https://journals.sagepub.com/doi/)
JSTOR (https://www.jstor.org)
Law Canvas (https://lawcanvas.in/)
Law Cat (https://lawcat.berkeley.edu/)
LawyerServices (https://lawyerservices.in/)
Levin Center, Wayne Law (https://www.levin-center.org/)
Library of Congress (www.loc.gov)
Librivox (https://librivox.org/)
LinkedIn (https://www.linkedin.com/)
Logical Indian (https://thelogicalindian.com/)
Malaysian Institute of Accountants (www.mia.org.my/v2/)
Malaysian Institute of Certified Public Accountants (www.micpa.com.my)
Mary Ann Liebert, Inc (https://www.liebertpub.com/)
McKendree University (https://www.mckendree.edu/)
Ministry of Trade and Industry, Singapore (https://www.mti.gov.sg/)
Munich Personal RePEc Archive (https://mpra.ub.uni-muenchen.de/)
National Archives, UK (https://discovery.nationalarchives.gov.uk)
National Archives, UK (https://discovery.nationalarchives.gov.uk)

National Digital Library, IIT Kharagpur (ndl.iitkgp.ac.in/)
National Herald (https://www.nationalheraldindia.com)
National Library of Australia (https://www.nla.gov.au/)
National Public Radio (https://www.npr.org/)
National Public Radio npr (https://www.npr.org/)
National Society of Accountants (www.nsacct.org/)
NaturalGas (http://naturalgas.org/)
Nature (https://www.nature.com/)
New Humanitarian (https://www.thenewhumanitarian.org/)
New York Public Library (https://www.nypl.org)
New York Times (https://archive.nytimes.com/www.nytimes.com)
New York Times Archives (https://archive.nytimes.com/www.nytimes.com)
New York Times (https://www.nytimes.com)
New Yorker (https://www.newyorker.com/magazine/)
News & Record (https://greensboro.com)
Newspaper SG (https://eresources.nlb.gov.sg/)
Newspapers.com (www.newspapers.com/)
Newton Project (https://www.newtonproject.ox.ac.uk/)
Old Bailey Online (https://www.oldbaileyonline.org/)
Open Library (openlibrary.org/)
Outlook (https://www.outlookindia.com/)
Oxford Dictionary of National Biography (https://www.oxforddnb.com/)
Perseus Digital Library (http://data.perseus.org)
Princeton University Library (https://library.princeton.edu)
Professional Risk Managers' International Association (www.prmia.org/)
Project Gutenberg (www.gutenberg.org/)
Proquest: https://www.proquest.com/openview/)
Radiant Blog (https://www.radiantcu.org/blog/)
Refdesk (https://www.refdesk.com/)
Research Gate (www.researchgate.net)
Resurchify (www.resurchify.com/)
Royal Museums Greenwich (https://www.rmg.co.uk)
Sahara Reporters, New York (https://saharareporters.com)
Saudi Anti-Fraud Association (www.saudiantifraud.org/fraud-resources-library/)
Scamleaks (https://scamsleaks.blogspot.com/)

Scholarpedia (http://www.scholarpedia.org/)
Scoopwhoop (https://www.scoopwhoop.com/news/)
Scopus (www.scopus.com/)
Scrolldrol (https://www.scrolldroll.com/)
Securities and Exchange Commission, United States (https://www.sec.gov/)
SHERLOC, United Nations Office on Drugs and Crime (https://sherloc.unodc.org/)
Singapore Business Review (https://sbr.com.sg/)
Singapore Government Online Platform (www.gov.sg)
Smithsonian Libraries (https://library.si.edu/digital-library)
Smithsonian Magazine (https://www.smithsonianmag.com/history/)
Smithsonian National Postal Museum (https://postalmuseum.si.edu/)
Snopes (www.snopes.com)
South African Institute of Chartered Accountants (www.saica.co.za/)
SSRN Electronic Journal (https://papers.ssrn.com/)
Stanford University(http://large.stanford.edu/)
State Library of Queensland (https://www.slq.qld.gov.au)
Sun (https://www.sunnewsonline.com/)
Sydney Morning Herald, Australia (https://www.smh.com.au/)
Taylor & Francis Online (https://www.tandfonline.com)
Texas Christian University (https://faculty.tcu.edu/)
The Register (https://www.theregister.com/)
The Royal Mint (https://www.royalmint.com/beta/)
Time (https://time.com/)
Time (https://www.thetimes.co.uk/)
Trove (https://trove.nla.gov.au/)
United States Department of Justice(https://www.justice.gov/)
Universal Digital Library (http://ulib.isri.cmu.edu/)
University of Chicago Press (https://www.journals.uchicago.edu/doi/)
University of Michigan Digital Library (https://www.lib.umich.edu/)
Villonova Law Review (https://digitalcommons.law.villanova.edu/vlr/)
Wall Street Journal (https://www.wsj.com)
Wiley Online Library (onlinelibrary.wiley.com/journal)
World Cat (https://www.worldcat.org)
World Digital library (www.loc.gov/collections/world-digital-library/)
ZDNet (https://www.zdnet.com)
Zee News (https://zeenews.india.com/news/india/)